Ben Robertson

Ben Robertson

South Carolina Journalist and Author

Jodie Peeler

Published by the University of South Carolina Press
Columbia, South Carolina 29208

www.sc.edu/uscpress

Manufactured in the United States of America

28 27 26 25 24 23 22 21 20 19
10 9 8 7 6 5 4 3 2 1

Library of Congress Cataloging-in-Publication Data
can be found at http://catalog.loc.gov/.

ISBN 978-1-64336-023-2 (hardback)
ISBN 978-1-64336-024-9 (ebook)

This book was printed on recycled paper with
30 percent postconsumer waste content.

Contents

Illustrations

Acknowledgments

This book is the end of a long journey. For almost two decades Ben Robertson has been in my life, in some form or another. Although I knew of him from his association with Edward R. Murrow, it wasn't until I was a graduate student at the University of South Carolina's journalism school that I really started researching the man himself. Eventually my efforts attracted the attention of Tom Poland, who had come across some of my work on Ben Robertson. Out of our conversations, and with his encouragement, I became interested again in the idea. It has taken a long time for this book to finally happen, but in a way I'm grateful for the delay. The years have given me a perspective I didn't have as a young graduate student and have opened up many marvelous sources of information I didn't have back then. Tom, for getting me interested again, for reminding me how much fun Ben Robertson was to research, and for convincing me to turn "someday" into "now," thank you.

I should begin where it all began, by thanking all those at the University of South Carolina, both in the J-school and in the History Department, who taught me through classwork and example the scholar's trade. I owe particular thanks to Dr. Rick Stephens, Dr. Kenneth Campbell, and Dr. Lacy Ford. I often think of my years in the J-school, where I was surrounded by a multitude of wonderful classmates and some of the best teachers and staff I could have had, as one of the happiest times in my life. To all of you who were part of that, I am grateful. And to the professors and instructors who taught me when I was in USC's graduate history program, and during my undergraduate days at Lander University, I thank all of you as well. I particularly want to thank my always cheerful and encouraging mentor at Lander, Dr. Robert Figueira, who taught me how wonderful it can be to practice the historian's craft. I also thank Dr. Marvin Cann, whose courses in Southern history taught me so much about the region that is my home, and Dr. Robert Stevenson, whose journalism courses helped me strengthen my love for the reporter's trade and reminded me what a privilege it is to be a journalist.

The first and most important stop for anyone studying Ben Robertson is the Special Collections unit of the Clemson University Library, where the papers of Robertson and others vital to his story are now housed. Over the years, whether doing research in person or requesting documents from far away, I have asked much of Special Collections. Always, they came through, and always with kindness. Thank you not only for your help to me, but for the opportunities you provided me to see and touch the remnants of Ben Robertson's story.

I thank as well the staff of the Thomas Cooper Library at the University of South Carolina, who retrieved obscure microfilm reels and bound periodicals from storage for me, helped me during endless scanning sessions, and made my task easier in at least a dozen ways. The South Caroliniana Library of the University of South Carolina, where the Narcissa Clayton Papers are held, also provided kind assistance. I also thank the Harry Ransom Center at the University of Texas, where the Alfred A. Knopf papers now reside, for its help from far away.

I am grateful to Clemson's Special Collections unit for permission to quote from the Ben Robertson Papers, the John Dewey Lane Papers, the William Wright Bryan Papers, and the B. O. Williams Papers, and for permission to use the photographs presented in this book. I am also thankful to the Harry Ransom Center for permission to quote from the Knopf Papers, and to the South Caroliniana Library for permission to quote from the Narcissa Clayton Papers.

Nathania K. Sawyer cheerfully shared with me her work and expertise on Harry Ashmore, and I hope she will soon turn her excellent research into a much-needed biography of a fascinating and forward-thinking man. Dianne Luce generously shared her examination of *Red Hills and Cotton,* which helped me better understand the book as a work of literature. I also thank A.R. Hogan, who has always had an encouraging word for me even as he has worked on incredible research endeavors of his own. And as with so many things in my life, I thank Rob Sherry, my trusted associate and general counsel.

There have been countless other people along the way who have helped. A complete list would be a chapter in its own right, but to those of you who helped in any way, large or small, I hope you realize how thankful I am.

I could not have completed this book without the support of Newberry College, which granted me the sabbatical leave I needed to complete this project. In particular, I thank our college's dean, Timothy Elston; my department chair, Patrick Gagliano; and my colleagues in the Communications program, Al de Lachica, Cayci Banks, and Larry Cameron, who ably kept things going while I was away. To the many colleagues who offered kind words while I was on sabbatical, thank you very much for your encouragement. I also thank my students for their patience during my absence, and for their support. You may not realize just how much that has meant to me, dear students, but it has reminded me why I love having you in my life, and why you so often make me believe I have the best job in the world.

Nor could I have done this without the support of my family. Even if they couldn't figure out more than 20 years ago why I was going on to graduate school, they supported and encouraged me in countless ways large and small. In their way, they helped me understand Ben Robertson. The values of honesty and decency and respect he was taught as a child, the virtues he praised in *Red Hills and Cotton,* were the same my family raised me with in my own rural childhood not so far from where Ben Robertson grew up. As his family did with him, you taught me about honor and things I should know. I love you.

The closest and most meaningful support has been from my husband, Ralph Nardone. He has been with me since this project was a pile of notes and source documents trying to become a dissertation. Both then and now Ralph has listened, encouraged, counseled, kept me steady, and has always reminded me that I am loved. I have also appreciated the guidance of my most trusted editorial assistants, Junior the Mighty Tiger and Smokey the Mountain Lion, who have always remained close at hand (and competed for my attention throughout this project). The three of you, and now Gilda too, are the world to me.

There's one more person who deserves particular thanks. More than two decades ago, when I began my graduate studies in USC's history program, I felt out of place, that I didn't have what it took. I thought about quitting. One afternoon that first semester, the professor who served as my adviser heard me out, talked me through my fears, and encouraged me to not give up. I don't know if John Scott Wilson ever knew before he passed away what a difference that conversation made, but I have never forgotten how he helped make possible everything that has happened since. He lives on each and every time I talk a student through a crisis, as he talked me through mine that day in 1996. Dr. Wilson, thank you.

I have saved two acknowledgments for last, to two people whose example made me a better educator and a better person. I first knew Dr. Henry Price when he served on my master's thesis committee. He refused to let me get by with any sort of intellectual or stylistic laziness, and he is without question the toughest editor with whom I will ever work. However painful the review process might have been, he encouraged me to do better because he *knew* I could do better. Out of it came not only a much stronger finished product, but a mutual respect. When he hired me as his graduate assistant the following semester, I learned as much from him as his students did. From Dr. Price I learned how to hold students to a higher standard, to lead them to be better than they were before—and to always push myself to be better, too.

What Walter Williams was to Ben Robertson, Ronald Farrar was to me—not only my teacher and adviser, but also my friend and champion. From my first semester in the journalism school, Dr. Farrar was a steady source of encouragement, always there when I needed him, guiding me through the ups and downs of my residency with calm, compassion, and good humor. As Henry Price taught me to set high standards in my classroom, Dr. Farrar taught me how to lead students and colleagues with mind and heart, reminding me that it's always more important to solve a problem than to win an argument.

Although my time with them was longer ago than I want to think about, Henry Price and Ron Farrar are with me every day. Through the examples they set, they taught me how to do my job, and do it well. Working with them was a privilege, and having had them as my mentors was a blessing. In the years since, I hope I have proved worthy. For what they have meant and will always mean to me, I dedicate this book to Henry Price and Ron Farrar with gratitude, love, and appreciation.

I lost count long ago of how many times Dr. Farrar said to me, "Jodie, make Robertson a book!" Now that I have, Dr. Farrar, I hope it's a book that would make you proud.

Prologue

As evening fell on Manhattan, Joe Wershba made his way to an imposing apartment building not far from Central Park. In his early thirties, the former newspaperman had been with the Columbia Broadcasting System nearly a decade. Presently working out of the network's Washington bureau, a summons from the network's headquarters had brought Wershba to New York this day. And an invitation from his boss brought him this evening to 580 Park Avenue.

Wershba's boss, Edward R. Murrow, was known to millions not only as the leading voice of broadcast journalism but also as its conscience. He'd made his name with wartime broadcasts from London during the Blitz, with first-person accounts of bombing missions with the Royal Air Force over Germany, with a haunting account of the liberation of the concentration camp at Buchenwald. With his deep voice, his masterful use of timing and dramatic pauses, his effective use of "little picture" scenes of war's effect on common people, Murrow had brought the war to American listeners in a way no one else had.

After the war, Murrow's nightly radio news broadcasts, which combined reporting with keen analysis and comment, helped Americans make sense of the day's events. As television began to weave its web across the nation, a somewhat reluctant Murrow brought his talents to a new documentary series, *See It Now,* in 1951. Among his first hires for the program was the Brooklyn-born Wershba, whose tenacity and plainspokenness had impressed Murrow.

The public Murrow, familiar to television viewers from *See It Now* and the celebrity interview series *Person to Person,* seemed straight out of central casting. He was tall and dramatic, with looks compared more than once to Humphrey Bogart, his trademark cigarette always close at hand, his deep and resonant voice lending gravity to his every utterance. Murrow seemed the living embodiment of his trade. But those who worked with him knew a different Murrow: shy, sensitive, caring, brooding, and never quite at home in his realm. Although his work often brought him in close contact with executives, celebrities, and political leaders, Murrow never warmed up to those circles. For Ed Murrow, who was born in rural North Carolina and had spent his youth laboring in the logging camps of Washington state, felt most at home with cameramen, soundmen, editors, reporters—the people who did the hard, unseen, and unsung work that made the whole enterprise happen. Cocktail parties and formal dinners with dignitaries, celebrities, and executives never meant as much to Murrow as an after-hours session at a favorite tavern with his reporters, a lengthy poker game with his production staff, or a long conversation with a trusted lieutenant. In their company, Murrow could relax and be one of the guys. And that's why he had summoned Joe Wershba to his door. Murrow knew his correspondent, exhausted after a battery of meetings, needed a place to spend the night. Better still, he knew Wershba was good company.

In the Murrows' luxurious tenth-floor apartment, the two men talked well into the evening, matters of work and current events giving way to the philosophical and personal discussions that cemented a friendship. As night settled in, they wandered into Murrow's book-lined study. The great broadcaster reached up to a shelf and pulled down a small hardcover volume, bound in red, worn from countless readings. Murrow placed it in Wershba's hands.

"Read this," Murrow said. "Only, please be sure to give it back."

A puzzled Wershba looked down at the weathered, well-loved volume: *Red Hills and Cotton,* by Ben Robertson.

"He was my best friend," Murrow said.[1]

More than a century after Robertson's birth, more than seven decades after his death, many people have the same puzzlement Joe Wershba had that evening in Murrow's apartment. Even among those who recognize the name Ben Robertson, it's all too often in connection with *Red Hills and Cotton: An Upcountry Memory,* the lovingly written 1942 hymn to his boyhood on his grandparents' farm in the South Carolina upcountry, a tribute that doubtless resonated with Murrow's roots in rural North Carolina.

Remembering Ben Robertson for *Red Hills and Cotton,* his most beloved work, is understandable. The little book is a classic of southern literature, to this day required reading in college literature and history courses, an entry on dozens of lists of essential books about the South. But it confines Robertson to a single work that, though heartfelt, is an exception to the kinds of writing on which he built an incredible and wide-ranging, if abbreviated, career.

The friendship Ed Murrow cherished was born in the fury of a Britain at war. In 1940 Murrow was only a few years into his reporting role for CBS, working out of London. There he befriended Robertson, covering the war for the New York daily newspaper *PM.* Together, they covered battles, faced danger, saw the horrors of war, and witnessed the invincible spirit of the British people. They faced the same struggles against wartime censorship and shared the same frustrations about American neutrality. In their quieter moments, Murrow and Robertson built a strong friendship, based not only on the hazards they faced and the frustrations they fought, but also on the genuine connection they had as two sons of the rural South who simply understood one another.

To his role Robertson brought a decade and a half of newspaper experience and a globetrotting past. From a little town in the South Carolina upcountry he'd set out to see what he could and to experience the world. From Clemson he had been to Missouri and then to Charleston, Australia, Java, New York, Washington, and London. He went on an odyssey at sea and covered stories as small as character pieces about telephone operators, as large as presidential elections, as significant as a continent at war, and everything in between. He fed a hundred curiosities and hobbies, read voraciously, and wrote prolifically.

Ben Robertson's journey had not merely been one of places. In his travels, in meeting other people and listening to them tell their stories—in seeing for himself how the world worked—Robertson had expanded his view. No mere reporter, Robertson had developed into a sensitive and perceptive observer of the human condition, becoming an advocate who sought action on the injustices he saw. At home, he wanted to see improvements in racial relations, despaired about the poverty he saw in the rural South, and he wrote and spoke passionately about how the South needed to modernize its economy—causes he believed in so strongly that he sometimes considered leaving journalism to run for office. In wartime, he condemned American neutrality in the face of Britain's lonely struggle to fend off the might of the Axis, and he urged the opening of a second front in Europe to defeat Hitler more quickly. In India, Robertson grew disturbed by the dismissive attitude the British displayed toward the people of India, and he chafed at British attempts to censor accounts of what was happening in that country. In his way, Robertson was living out the credo of *PM,* whose publisher famously declared "We are against people who push other people around." Even *Red Hills and Cotton* has been misremembered as mere nostalgia for times past; for buried within its fond remembrances of a Carolina boyhood is a critique of a socioeconomic system its author believed was outdated, a call for the South to reconsider its attitudes on race, and a proposal that the South should not dwell on its defeats but honor its past while moving toward a better future for all its people.

So many of the touchstones of Ben Robertson's world have vanished. The New York *Herald Tribune* and *PM,* the newspapers that gave his journalism its widest reach and greatest impact, are long gone. The South of cotton farms has given way to the South of manufacturing and industry. The Democratic Party that shaped the South Carolina of Robertson's time no longer holds power; now, after a seismic political realignment, the state has become a Republican stronghold. Farms have given way to industry. The trains that took him to places near and far stopped running long ago. Streams and valleys he explored are now submerged beneath an enormous lake. And the Clemson College that shaped Robertson's life in countless ways has grown into a major research university, a city unto itself, a campus whose modern facilities stretch for miles.

On the Clemson campus, however, there are still traces of the world Ben Robertson knew. The old main building still stands, as does the Calhoun mansion, in whose shadow Robertson attended grade school. The red hills of Robertson's childhood are still there. And a highway that winds along forested hillsides still leads to the town where the adventure of Ben Robertson's life began. It was an American journey, centuries in the making. On a misty morning, as the first light breaks over the red hills of Pickens County, it isn't difficult to imagine how it must have felt two hundred years before, as the wagons came to a halt and a wise old woman, tired from a long journey she had reluctantly taken, took her first look at a valley she had been promised.

CHAPTER I

American Pilgrims

From his earliest days, Ben Robertson was taught that being from South Carolina was an honor. There was a South Carolina before there was a Union, his grandmother Bowen taught him, and years later her grandson wrote of his belief that she thought God had chosen them for this country.

"A hundred and ninety years ago God had brought us into Canaan from eastern Pennsylvania," Ben wrote in 1941. Theirs was a family of twenty-one, a people of hardy Scots-Irish stock who entered America through Pennsylvania, migrating south on the first western trail. Their new Canaan was an English league of land from the King of England at six-and-a-quarter cents an acre.[1]

As a boy, Ben listened to his great aunt Narcissa Clayton tell the story of her namesake, his great-great-great-great-great aunt. The original Narcissa wanted to live her life in peace, dreamed of a quiet house with a flower garden. But her family didn't want to stay. "Three times her people got the moving fever," Ben wrote. "Virginia had struck their fancy in Pennsylvania, North Carolina in Virginia, western North Carolina in eastern North Carolina. For sixty years they had wandered and at the end of all that time all that Narcissa had to show for her life were graves of her loved ones scattered across six hundred miles of wilderness, a small yellow creek named with her name, somewhere in Virginia a grove of cedar trees of her planting, memories of tomahawks and scalping knives."[2]

Just when Narcissa thought she had finally found rest, her grandson and his family decided to move to South Carolina. The weary old woman tried to discourage him. She warned of natives that would hunt them, terrible wolves and wildcats and panthers that would frighten them, and of the constant fear in which they would live. But her arguments were in vain. She suddenly knew that her grandson's mind was made up, that something was drawing him into the unknown—that the urge to wander was too deep in his character.

Narcissa accepted the inevitable and bundled up the few possessions she could not bear to leave behind: a copy of the *Arabian Nights,* a bottle of bear-oil for snake bite, volatile drops for her heart, peach stones, hollyhock seed, rose seeds, watermelon seeds, knitting needles, and a Bible. She also carefully wrapped up her most cherished possession: a sugar bowl, a piece of yellow crockery with a gold band, that she had received as a bride in Pennsylvania. It had made each move with her, and somehow it had survived. To Narcissa, it was a symbol.

The next morning, after her grandson led the group in prayer, the caravan headed out, leaving behind all that had become familiar. For a moment Narcissa felt some excitement at heading off into the unknown. Then she felt her great-grandchild, ill with fever, stirring in her arms. Despair again washed over her, and she cried, "What chance have we got on a journey like this? A helpless old woman and a baby?"

The caravan went on for several weeks, stopping at night and resuming in the morning, rolling over hills and through groves and wilderness, fording streams. A fierce thunderstorm came up, making a stream rise three feet in an hour. The caravan held up for most of a day until the storm passed and the stream could be crossed.

In the evenings they sat by a campfire. Narcissa told the children stories from the Bible, from the *Arabian Nights,* and stories about the life she had left behind in Pennsylvania. Sometimes, alone, Narcissa wandered off through the woods. Her mind filled with thoughts of all those who had come before and left no mark, whose dreams had amounted to nothing, and of how lonely the wilderness was. "She saw the wilderness as a great barren rock upon which a million settlers would have to lay down their lives like leaves, one upon another," Ben wrote.[3]

At last the party came to the crest of a high hill, overlooking a deep, tree-lined valley with a creek rattling through the middle of it. A light rain fell, and mists filled the valley below. Narcissa's grandson spread his arms grandly. "This is the valley I was telling you about," he said. "Here we are." Narcissa looked out and, as she cast her view across the valley, her skepticism gave way to hope and relief. The valley was as beautiful as her grandson had promised.

Once the family had settled in the valley, Narcissa planted half of her peach kernels and hollyhock seed, and a quarter of her rose seeds. The wise old woman knew not to risk everything at once. As the seeds sprouted, Narcissa turned her attention to the children, teaching them proper manners, helping them memorize her favorite Psalms, and instructing them to obey the Ten Commandments. Her efforts to teach them arithmetic weren't hampered by the lack of a book. Instead, Narcissa spent weeks writing one of her own. When it was finished, it spanned more than a hundred pages.

When Narcissa wasn't composing arithmetic problems, she wrote instructions on the children's proper upbringing. "A family of well-regulated children is a charming sight," she wrote on one page. On another: "Good breeding is often a surface without depth but politeness is the sunshine of the soul." Narcissa wanted the children to make something positive of themselves. "Settle down, become a credit to your kinfolks," she taught them.

One day soon after her family had settled in the valley, Narcissa went to the creek. As she bent down to fetch a pail of milk that had been cooling in the rushing waters, she was struck on the head and Cherokee arrows pierced her side. "She met life with calmness, resignation and the firmness of a Christian martyr," her grandson said at her funeral. "Disappointment did not change her, and no matter what happened, she always heard the birds singing and saw the beautiful wild flowers." Her family buried her among pine trees on top of a hill, in a coffin made from the valley's cedars. Two centuries later, Ben would write of his ancestor, "She was courage and faith. She was sacrifice. She was our holy mother—the great mother of everyone who is born in the United States."[4]

Robertson's ancestors had settled around the Pea Ridge area, nestled between Glassy Mountain and Six Mile Mountain near what is present-day Pickens, South Carolina. There they made their own treaties with the Cherokees on Big Cherokee Creek. "We took our land from the Cherokees who had taken it from the Creeks years before," Robertson wrote nearly two centuries later. "Sometimes in Twelve Mile Valley we forget about the Puritans and Pilgrims; sometimes we have a feeling that we have come down the dusty ages through the red men, that we have been in America forever."[5]

Since 1750, Robertson's ancestors had occupied the same land in the undulating clay foothills of Pickens County. Marriages had joined the Robertsons with other upcountry families, including the Claytons, Bowens, O'Dells, Craigs, Allgoods, and Boones; these relationships spun a familial web over the region. Many years later a family genealogist wrote that Ben Robertson was "blood-kin to half of Pickens County and linked somehow to the rest." Sometimes these family connections meant proximity to historical figures; Hattie Boone McKinney, Ben's great-grandmother, was the great-niece of Daniel Boone, and throughout his life Ben took great pride in his kinship to the legendary frontiersman. Another pioneer in the Robertson lineage was James "Horseshoe" Robertson, the great Revolutionary War soldier whose exploits inspired a novel by John P. Kennedy.[6]

The heroism of his ancestors didn't stop with Daniel Boone or Horseshoe Robertson; in his childhood Ben thrilled to hear stories of his relatives who had fought in the Civil War. His paternal grandfather, Thomas Lafayette Robertson, had enlisted in the Confederate Army at age twenty-two. As part of "Orr's

Rifles" in the 1st South Carolina Rifle Regiment, Robertson fought for the Army of Northern Virginia, spending most of the war in that state, and was wounded in action.

Two weeks before Lee's surrender at Appomattox Court House, Robertson was captured at Petersburg, Virginia. He was sent to Hart Island, between the Bronx and Long Island, where the Union had established a prison camp. Robertson was interned along with more than three thousand other prisoners. They had very little in the way of shelter or facilities, and diarrhea and tuberculosis were rampant. More than two hundred prisoners died during the four months the prison was open. Soon after the war's end, Thomas Robertson won his parole from Hart Island. According to family legend, he walked from New York all the way back to Pickens County.[7]

Soon after his return to South Carolina, Robertson married Artemissa Clayton, a member of a family "old and influential in the upcountry." The Claytons had come south from Virginia, settling near Twelve Mile River in what became Pickens County. Ben Robertson would write that the Claytons "were great landowners—owning bounty, grant and bought land—and there are many records of them in the courthouses at Walhalla and Pickens." Artemissa was one of thirteen children born to Philip and Katy Clayton; some lived to old age, while others died in childhood. Some of the children succumbed to illness, and one was shot to death in a brawl. The family home, a large house called Forest Mansion, was handed down to Thomas and Artemissa Robertson after the Civil War. Artemissa, who according to Ben "wore silk dresses and smoked a pipe," bore three children. The youngest, Benjamin Franklin Robertson, was born in the farmhouse in August 1873. He was raised in their own mold, a devoted Baptist and ardent Democrat.[8]

According to an old family story, when Benjamin was sixteen, his father gave him a choice. Benjamin could inherit and farm half of the family's nine hundred acres, or he could enroll in the new Clemson Agricultural College that was being established nearby. Benjamin packed a bag, rode on horseback to the rail station in nearby Liberty, and took a train to Calhoun Station near the Clemson campus. A chemistry major, he was part of Clemson's first graduating class in 1896. After graduation, he accepted a position in the chemistry department, and with it an apartment the college provided on nearby Hotel Hill.[9]

Not long after his graduation from Clemson, the young chemist fell in love with a young woman who had an impressive family tree of her own. Mary Iola Bowen was the daughter of one of Pickens County's most prominent citizens. Born in 1843, William Thomas Bowen had served with the "Pickens Guards" of the 4th South Carolina Infantry during the Civil War. After the war, he married Rebecca Allgood. They settled on a farm in Pickens County and had six children.[10]

After the Civil War, Bowen was among the South Carolinians resentful of Reconstruction policies. He believed the postwar Republican government was corrupt and saddling the state with immense debt, and that the legislature was full of "carpetbaggers" and "scalawags" intent on imposing their way of life on a defeated state. In resistance, Bowen and scores of others joined the Ku Klux Klan, one of the vigilante groups that had sprung up in protest of Reconstruction policies, which sought the return of Democrats to power. The Klan's tactics against blacks and white supporters of Reconstruction grew so brutal that in 1871 Congress passed legislation to fight the Klan. When the South Carolina Klan proved especially difficult to contain, President Ulysses S. Grant used a provision in the new legislation to suspend habeas corpus in nine South Carolina counties. With the help of federal troops, marshals arrested hundreds of Klansmen.

As the federal government pursued the Klan, its influence waned. Many of its members joined other organizations that sought the overthrow of the Reconstruction government, but they tried to distance themselves from the secrecy and brutal tactics that had prompted federal action against the Klan. More than twenty thousand South Carolinians joined these groups. Bowen shifted his allegiance to one of these groups, the "Red Shirts," whose professed slogan was "force without violence"—although in reality they were known to use violence against their opponents. Bowen was hardly alone in the family; as his grandson wrote years later, "All of my kin folk were Red Shirts."[11]

The Red Shirts achieved their ambition with the 1876 election of Wade Hampton as governor, thanks in no small part to massive election fraud committed by the Red Shirts and other supporters. When the disputed election was resolved by the South Carolina Supreme Court in favor of Hampton and the Democrats, and when the Compromise of 1877 signaled the end of the Reconstruction Era, Hampton and his fellow "Redeemers" began reshaping South Carolina's government.

In time, some southerners who worried that the sharecropping system that had emerged in the postwar era had created a different form of slavery; that bankers, merchants, and monopolies were taking advantage of poor farmers who were trying to make a living; and that elected officials were looking out only for the wealthy joined in the Farmers' Alliance movement. Bowen became active in the Alliance, which was highly instrumental in the 1890 election of former Red Shirt "Pitchfork Ben" Tillman as South Carolina's governor. Bowen himself entered government when he was elected to two terms in the state house of representatives, then to a term as a state senator. An ally of Tillman, who was called "the Agricultural Moses" for his advocacy on behalf of poor farmers, Bowen was a proponent of Tillman's proposal for a state dispensary system, which put the state in charge of bottling and selling liquor. "One thing which he did while in the legislature and of which he was particularly proud was putting through the bill which abolished saloons in Pickens County," Bowen's obituary noted. "It was only after a hard fight that he was able to get the bill passed." Bowen was also an advocate for education, and he served as a Pickens County delegate to the state's constitutional convention in 1895 where he worked hard to ensure the new constitution forbade divorce.[12]

During Tillman's governorship, the South Carolina General Assembly established the South Carolina Industrial and Winthrop Normal College, which grew out of a small school established in 1886 to train women to become public school teachers. As Clemson was founded to train young men for agriculture and industry, Winthrop was considered the counterpart for women. It was only appropriate that Mary Bowen, who inherited her father's Tillmanite sympathies, became a Winthrop graduate.[13]

In time Mary, "a young woman of grace and accomplishments," met and fell in love with Benjamin Robertson of Clemson College, "a young man of promise." During a ceremony in the main parlor of the Bowen home one afternoon in August 1901, surrounded by friends and family members, they were married. The two embarked on a train tour of Asheville and mountain resorts in North Carolina, then returned to the little apartment on Hotel Hill. It was there on June 22, 1903 that Mary gave birth to a boy they named Benjamin Franklin Robertson Jr. The child inherited not only the family name, but also its adventurousness.[14]

CHAPTER 2

A Childhood in the Red Hills

Just as Ben Robertson could trace his ancestry to the settlers who made their way south from Pennsylvania to the upper Piedmont of South Carolina, so could the origins of Clemson Agricultural College be traced to another Scots-Irish family that moved from Pennsylvania to South Carolina in the mid-1700s and settled near the Keowee River. There, the Calhoun family eventually took over several hundred acres of land that came to be known as Fort Hill. The family built a large, white house on the property. In 1836, it was under the control of John C. Calhoun, then a United States senator. Two years later Calhoun's daughter Anna married a young mining chemist from Philadelphia, Thomas Green Clemson. In time, the Fort Mill estate was bequeathed to her.

Both Thomas Clemson and his wife had taken an interest in scientific education. Thomas had seen the methods farmers used in Europe, and he had used his farm in Maryland as a proving ground for new techniques. He had been instrumental in the founding of Maryland Agricultural College, which opened in 1859. Clemson was also a strong advocate for the "land-grant" proposal, which set public land aside to establish universities and colleges.

When Anna died in 1875, the Fort Mill estate was in Thomas Clemson's hands. As it happened, sentiment was growing in South Carolina for establishing a college that focused on agricultural and mechanical subjects. In 1886, Clemson had a new will drawn up that would offer Fort Hill's 800 acres to the state of South Carolina as the site of a new agricultural college. A year and a half after Clemson's 1888 death, the state formally accepted Clemson's bequest. With federal help, Clemson's gift provided the foundation of the Clemson Agricultural College, which opened in July 1893 with an initial enrollment of 446 students. One of them was Benjamin Robertson Sr., who was one of the 37 graduates of the Class of 1896.

As the college grew, as big buildings made of brick rose on campus, as the cadets of the all-male military-style school performed drills and attended classes, a little community grew nearby. On a hill, a hotel soon sprung up. Those who worked for the college started building homes. Many of the college's faculty and staff members were young, and their children needed an education too. In a schoolhouse near John C. Calhoun's old mansion, Benjamin Robertson Jr. began his formal education. From the start, young Ben was not only surrounded by the college that employed his father, but by the reminders of the history of South Carolina and its most famous men.[1]

While Ben Sr. worked in the college's fertilizer laboratory, Mary looked after Ben Jr. and their daughter Mary Bowen Robertson, born in 1905. Nearby lived grandparents, aunts, uncles, and other relatives, the family line never straying far from the ancestral grounds, their roots deep in the Carolina clay. Wright Bryan, Ben Jr.'s lifelong friend, wrote that the senior Robertson was "gaunt and laconic but always had a twinkle in his eye and a dry jest on his tongue," while his wife was "plump and jolly."[2]

The Robertsons were active members of the community. The senior Ben assisted with Clemson's alumni association and worked with the college's new extension service, and later served as the state's chief toxicologist, often assisting law enforcement officials and providing expert testimony in legal proceedings and murder cases. Mary was one of the founders of the Tamassee Daughters of the American Revolution Industrial School; she had donated a hundred dollars to help the new school in its mission of educating girls. The Robertsons also helped to establish Clemson's First Baptist Church, where Ben Sr. would teach Sunday School for many years.[3]

His mother, Mary, fought health problems. In the summer of 1906 she contracted typhoid fever, and for a time was confined to a room at her parents' home. Though she recovered enough to return home, her health was never as good after. In December 1910, Mary busied herself in the kitchen making pies, pastries, and other sweets for the holidays. According to family lore, Mary tasted each as she made them, not knowing she was diabetic. Three days before Christmas she fell ill, and on Christmas Eve she died. "Mrs. Robertson was a most excellent Christian woman, and her death was a great shock to her many friends," her obituary read.[4]

While Ben Sr. dealt with the aftermath of Mary's death, the two children went to live with their uncle Wade C. O'Dell—a farmer and rural mail carrier—and his family at their home on Commerce Street in Liberty. O'Dell, and his wife had a son four years Ben's senior, and together they looked after the Robertson children. In 1913 Ben Sr. married twenty-eight-year-old Hattie Boggs of Liberty, and Ben Jr. and Mary returned from living with the O'Dells. The family moved into a new home in a subdivision that Ben Sr. had helped create in Clemson. The

Robertson family grew with the birth of Hattie Boone Robertson in 1915. Ben and his sister grew close to their "Momma Hattie" and to the baby sister they nicknamed "Booney." But while his parents, his uncle and aunt, and other family members helped raise young Ben, another relative who lived nearby captured his imagination and fed his sense of adventure. Ben Robertson would carry warm memories of all his relatives, but few would influence him like his Grandfather Bowen.[5]

After his service in the state legislature, William T. Bowen had returned home to his farm in Pickens County, a short train ride from Clemson. During the summers Ben and his sister would ride a train from Clemson to Pickens. There, they would catch a train called the "Pickens Doodle," which ran the short route to Easley. Since Grandfather Bowen had granted the railroad right of way through his property for the spur line, the Doodle's conductor was happy to stop the train near his home to let the children meet up with their grandfather. The children would stay for weeks at the large, white, two-story house at the top of a hill near Wolf Creek. There, Ben not only learned the rhythms of farm life, but gained lessons in history and character that forever shaped him. Decades later, those memories became some of the warmest passages of *Red Hills and Cotton.* At that house high on a hilltop, Ben wrote, "We always found great love and affection and repose. There was a deeper rest about that happy house than about any other house in our valley."[6]

To the young Ben Robertson, his grandfather was a hero. Ben remembered him as "a dignified man, solemn, courtly, severely grave." In his grandson's eyes, the four years Bowen had spent in the Confederate Army had tried him and made him gentle and good. "Sometimes I think my grandfather got more by goodness than others in our family got by even the shrewdest guile," Ben wrote. Bowen doted on his grandchildren, taking them to wade in the creek, giving them pets, and winding twine balls for them to play with. He talked with them for hours, telling stories and giving the children a gentle education in proper values.[7]

Ben's favorite stories involved Bowen's service in the Civil War and his reminiscences about family history. Rapt with attention, Ben listened eagerly and absorbed the dates, names, and lessons that would pop up in his writings for decades to come. Just as the ancestral Narcissa had taught her grandchildren soon after the family had arrived in South Carolina, so did Grandfather Bowen teach his grandchildren the values with which he was raised. And although the family's Baptist faith spoke of God's forgiveness, those who practiced that faith believed that people should live their lives in a way that was as worthy as possible. "It is essential to my kinfolks that they live by an ethical code, that they live their lives with dignity to themselves, that they live them with honor. A Southerner who loses his honor loses all," Robertson later wrote.[8]

The parables Grandfather Bowen shared were part of a longstanding tradition in the rural South. Family elders often talked about the past to their children and grandchildren. Not only did this pass along family lore, but it helped to build and reinforce the values of an honorable life: honesty, hard work, and respect for one's ancestry. The evenings the Robertson children spent listening to family lore were what historian Tony Stanley Cook described as "a long, patient introduction in the background and ways of his people . . . Children are rarely given the opportunity to speak, but the older folks around them realize the young ones are like dry sponges, and they like to fill them up."[9]

Robertson observed that his kinfolks believed that "culture could be acquired but character had to be formed. Character had to be hammered into shape like hot iron on an anvil." As he wrote, "The library of early American knowledge was the principal theme of my kinfolks' conversation—the passing on from one generation to the next of histories, codes of laws, prophecies, some memorized songs and proverbs, and letters. Biblical, Puritan, Southern, it was a variation on a single constant driving theme, rich and homely and timeless, of backwoods people trying in the backwoods to set up a certain sort of life."[10]

Through it all, Bowen hoped to educate his grandchildren about living an honorable life, to teach them right from wrong. Only twice, Ben remembered, did his grandfather punish him: once when Ben got into a fight with a black boy—and once when Ben bit his cousin Ira, who then hit him with a brick. When Grandmother Bowen punished the children, she did so with the swift stroke of a switch. But to Ben, his grandfather's form of reproof was far more devastating. He "would just take us into the parlor and sit for a while and say nothing. A hurt look would come over his strong stern face and that would bow us down with remorse. It was better to be switched than to sit there in that sort of silence—it was quicker, less accusing."[11]

A tremendous part of the education young Ben received from his family related to the Civil War and the many stories of the sacrifices the people of the South, including several members of his family, had made. The "lost cause"—the loss of the life that white Southerners felt they had created out of the American Revolution, the feeling that so many young Southern men had given their lives in a losing effort, and the veneration of those who had served in the Confederacy—haunted much of Ben's youth. The idea of the "lost cause" emphasized the belief that the principles for which the South had fought were both noble and constitutional, lending the South a means of coping with its defeat and holding onto its regional identity. “Our Southern country and all of our older people were still grieving,” Ben remembered. “Among our own kinfolks our Confederate soldiers could not bear to think that so many of our fine and promising and dear relatives had died on the battlefields for nothing more than failure . . . so they resurrected all the dead.”[12]

Grandfather Bowen, who had fought all the way from First Manassas to Appomattox, and Great-Uncle Bob, who had been shot in the hip at Missionary Ridge, sat on the porch at night and told the children about their relatives who fought in the War between the States. The result of these vivid reminiscences, Ben wrote, was that he sometimes felt he had taken part himself in half the campaigns of the Confederate Army. Years later, visiting Chickamauga and Manassas, Ben’s eyes filled with tears as he remembered tales he was told as a boy. During a stop at Appomattox, Ben remembered how his grandfather had felt hungry and defeated; and standing there more than half a century later Ben himself felt overwhelmed. “Always and everywhere as I was growing up, there was the lament: we had lost, we had lost.”[13]

When he wasn’t telling stories of the war, Bowen taught his grandchildren about treating others with kindness and dignity. Ben wrote that his grandfather “believed literally that men were born equal, he stood for their retaining their equality after their birth—for all being given equal opportunity. . . . Always my grandfather was for more knowledge—for the rich man, the poor man, the black man and the white.” This was an interesting assertion, given that Bowen had been a political ally of outspoken white supremacist Ben Tillman, and after the Civil War he had affiliated with the Ku Klux Klan and with Wade Hampton’s Red Shirts, resisting Reconstruction efforts to integrate government and society. Years later, nostalgia and deep affection no doubt kept his grandson from exploring these deeper aspects of his grandfather’s politics; instead, he focused on his grandfather’s calls for dignity and equal opportunity. And as Ben grew up, his family lived closely with blacks—as servants, as sharecroppers, and as playmates. But this proximity did not mean equal standing with whites, as the legal and social codes of the day forbade it.[14]

Although proximity did not mean equality, it did quietly influence Ben, and in a lasting way. He later wrote of the blacks who helped around the farm as if they were family members, remembering the stories they told and the wisdom he learned from them, and seeing the essential humanity and dignity within them. He would write of the tales one of them, Windy Bill, told of his time in the penitentiary, serving a sentence for a murder he didn’t remember committing and probably didn't. Eventually pardoned, Windy Bill returned to the family farm where, as Ben recalled, Bill "fed the mules, cut stovewood, played on a banjo, drank lightning liquor, hunted possums, talked about the world and everything on the broad piazza." Young Ben enjoyed visiting Windy Bill at his cabin, loved hearing him sing and tell his great stories, and sometimes Ben would sneak off to go hunt possums with him.[15]

Throughout his life, his father's household was assisted by two black servants, Jim and Mary. Jim handled manual labor while Mary saw after domestic tasks. Ben spent so much time around them when he was growing up that, as he later put it, "they raised me." He listened to them tell stories and kid each other, got to know their deep faith, and found wisdom in their words. But Ben remembered their relationship as both "intimate and personal, and at the same time strict." Long memory, he wrote, reminded them of why it was so. In time, Robertson began to question the system that kept the races apart and became a vocal advocate for anti-lynching legislation and racial equality.[16]

Although the code Robertson was raised with stressed independence and self-reliance, it also demanded responsibility towards one's fellow human beings. Robertson's family felt an obligation to those who worked on the farm, both to the white tenants and the black laborers, all of whom worked for the farm's benefit as well as their own. This philosophy of basic equality and interconnection became one of Ben Robertson's dearest values in life, and he would bristle at rigid class systems of the sort he associated with the South Carolina lowcountry.[17]

And just as Robertson learned to dislike class systems, he learned to be skeptical of banks and business interests. Bowen warned his grandchildren never to mortgage even a tiny amount of their land: "No matter what happens, don't mortgage it, and if you haven't cash money, don't buy; and if times are hard, do without." For land meant security, and Bowen believed America would come back to the Southern way of doing things, if only they were patient; with the security of land, the family would be prepared for that moment. Land meant security and comfort, it meant connections to one's familial and emotional roots, and it also meant self-reliance—critical to keep a family secure and prosperous in an isolated, rural area.[18]

Between the stories of the Civil War and the religious lessons handed down by his grandmother, Robertson wrote that the goal of all this indoctrination was simple: his family intended "to make me a Carolinian, a Democrat, and a Baptist. Once they had accomplished that—well, hell and high water could try as they liked." His Grandmother Bowen told them that it was an honor to be born in Carolina. "She said we and all of our kissing kin were Carolinians, and that after we were Carolinians we were Southerners, and after we were Southerners, we were citizens of the United States."[19]

Ben described his people, the people of the upcountry, as people who contained multitudes:

> We are farmers, all Democrats and Baptists—a strange people, complicated and simple and proud and religious and family-loving, a divorceless, Bible-reading murdersome lot of folks, all of us rich in ancestry and steeped in tradition and emotionally quick on the trigger. In many peculiar and particular ways my kinfolks and I are quite remarkable people. Anyhow, we think we are. . . .
>
> We and the ten million like us call ourselves the backbone of the Southern regions, the hickory-nut homespun Southerners, who while doing a lot of talking have also done a world of work. We are of Scotch-Irish stock, improved Scots of Ulster extraction, and it has never been said of any of us that we have held back from sounding our horn. We are forthright and outspoken. We are plain people and our houses are plain—you will not find on our front piazzas tall white columns holding up the roof. We are the Southern Stoics. We believe in self-reliance, in self-improvement, in progress as the theory of history, in loyalty, in total abstinence, in total immersion, in faithfulness, righteousness, justice, in honoring our parents, in living without disgrace. We have chosen asceticism because all of our lives we have had to fight an inclination to license—we know how narrow and shallow is the gulf between asceticism and complete indulgence; we have always known much concerning the far outer realms, the extremes. We have tried throughout our lives to keep the Commandments, we have set for ourselves one of the strictest, sternest codes in existence, but our country is Southern and we are Southern, and frequently we fail. In the end we stake our immortal souls on the ultimate deathbed repentance. We put our faith in the promise of Paul the Apostle that in a moment, in the twinkling of an eye, we shall be changed.[20]

Robertson's upbringing emphasized character and values, lessons meant to teach him to stand for something. "My kinfolks said any person with any kind of background could acquire a city civilization, but that few city people could ever learn the culture of a rural country," he wrote. Robertson's family sought to instill in him a permanent belief in how hard work and honor would build a strong character. "They wanted to instruct me in the rural beauties, to ground me in the Southern fields, to give me an anchor that no storm could ever loose." One day Great-Aunt Narcissa took the children to a high cliff. Below them, the red clay of Twelve Mile Creek flowed into the Keowee River. As they watched the little creek darken the clear waters of the river, Great-Aunt Narcissa called it "a wonderful example of sin."[21]

Around Ben were structures: the rules of his upbringing, the tenets of belief, the cycles of the growing season. Some of those constraints were loving, others demanding; but even considering the more demanding rules, Ben wrote that his childhood did not feel harsh. "I was surrounded by all sorts of restrictions—by the rules of the church, by all the personal rules of my kinfolks, by the rules of the white and colored races, but I was not aware of restrictions. I thought I was free."[22]

One of the structures that shaped Robertson's life in those years was the yearly cycle of nature, which dictated life on the family's farm. March meant planting cotton; April meant planting corn; and May and June meant tending the plantings, thrashing oats and wheat, and planting pea vines and sorghum cane. July meant more plowing and hoeing. The hot weather of August was prime cotton-growing weather. "Cotton liked the blazing heat, chilled now and then by a short sudden August shower. The fields blossomed like islands in the South Seas, white and red splotches on a glorious green and crimson—the white and red hibiscuslike cotton flowers on the green cotton plants that spread away in long curving rows across the silky vermilion of the fields." As the cotton grew, Ben and his family went to family reunions and all-day singings and went fishing "and enjoyed ourselves to the fullest."[23]

Those happy days lasted until the heat of summer yielded to the cool of autumn. When a chill came in the air, it was time for the cotton harvest. Years later Ben remembered families in the fields, sacks slung over a shoulder, singing hymns as they picked cotton with both hands. Since they were paid by the pound at sundown, they started early in the morning while the cotton was still heavy with dew. "Everything was fair in cotton-picking," Robertson remembered, "even rocks in the sack."[24]

Each day as the sun rose, Ben helped feed and milk the cows, and checked the rabbit traps before the family gathered for breakfast. The schoolhouse occupied his days during much of the year, and in summer months he helped on the farm. Noon brought the family together for dinner—and then it was back to work. On weekends, Ben tended a garden. On evenings in the cooler months, Ben split kindling and brought in wood for the fire, then tended and milked the cows again. At dusk, tired from the long day, the family gathered again for supper. At night the children sat with their grandparents on the porch and listened to stories, or sometimes they enjoyed nature through the peace and silence.

"Sometimes at night we seemed the only people in existence," Robertson later wrote. "At our grandfather's house we had time of our own to find ourselves, time of our own to think."[25]

Ben used some of that time, both at his grandfather's house and at his father's home, to explore the countryside. He swam where Twelve Mile Creek and the Keowee River converged to form the Seneca, and in the rolling hills nearby he learned to identify the plants and animals in the area. Inspired by advertisements in the *American Boy* and *Boys' Life,* Ben dreamed of turning his knowledge of the surrounding wilderness into a fortune by becoming a fur trapper. With his friend Woots Klugh, Ben wrote to fur houses for booklets on how to trap minks and bears. The boys spent all their money on two dozen steel traps, setting them up on logs along a path in the woods, sure a bonanza was in the making. But a spring thaw ruined their plan to become millionaires. "We lost the whole business in the first freshet—the last of Klugh & Robertson, Inc."[26]

On a fine March morning, Ben went out into the woods with a friend named Harve, son of a tenant on his Grandfather Bowen's farm. With them was Popcorn, the son of one of the black families that also lived on the farm. The boys adopted Cherokee names and went off roaming through the hills and woods, exploring the gullies for quartz crystals, examining a hole in which a skunk lived, and carving their names into a beech tree. They emerged on a high ledge above the river and lay down on it, the fields far below them, and talked about their hopes for adulthood. Harve predicted that he would travel the world to find the right country, then settle down and make $100,000. Popcorn said that when he grew up, he wanted to get a job in an Ohio automobile factory and make $18 a week. Ben vowed that he would travel around the world and see the Pacific Ocean before he came back.[27]

One of his closest friendships was with the son of another Clemson instructor. William Wright Bryan, born in Atlanta, came to Clemson with his family when his father was hired to teach English at the college. Wright, two years younger than Ben, forged with Ben a strong friendship that would last Ben's lifetime. Together they played baseball on rocky hillsides, served as batboys for the college baseball team and water boys for the college football team, and explored the countryside. From their classroom windows they could watch the Southern Railway trains, headed from Atlanta and New Orleans to Charlotte and New York. Sometimes they could give in to their wanderlust, catching a train to Greenville or Anderson for a circus, or to Walhalla or Pickens for a high school field day. Once they went by rail to see Woodrow Wilson speak in a nearby town. There Ben, the future Washington correspondent, got his first glimpse of a president of the United States.[28]

The boys explored the campus near their home. They discovered libraries—first the small library in their school, and then the large university library. On occasion the boys caught a glimpse of Ben Tillman, who served as one of the college's trustees, visiting the campus. Aged and worn, hobbled by a stroke, the sight of the grim-faced, one-eyed Tillman startled the youngsters. On fine days, they watched as Shakespearean players set up a tent near the campus greenhouse and regaled audiences with performances of *Richard III* and *King Lear.*[29]

To young Ben, there was no finer place to be. Years later, he recalled his grandmother's insistence that "heaven would be like Carolina in the month of May in the early morning. The sun would never rise more than an hour high, and there would be peace and rest forever." The upcountry he would carry in his heart the length of his life was

> a land of smokehouses and sweet potato patches, of fried pies and dried fruit and of lazy big bumblebees buzzing in the sun—a country of deep dark pools, of the soaring spirit, of little rooms stored with apples, and of old Confederates and tenant farmers and colored people and swarms of politicians and preachers. An ideal country for cotton farmers and dreamers; a brooding great country that had caught the sight of God. You can see a wedge of sheldrakes, a cloud drifting in southern space, and there before you are the old, contemplative mountains, a long range sifted with a powder that was blue. Sometimes the valleys are filled with showers, melting into yellow light, and in the evening in the depths the woodthrushes sing. It was a disturbing country that rested us and somehow never let us rest. There seemed to be a divine discontent, a searching for its soul.[30]

With his wanderings, his adventures on the Clemson campus, and the days and weeks he spent on the family's farms, Ben Robertson's childhood years both informed the life he would lead and provided warm memories that would fuel a lifetime's work. And yet, as he and the family sat and talked and thought on the porch, tired after a long day of farm work, things were changing around them. The world they loved was fading into history.

Cotton had been the South's key crop for almost a century, and Pickens County's economy was centered around the crop, based on both the farms that grew cotton and the textile mills that turned it into fabric. But cotton was not only becoming a sign of the past; it was also keeping farmers from prospering. As Ben noted, while cotton had saved the South's economy after the Civil War, as a stopgap measure the crop had become a habit that was difficult to break. Though cotton farmers had been prosperous in the early 1900s, and though there had been a period after the First World War when cotton went to 40¢ a pound, farmers were not finding much profit in their crops. Sometimes, they didn't make anything; and to make matters worse, cotton farmers spent a large part of their income on fertilizers to replenish their acidic soils. Compounding all that was the devastating effect the boll weevil, an insect that began invading American cotton crops in the early 1900s, had on cotton production in the South, driving many farms out of business. Advocates of crop diversification tried to persuade farmers that planting different crops would replenish depleted soil and provide new sources of income. But many farmers refused. Cotton was familiar—too comfortable to give up as a staple crop. Ben wrote that cotton was seen as "a heaven-given crop," noting that "cotton is a state of mind with us, a philosophy, and we continue to plant it in spite of the fact that we have not made money on cotton more than once in about every ten years."[31]

In spite of hard times and falling prices, cotton farming—according to the system handed down from generation to generation—still ruled. "Cotton, with us, is almost human," Ben wrote. "Cotton is like some member of the family that the folks have had a lot of trouble with, but in whom they still believe." There were sound reasons why farmers didn't want to give up cotton. Its longevity provided farmers with a measure of comfort. Unlike food crops, it didn't perish, and a barn full of cotton meant security in hard times. While other crops could provide more money, Ben noted: "Cotton is cash to us, it is faith, it is hope." Cotton was also a six-month crop, which meant that only half the year was given over to the hard labor of agriculture; the rest of the year could be devoted to train trips to distant places, days fishing at the creek, or pursuing other interests or adventures that might beckon. Cotton meant being in charge of one's own time; but as economic situations changed and the price of cotton fell, Robertson noted that farmers' dependence on the crop "seemed to result in an economic defeat." Tenant farmers and black workers hit bottom and ultimately gave up. Grandfather Bowen, as much as anyone else in the upcountry, knew the allure of cotton, knew the feeling of sureness it provided. He also knew, however, that other measures were needed. When he spoke during meetings at the courthouse, Bowen urged his fellow farmers to diversify—to raise livestock and feed, to raise other crops, and to use lime to replenish depleted soils—for only those kinds of measures could help rural farmers retain their independence.[32]

The cherished rural way of life this independence brought came to be threatened by more than just agricultural challenges. Industrialization was moving into the region as cotton mills sprang up around the upcountry. They had started arriving in South Carolina during the 1890s, and within a decade there were more than seventy around the state. Pickens County was no exception. Its first cotton mill opened in 1895, and by 1900 there were two more. Young Ben could hear their whistles summoning employees long before daybreak, and the haunting sound filled him with unease. "There was something alarming in being ordered to rise by a factory whistle," he wrote. "It was the command that frightened, the imperative in the note. It was a sound that we had never heard before in the valley."

Although the mills came in with the promise of work and a regular paycheck (tempting for tenant farmers who were struggling to get by) to Ben the choice to "swap the furrow and the open for the cash of a daily wage" seemed like a sentence served in the gloom of a windowless factory. The industrial boom shook the faith of those in the valley. "My grandfather believed in the freedom of the spirit," Ben wrote. "The engineers believed in a standard of living." His grandmother likewise didn't care for the Northern industrial mindset. She insisted that Northerners made a living off the sweat of others.[33]

Ben's great-aunt Narcissa Clayton also recognized the problem of an industrial economy making inroads in an agricultural society. Unlike most in her family, however, she argued that the South needed to adapt rather than fight. Narcissa, in whom Ben saw depths, held her own point of view about many things. She had taught herself French and, while working as a spinner, she had passed the time by memorizing Walter Scott's *The Lady of the Lake.* A longtime teacher, she had once been offered a professorship to teach mathematics at Sweetbriar College, but she decided against it. Ben called Narcissa "one of the remarkable women of her time in the upcountry" and compared her to a cathedral, untouched by eighty years of struggle. Although she shared the Baptist and Democratic values of Ben's grandparents, Narcissa didn't believe that the United States would come around to the Southern way of doing things. The pragmatic Narcissa, who Ben remembered as someone who prepared for what could happen, believed that the South should adapt, balancing agriculture with more industry. The Bowens believed that the South's economic system would win out if only they had patience. But Narcissa pointed to "our lost opportunities, to our poverty, to the fields that were washing into the creeks." Grandfather and Grandmother Bowen disagreed, but they would hear her out, sometimes telling the children, "Your Great-Aunt Narce is like all the Claytons. She is actually proud of being peculiar." These debates—the Bowens' belief that the Southern way would prevail, Narcissa's criticisms of the region's economic and agricultural systems—lingered in Ben's mind, finding their way into his critique of the Southern economy years later.[34]

The Ben Robertson who listened to these family debates and absorbed these lessons was growing into a bright and perceptive young man. Thin and strong from working on the family farm, his adventurousness mingled with a shy and introverted nature, a love of reading, a curiosity that led him to explore, an observant eye sensitive to fine detail, and an unusual talent for the written word. Surrounded by a loving family, rooted in the familiar hills that were like a cradle, it seemed a happy way to grow up. But events unfolding half a country away, prompted by events half a world away, were about to shake Ben's life once again.

In 1917, the United States entered the First World War. Around the country, training camps for the armed forces opened. One such camp opened on the Clemson campus, and students not enrolled at the college were trained to become officers or specialists under the Student Army Training Corps. In the spring of 1918, an outbreak of influenza hit a military encampment in Kansas and spread around the United States. That September, additional cases of influenza were reported in the Boston area, as ships returning from Europe brought people and cargo that unknowingly carried the virus from outbreaks there. With the war mobilization effort spreading people around, a public health disaster was in the making. An illness that seemed to come on as a common cold rapidly turned into a killer, often developing into pneumonia, and had a high mortality rate among those aged 20 to 40. By the time the pandemic ended in 1919, it had killed 675,000 Americans.[35]

South Carolina's board of health ordered educational institutions closed as a precaution. But more than 150 cases of influenza were reported near the Clemson campus. Three buildings at the college became emergency sick wards. Campus physician Dr. Alexander May Redfern called on several local physicians and the town pharmacist to help him treat the stricken. He also enlisted the help of several women on campus to help care for the ill and dying.

Hattie Boggs Robertson answered the call. Assigned to the upper floor of the Textile Building, she helped care for the seriously ill. While tending her patients she contracted influenza, and it developed into pneumonia. She succumbed on October 19, 1918, one of two Clemson people to die in the outbreak. She was buried in the family plot, in a cemetery in nearby Liberty. On her tombstone were carved the words "Died for Humanity." For the second time in his young life, Ben mourned the loss of a mother figure.[36]

CHAPTER 3

An Education

Ben Robertson, bright and interested in the world around him, had an unusual ability with words. As he completed Clemson-Calhoun High School, he won an essay contest sponsored by the Daughters of the American Revolution. It seemed natural that a student so talented would continue his education beyond grade school.[1]

The college that had been part of his life from the beginning was nearby, and although an agricultural and mechanical school offered no majors that would allow Ben to build on his writing abilities, nevertheless he matriculated at Clemson. It was there, and it was home. "It was natural that we go to Clemson," Wright Bryan remembered. And Robertson opted for a major in horticulture. "There were no liberal arts at that time, so the student who was bound to go to Clemson was bound to choose from the courses they had," Bryan said. Since Ben had spent a childhood exploring the wilderness, learning the names of local plants, horticulture was a logical and highly accessible field of study for him.[2]

At the time the all-male Clemson was run according to a military-style regimen. Students were referred to as "cadets," lived in barracks, and were regulated according to a strict code of conduct. "The organization of the corps of cadets shall, as far as practicable, conform to that of a regiment of infantry of the Regular Army," read the *Regulations for the Government of Cadets;* and the code of conduct enforced military-style discipline and issued demerits for misbehavior.[3]

The day began with reveille at 6:30 and cadets had to be cleaned up and in uniform, with their rooms in order, by 7:20. They marched to breakfast, followed by roll call and chapel. Classes and labs occupied the morning and early afternoon, with a midday meal served family-style at 1 P.M. Cadets drilled later in the afternoon, and then had a brief period for recreation before the evening meal. The cadets then returned to barracks for study until 10 P.M., when taps signaled the end of the day and a strict lights-out policy took effect. On Saturday mornings cadets endured room inspections, then spent the afternoon meeting in literary societies or practicing public speaking before members of the faculty. Only on Saturdays did they get time for recreation. On Sundays, cadets were expected to attend services in the Memorial Chapel.[4]

All students had to take three hours of military instruction each week, and all physically-capable students were required to take Reserve Officers Training Corps (ROTC) their first two years, participating in drills and basic military training. If they passed a physical after the first two years, they took two more years of ROTC. Cadets were required to have military-style uniforms, an olive-drab uniform for drills and a dress uniform for special events.[5]

With its military-style discipline, with its strict rules and regulations, Clemson was a challenging place to continue an education. But none of it was new to Ben Robertson, who had known the college's culture all his life, and whose respect for the military had been handed down from the old soldiers whose stories had fired his imagination. In his way, he was carrying on a family tradition of service. Robertson applied himself and took his drills and his classes seriously. In his courses, Robertson used his eye for detail and his knowledge of vegetation to produce very precise detailed descriptions of plants. There were also plenty of English and literature courses available, and Ben took as many of those as he could. A hard-working student, Robertson made the honor roll in his freshman and junior years. And ever the devoted reader, he explored the huge library in the college's main building, browsing the thousands and thousands of volumes on its shelves, reading books on all different subjects. "Anyone who could learn a small part of the knowledge in that library," he told Bryan, "could set the world on fire."[6]

There were extracurricular opportunities at Clemson for a young writer, including literary societies—the Calhoun, the Columbian, and the Palmetto—the three of which together produced a magazine. The *Clemson College Chronicle,* first published as a monthly in 1897, had started out as a combination news publication and souvenir for the graduating class. Over time it evolved into a literary magazine that published student-written articles about a variety of subjects. Soon after Robertson began his studies at Clemson, the *Chronicle* published an appeal for students to join the magazine, challenging them to build their skills with words, the better to be successful in business as well as life. "Cultivate your latent powers, become a master of your language," it urged. "Your college is not a literary college. That is all the more reason for taking advantage of the chance you have before you."[7]

Robertson joined the staff of the *Clemson College Chronicle* as Junior Literary Editor, and he published his first piece in the May 1921 issue. In an essay titled "The Part South Carolina Played in the Confederacy," Robertson wrote of the heroism he found in the stories of a state at war. Inspired by the tales he'd heard as a boy, informed by his love of history, and with a dash of youthful idealism and hero worship, Robertson explored themes passed down from his elders, themes that later formed the cornerstone of his most famous work: pride in South Carolina, a sentimental and romanticized view of Confederate strength and values, balanced with pride in being part of America. True to what Grandmother Bowen taught him, Robertson's allegiances in the piece were first to South Carolina, then to the South, then the United States. He concluded with an appeal steeped in both regional and national pride, veneration for his Confederate ancestors mingling with a call to move ahead: "Time has passed and has healed the wounds of Confederate defeat. Time has also shown that Southern defeat has ended for a greater national glory. We believe that South Carolina was justified in her stand. It is now to us to live so that we may maintain the glory and valor of our state as well and as magnificently as did our grandfathers of the Confederacy. South Carolina, though defeated, has nothing of which to be ashamed, and she has resumed her position not only as a leader of the old South, but also as a prominent member of the forty-eight American Commonwealths."[8]

Robertson wrote more pieces for the *Chronicle.* One told the story of what Clemson was like in 1776, when "the forest around the junction of the Keowee and Seneca Rivers was the seat of one of the most powerful tribes in the southeastern part of the New World," only to be taken over by colonial forces after battles with the Cherokees. Robertson wrote that a monument, built on the site where Fort Rutledge had stood, marked "the supremacy of one civilization over another less progressive and less able to endure. It is only one example of the accomplishments of our far-seeing ancestors."[9]

In another *Chronicle* piece, Robertson told stories of the Old Stone Church near the Clemson campus, of the historic figures who had worshipped there and of those buried in its cemetery, including some of the legends that had been told about the place. One of the stories Robertson included in this essay signaled the region's ongoing resentment of carpetbaggers and scalawags, as well as the prevailing racial sentiments of the times:

> The Old Stone Church has been a topic of much superstition among the illiterate folks of this region. There is a story related in "The Maid of the Foot Hills" which places the scene in this old church. It was just after the War Between the States, that some carpetbaggers had called all of the negroes from the surrounding plantations to meet at the church on a particular night. The renowned Mance Jolly, hearing of their plans went to the church with a few white supporters and there concealed themselves in the gallery. Just as the negro assembly was preparing to begin its session, these men, masked as Ku

> Klux ghosts rose from the gallery and began to moan in a deathly fashion. Instantly, the horror-stricken slaves left in every conceivable direction, and for years would not think of approaching the cemetery at night. Some old darkies have sworn that on certain nights, ghosts of the dead still ride through the cemetary [*sic*].[10]

The Fort Hill mansion on the Clemson campus formed the basis of another *Chronicle* piece on local landmarks. Robertson outlined the home's history, writing that as John C. Calhoun's house it served as "a brilliant social ceinter and an economic one." Robertson told of the many historic speeches and documents Calhoun wrote in the study behind the house, and then described some of Fort Hill's interior features and some of the artifacts on display: Mrs. Calhoun's spinet, a cape made of otter skin that Mr. Calhoun often wore, a plush chair presented to Calhoun by King Leopold of Belgium, and the home's huge mahogany dining table. "It is not a lonely place," Robertson wrote, encouraging visitors and cadets to visit the house's relic room. "The mansion has the simple air of respectability and peace that so characterized the colonial home of the South."[11]

Other pieces Robertson wrote for the *Chronicle* looked at local heroes, such as the county's namesake, Revolutionary War hero General Andrew Pickens, "one of South Carolina's most sterling citizens. He stands as a shining light in the early days of statehood. He was a leader politically and socially." A lighter piece, in the December 1921 issue, provided a brief overview of Christmas traditions from around the world. Robertson's efforts, which revealed a talent for detail, combined with his devotion to the *Chronicle* earned him both a position as an editor and membership in the Palmetto Literary Society.[12]

The *Chronicle* had spawned two more campus publications. A demand for more frequent updates on happenings around campus and around town prompted students to create a college newspaper. Named the *Tiger,* the paper's first issue was published in January 1907. In 1921 Robertson joined the *Tiger* staff and the Reporters' Club. That December, he was one of four staffers who attended a meeting of the state press association in Greenville. Another outgrowth of the *Chronicle* was a yearbook, eventually called *Taps.* In February 1922, Robertson was elected editor-in-chief for the 1923 edition. "This young man is known by everyone at Clemson," read a story in the *Tiger,* "and all wish him well. If 'Ben' is as good an editor as he is a friend he will certainly make good."[13]

Clemson afforded Ben the chance to explore other areas of his creativity. As a child he had taken piano lessons, and his love for music had only grown in the years since. When he could, Robertson played the piano in Agricultural Hall's gymnasium. His musical abilities opened doors, earning him a place in

Clemson cadet Ben Robertson, Class of 1923. Special Collections & Archives, Clemson University Libraries, Clemson, South Carolina.

Clemson's Glee Club and as a founding member of the Jungleleers, also known as the "Jungle Seven," a small combo that played at local functions. Campus clubs also invited him to play the piano at their events. While with the Glee Club, Robertson set new words to "As the Caissons Go Rolling Along," turning the Army song into a tribute to the Clemson football team. But "Down by The Old Mill Stream"—according to his sister, Mary, the first song he learned how to play—remained his favorite. His fondness for that song earned Robertson the nickname "Millie" from fellow Clemson students. His music teacher, Mrs. Frank Dargan, said he could make a career of music. News of his talents at the keys spread, and at one point an offer came his way to be a pianist aboard a transatlantic liner for the summer. It was a perfect offer for a young man who loved to travel, but he had to turn it down due to a six-week infantry training course at Fort McClellan, Alabama, which was required of students in advanced ROTC.[14]

Robertson's musical abilities extended to other realms. He joined the dancing club, becoming its secretary and treasurer, and often popped up at social events around Clemson. The once-shy country boy grew gregarious, and people enjoyed his company. "He made more friends, young and old, high and low" than other students, Wright Bryan recalled years later. "He never cared whether a friend was simple or complex, poor or rich, weak or powerful. He simply loved people and they loved him." The 1923 edition of *Taps* described "Millie" as a "gossip fiend" for whom "tales of intrigue are like music to his ears," but summed him up as "a mighty fine chap. To know him is to like him."[15]

The likable Ben Robertson had grown into a handsome young man. By this time he had reached his full height of five feet, ten inches. While the life of a cadet kept him thin, Robertson eventually filled out to a weight of about 165 pounds. Broad at the shoulders and slender at the waist, he had a long face, which fleshed out in later years. It was punctuated by blue, slightly sad eyes that twinkled when he broke into one of his frequent, friendly, sometimes mischievous smiles. His head was topped with black hair that, in later years, started to recede. Though he had a soft Southern voice, his sister remembered that he pronounced all his words clearly.[16]

While at Clemson, Robertson further explored his wanderlust—an attribute of his character that he believed ran in his genes, and that he would explore in many of his adult writings. "We can forget time in our country and be contented," he wrote, "and then the old restlessness will stir again, like a wind rising; and we have to travel. We are all like that."[17]

Travel was in his genes, in the stories of family lore, and in his youth. As a child, he and his sister Mary had made countless trips on the Pickens Doodle to visit their grandparents. In the fall, when the cash came in from selling the cotton crop, Ben and his family would board the Southern Railway excursion trains, off to see sights in Georgia or Tennessee or Virginia or whatever destination sounded interesting. Even when the trains were packed with other travelers, the family enjoyed the trip. "We did not care much where the excursion went nor what was the occasion," he remembered. "We went along for the ride, for the joy of traveling on a train." In later years Robertson wrote that traveling as the miles passed along on a train or sailing on a ship counted among his favorite things, and he would seldom pass up an opportunity to take to the rails or put to sea.[18]

The love of travel, deep in his genes, never let up. A cousin once floated the idea of driving to California to see the Pacific Ocean. It struck Ben as a strange notion. "I have no business at the Pacific Ocean," he replied. But his Grandmother Bowen, sitting in a corner, disagreed. "Go ahead," she said. "Go while you have the chance." Ben and his cousin set out for California the next day, by way of Virginia.[19]

The need to travel carried on through his years at Clemson. One summer break, Robertson traveled to Kansas and Oregon, working in wheat fields and orchards to earn his keep along the way. Yet no matter where he went, no matter how far away, Clemson always called him back. One lazy day late that summer, piano music started wafting from the open windows of Agricultural Hall, and within minutes, from house to house, the news spread: "Millie is home." And just as quickly, so many of his friends gathered around the piano, glad to welcome their friend back to Clemson.[20]

Ben Robertson graduated from Clemson in the Class of 1923. With his horticulture degree, he could have easily turned toward a degree in agricultural science. With his ROTC training, he could have accepted an Army commission and started a military career. But his experiences on the *Tiger,* the *Chronicle,* and *Taps* had reinforced a love for chronicling what he saw and sharing it with a larger audience. In its way, it was an extension of the storytelling with which he grew up. It was natural for a young man who years earlier had haunted the local drug store seeking the latest news on the developing war in Europe. And better still, journalism provided opportunities to travel far, see new places, and gain new experiences.

In 1923, more than two hundred colleges and universities in the United States offered some form of instruction in journalism. The most prestigious was at the University of Missouri, whose journalism school had been established in 1908 by Walter Williams. It was where the quietly ambitious Robertson wanted to go. What his family's stories had inspired, and what his experiences as a Clemson student had helped him build, Missouri would refine.[21]

As the young editor and part-owner of a small weekly newspaper, the *Boonville Advertiser,* Walter Williams had grown disgusted with the "newspaper wars" in which competing publications hurled invective at one another. Instead, he wanted to build a journalism profession in which reporters and editors got along. In 1889, as the twenty-five-year-old president of the Missouri Press Association, Williams visited newspaper offices all over the state and urged that the press should "stand for the noblest in thought and deed."[22]

Williams became an advocate for formal education in the journalism profession. It wasn't a new idea in Missouri. For years the state legislature had considered proposals to establish a journalism program at the state university. None of those efforts had succeeded. But in 1898, Williams was named to the university's Board of Curators. As a board member, he befriended the university's young new president, Richard Henry Jesse, and sold him on the idea of a journalism school. But greater support was long in coming. As time passed, other states considered journalism programs for their universities, and Joseph Pulitzer, feeling remorseful for his part in escalating "yellow journalism," proposed a journalism school at Columbia University. When it was clear that the idea of a journalism school at Missouri wasn't an isolated idea that would quickly become an afterthought, Williams' efforts finally gained traction.

Missouri's journalism program, with Williams as its dean, held its first classes in the autumn of 1908. The program combined a series of courses in journalism fundamentals with the production of a newspaper, the *Daily Missourian,* a community newspaper which served as a laboratory for students to practice what they were taught. Classes in the journalism program began at eight o'clock each morning and were dismissed by ten, when the students went to work on their assignments for the newspaper.[23]

By 1923, the Missouri program was well known; and for Ben Robertson, it was an opportunity to get the kind of education that Clemson's agricultural focus could not provide. Years later Robertson's friends couldn't pinpoint why he wanted to enroll at the University of Missouri, but Wright Bryan suspected the reputations of both the school and its founder played a role in the decision. It also didn't hurt that the Missouri campus was hundreds of miles from his South Carolina home, giving new opportunities for adventure to a young man who always loved experiencing new places. Whatever his reasons for leaving Clemson and heading west to study, Robertson's studies at Missouri profoundly shaped not only his career, but also his view of the world. (And whatever Robertson's reasons for attending Missouri's journalism school, they apparently influenced Bryan to follow him there in 1926.) As he began the journalism program in 1923, the twenty-year-old Robertson would come to know Williams well—the man who would not only help Robertson launch his international journalism career, but who also forever influenced his views on the mission of journalism.[24]

Each incoming journalism student was required to take "History and Principles of Journalism," a course Williams developed and taught. Although Missouri's catalog stated that the course was designed to "present the main facts of the history of newspaper making, of journalism in various periods and conditions, the meaning and aims of journalism and its fundamental principles," Dean Williams saw the course as something more. As Williams' biographer Ronald Farrar wrote, the dean felt he must "sell his students—sell them on the task ahead, on the worth of their chosen major, and indeed, on the worth of journalism itself." The class was not so much a class, Farrar noted, as "professional indoctrination, the critically important first step in shaping the visions of those who could have an impact on their, and his, profession." Williams required all students to memorize a lengthy creed he had written, a statement of values for journalists that one editorial compared to the Hippocratic Oath. In it, Williams stated that "the public journal is a public trust; that all connected with it are, to the full measure of their responsibility, trustees for the public; that acceptance of lesser service than the public service is a betrayal of this trust." It condemned suppression of the news; disapproved of taking bribes; stated that advertising, news, and editorials should serve the good of the readers; and made clear that "the supreme test of good journalism is the measure of its public service." To drive home the importance of the creed and all it stood for, Williams tested students on it soon after they joined the journalism program.[25]

As Robertson sat in Williams' lectures at Neff Hall, the great teacher discoursed on the names, places, and events of journalism history. Though Williams commanded respect, as Farrar notes, some students found his lectures "platitudinous and dull"; a few complained that he would "preach instead of teach," right down to using Biblical material in the lectures, some of the same material Williams used in his Sunday school class. And though Robertson tried to be attentive and took careful notes in his bold cursive, sometimes Williams segued into one of his trademark sermons. His focus wandering, Robertson sketched in the margins of his notebook.[26]

When not in class that first semester or working on assignments for the *Daily Missourian* under its manager, Frank Martin, Robertson investigated the university's social opportunities. According to one story, a letter of introduction from a Clemson friend earned Ben an invitation to the Phi Delta house near the end of rush. The visit had been a little awkward, as the quiet Robertson had trouble hitting it off with the brothers. But over in a corner of the room, Robertson saw a piano that appeared to have sat idle for some time. As the conversation went on, his host mentioned that the fraternity needed musicians. "Do you play the piano?" he asked. "A little," Robertson replied. With eight of the brothers in tow, he sat down quietly at the keyboard, and the music began to speak for him. According to one account, the music "could be heard all the way up to the third floor." That quickly, Phi Delta had a new pianist, and a new brother.[27]

Robertson was an apt student; during his first semester at Missouri, he took six courses and managed average marks in Journalism, Principles of Advertising, Psychology, and Elementary French; above average marks in History and Principles of Journalism; and an Excellent mark in English. But as soon as classes were over he was on the road again, spending part of the winter at the home of a friend in the mountains of Oregon.[28]

After a year at Missouri, Robertson took a year off to return to South Carolina, gain some experience in the practice of journalism, and earn a little money to pay for his next year of school. Robertson joined the staff of the Charleston *News and Courier*. He first worked the sports beat, but soon earned general assignments from the city desk: hiring of new professors at area colleges, meetings of civic and business organizations, and stories dealing with agricultural meetings and events. Often these stories brought him in contact with the powerful and influential of Charleston. Robertson built connections with Herbert Ravenel Sass, who became an author of renown in the South, and city editor Tom Lesesne, whose editorials held great influence throughout the state. Robertson also developed a friendship with a young businessman, Burnet Maybank, who had his eyes on the mayor's office.[29]

Throughout his assignments, Robertson reported in a personal, folksy storytelling style that painted in vivid detail—"Mush, slush, ooze and rain were there in abundance and throughout the afternoon the players dove and wallowed like pigs in a mud pen," he wrote of a football game played after a downpour. Robertson also began writing human-interest stories, showing a particular talent for character sketches, fine detail, and the unusual qualities that became a professional hallmark.[30]

Whenever his stories appeared, Robertson clipped and pasted them into a ledger for posterity. Not only did he save his own stories, but he clipped other stories of interest by his fellow staff members. Sometimes those stories were about Charleston's shipping industry and the great ships that called at the busy port. Other clippings spoke of places far beyond, such as Honolulu and Tahiti, exotic ports that beckoned the inquisitive spirit of a young journalist and the curiosity of a born wanderer.[31]

In 1925 Robertson resumed his studies at Missouri, and he completed his degree requirements the following year. From Dean Williams, who had mentored Robertson as a journalist in much the same way Grandfather Bowen had influenced him as a person, Robertson had learned important lessons. He had learned that to be considered a profession, journalism had to matter. And he also knew Williams's belief that "he who has not set eyes on the outside world is not a journalist." With his mentor's help, Ben Robertson was about to see the world.[32]

CHAPTER 4

In Exile

In his many travels, Walter Williams had become well connected. During his visits to news organizations around the world—in Latin America, Europe, South America, and the Pacific—he took care to cultivate good contacts with editors and publishers. With this network of acquaintances the world over, Williams could easily arrange for his students and graduates to get positions with newspapers and press organizations. His friends in the trade trusted Williams' judgment and were glad to hire his students, knowing they had been trained well and that they would work hard. In the process Williams could not only help fledgling reporters, but also he could build the Missouri program's reputation as a source of bright and able journalists.[1]

Dean Williams helped many students in this way. One of them was twenty-three-year-old Ben Robertson, eager to start seeing the world, for whom Williams arranged a job with the *Honolulu Star-Bulletin* in mid-1926. Robertson publicly said nothing about his dean's intervention, but to Wright Bryan he admitted that Williams got him hired in Hawaii. "I know from personal experience while at Missouri that Dean Williams had numerous contacts in the Pacific area," Bryan told an interviewer decades later, "and it would have been easy for him to arrange the job."[2]

Robertson set out for San Francisco, where he began a five-day voyage to Honolulu. The new graduate, who barely had the money to make the trip, arrived at the *Honolulu Star-Bulletin* offices. The staff needed a financial reporter. "Sure, I could do it," Robertson told them. He knew how to cover cotton, but tropical crops were new to him, and he needed help. His editor, Riley Allen, gave him information on some contacts who could help. "I picked out one in pineapples and one in sugar and confided my predicament," Robertson later said. "Each said he would help me." For six months, as he built familiarity with Hawaii's economy, Robertson let the two men review his copy before he submitted it to his editor.[3]

Although agricultural markets were his primary beat, Robertson did a little of everything, working as a general assignment reporter and even contributing book reviews. As he covered events wherever Allen needed a hand, Robertson built a talent for stories that demonstrated the human side of big events. When Mount Kilauea rumbled back to life in the summer of 1927, Robertson's account of visiting the site focused as much on visitors' reactions to the volcano and what it meant for increased tourism as it did on the eruption itself:

> Many Honolulu people were at the Volcano house during these days. Hundreds of people, representative of this greatest age of civilization, gazed at the boiling fire a quarter of a miles below. They were as afraid and as silent as the first man who saw the first fire and was afraid.
>
> A pillar of cloud hung over the pit by day. A pillar of fire, a rose-colored reflection, hung over it by night.
>
> The crowd arriving Saturday rushed straight to the pit. It returned to the Volcano House in time for dinner. Dinner was to be served at 6:30 o'clock. By 6:15 P.M. these civilized people began to gather at the door. At 6:30 they made a mad rush. Again the strongest and the longest survived. In a few more minutes in modulated style they were ordering a perfectly proper meal, fingering napkins, and picking up silver knives, forks, and spoons.
>
> They had come to see the volcano, they had seen it, they were enjoying their meal—very satisfied.[4]

As Robertson explored the islands, he came to love their exotic beauty. And he developed an admiration for Hawaii's people, in whom he saw a "friendly disposition" that "struck the happy medium of existence." As he later wrote, "Few people in modern times have developed a State with more intellectual wisdom, with greater industrial possibilities or with finer social understanding than the people of Hawaii . . . they have established order, set up and carried on a government, organized industry and finance, established political aid and religious freedom, and to a degree almost unparalleled in contemporary history have learned to respect a neighbor's right of dissent."[5]

Robertson wasn't the only Missouri student to make it to Hawaii. His classmate and friend Edgar Snow came to the islands on the first leg of what he hoped would be a round-the-world adventure, and the friendship between the two men strengthened. And Dean Williams, en route to the Orient, had visited Robertson during a stop in Hawaii, happy to see his former pupil flourishing in his new job. After a year, however, Robertson wanted something new, and he wrote to his mentor for help. Again drawing on his network, Williams contacted J. E. Davidson, publisher of the *News-Limited* in Adelaide, Australia. The *News-Limited* was expanding and Williams knew Davidson needed more reporters, so he gave Robertson a hearty recommendation. Davidson, heeding his friend's

Robertson (reclining, at left) and friends enjoying pineapple on an adventure somewhere in the Pacific during the 1920s. Special Collections & Archives, Clemson University Libraries, Clemson, South Carolina.

"sound judgment of men and journalists," offered the young man from Clemson a position on the reporting staff. With an added recommendation from Riley Allen, Robertson took the job and sailed for Australia at the end of the year. His friends at the *Star-Bulletin,* sad to see him go, threw a farewell dinner for him and fellow staffer Robert Unseld. Though Robertson was en route to new adventures, he admitted that "it's hard to say aloha to Hawaii," and for the rest of his life he would think of the islands with fondness and vow to come back.[6]

Robertson sailed to Adelaide and began his new job with the *News-Limited.* In between assignments, he explored the fascinating new land around him, feeding his endless curiosity and thirst for adventure. "I'm afraid I'll never make a successful tourist," he wrote on a postcard to his father from Hobart, Tasmania, in February 1928. "While the people on the boat were off on a trip, I have spent the morning inspecting a Norwegian whaling ship in from the season in the Antarctic—odor like the place where they burned horses."[7]

He began gathering material which formed the basis for freelance articles he later sold, noting with some amusement that Australians' three major enemies were dingoes, kangaroos, and rabbits. Out among the bush people, Robertson met people whose independence and spirit reminded him of his family's journey, and he described the bush people as "a Saxon folk." Fighting dust storms and droughts and flies and heat to make their lives, Robertson wrote, the bush people had "scorn[ed] the luxuries of effete cities. In their boots they have lived and in their boots they will die."[8]

In early November Robertson visited the Western Australian town of Broome, whose shoreline on the Indian Ocean yielded "the shell for seventy-five per cent of the pearl buttons of commerce," a bustling little town with two banks, several pearl buyers, and a reputation as "the drunkenest town in Australia." Robertson talked to locals and observed the native pearl divers who competed with those who came from other countries to harvest the valuable prizes from the deep. In the sweltering evenings, he sometimes cooled down in one of the town's many pubs. One night he met a man, originally from Kansas City, who had deserted from a battleship two decades before. The man sat down with Robertson, commenced "a gin-ordering barrage with the bar below" and, after two hours of Australian hard gin, had told much to his fellow American.

A few days later Robertson was boarding a ship to return to Adelaide. The exiled American whom Robertson had met at the pub came by to see him off, carrying a copy of Broome's weekly newspaper. In it, Robertson read that Herbert Hoover had been elected President of the United States, defeating Democrat Al Smith. "A bloody shame, I reckon," the man said. "I had hoped to see Al get it. Maybe then the country would have opened again and flourished. We will never have prohibition in Australia. We've got too strong a government."[9]

Soon Robertson again grew restless. Eight months after arriving in Adelaide he left the *News-Limited,* bound for Java in the islands of Indonesia. His mind set on a newspaper job there, Robertson found himself frustrated when he discovered there were no English-language papers in Java. His friend from Hawaii, Bob Unseld, had become vice-consul for the American Consular Service in Surabaya under Consul General Edward Groth. So with Unseld's help, Robertson went to work at the consulate.

The Americans were headquartered in an old mansion, No. 2 Kroesenpark, once occupied by Dutch traders and then sold to the Americans by a sugar estate official who retired back to Amsterdam. Its stucco yellowed by years of blazing sun, the house was surrounded by tall mango trees whose fruit frequently landed on the roof "with the sound of a minor cannon." Nearby was a pavilion that served as living quarters for Robertson, Unseld, and two other men.[10]

There was much for the consulate staff to do. Under Dutch colonial rule, Surabaya had become an important center for industry and trade, and its port was of vital importance. In the late 1920s, trade with Java was booming. American ships came with manufactured goods and took home such commodities as tea, rubber, and quinine. There were invoices to review and approve, visiting businessmen to advise, tourists to look after, the occasional crisis to resolve. Robertson was surrounded by an interesting variety of scenes and characters; and in between writing reports and providing assistance to visitors and residents, Robertson kept a journal of what he saw, stockpiling stories, anecdotes, and character sketches for use in later pieces. The most memorable of the characters he met was the consulate's resident cook, an older woman the staff called Aunt Ella. A native of Java, she had worked for the consulate since it opened and had accumulated countless stories about previous consuls, anecdotes she readily shared. Although she had never left Java, Aunt Ella had learned how to make dishes that made the staff feel like they were at home: Maryland-style fried chicken, Boston baked beans, cornbread, and biscuits.[11]

Surabaya was a strange place to the young man from South Carolina. The long Dutch presence in the port city meant European colonial architecture in the midst of the Asian tropics. The temperatures were warm year-round, with high humidity and strong breezes from the harbor, and a rainy season lasting roughly half a year. In those hot months, Robertson could watch the clouds stack over the valley until rain poured in mid-afternoon, almost as if on schedule. In the center of Surabaya, a red bridge spanned the Kali Mas, the river that flowed through town. Robertson watched the thousands who traveled back and forth across the bridge carrying all kinds of goods, the cars and carts that jockeyed for space on the bridge and in the crowded thoroughfares, the policeman on a striped iron stand who directed traffic with wild arm gestures, the boats passing on the river, the peddlers and their carts on the streets. People from Japan, China, India, the Netherlands, Portugal, and America mingled among the local residents, "a lively and thronging multitude of races."[12]

Years later, Robertson remembered his months in Java, and the feelings he and his coworkers had in this fantastic land, seized by a "remote and curious feeling . . . wonderfully excited by so much strangeness about us yet homesick all the time and lonely for another land." To him and the other Americans, he wrote, "it was a foreign, alien, faraway scene and like all Americans who are forced by their business to live long abroad—we grieved. We were exiles from home and we knew it."[13]

The men of the consulate weren't alone. Every so often, some American oil drillers came down from Borneo. They often met up with the consular staff at the Hotel Oranje, desperate to connect with fellow countrymen and talk about all the things they left behind in America. As the oilmen talked about how much they missed their homes in California, Robertson's thoughts drifted back to South Carolina. Other times, the homesickness could be prompted by a random encounter with a visitor. One day a traveler from Georgia passed through the consulate, speaking in what Robertson described to Wright Bryan as "the most Southern dialect ever heard in this consulate before." And even an investigation into the gathering of kapok pods, whose fiber was harvested to make mattress stuffing, could make him yearn for home. Not only did the fluffy mounds of harvested kapok fiber look like cotton, but the length and rhythms of the kapok season reminded Robertson of the cotton season he knew well from his Pickens County childhood.[14]

Robertson and his colleagues spent their days at the old mansion "to keep office hours from nine to five and to eat cereal with canned cream for breakfast and to talk, during the sultry evenings, of the tariffs on coffee and spices and of the poor chances of the Democratic Party." Homesick, he read old newspapers and wrote letters back home. His yearning to be back in South Carolina only worsened. He begged Bryan for news from Clemson, reminiscing about funny moments from the childhood they shared there. A Clemson professor who sent along a book about the college's namesake triggered more nostalgia and longing. "I am anxious to get back," Robertson wrote. "It will be a gold day when I shall again see home and all of you." And even some of Robertson's friends from back home were astonished by his frequent changes of venue. "How many more countries are you going to before coming home?" wrote one. "I thought you were back on native soil and there comes your letter from Java."[15]

During his time in Java, Robertson came down with a tropical illness. Too weak to work, he lay on his bed in the pavilion, a stack of books nearby. One day during his convalescence, he started on *Leaves of Grass.* As he read through Walt Whitman's songs of the American spirit, he later wrote, he had a revelation, that he "for the first time saw the vision of our people . . . all moving through American time and the vast territories of American space, homesick themselves and lonely; an American exodus, a long westward search for a way of living, for spiritual rest." It connected with the same impulse he had felt, the exodus that had led him to Missouri, then Hawaii, then to Australia, and to Java—and the same yearning he now felt to return to South Carolina.[16]

Robertson decided then that he wanted to capture that spirit somehow—to "catch the glimpse I had of a plain family making its way in America . . . to show a group of Americans as they had been from the beginning, as their children were, as surely their children's children would be—a people almost always living for the future." It would take time to make a reality, but the seeds for a southern literary classic were planted during his time in Java.[17]

In the meantime, Robertson did his work on behalf of the consulate, using spare moments to capture his impressions of what he saw, filling notebooks with the raw material for future articles. Already looking ahead, he compiled a listing of addresses for publications that might buy some of these pieces.

After five months working in Java, Robertson headed for home. With money saved from his salary and proceeds from freelance work, he came home the long way: via Borneo, India, Europe, and England, completing his global circuit with a voyage across the Atlantic aboard the *Berengaria.* He returned to Clemson with full notebooks and countless memories—plenty of raw material for future articles. And deep within, he returned with an idea for a lasting memorial to the people he came from and to the spirit that drove them.[18]

CHAPTER 5

The Hope of the Herald Tribune

Having seen the world, Ben Robertson hoped he could make a living from Clemson as a freelance writer. But it didn't take long for him to feel frustrated in the little college town. Late in 1929 he was off again, this time moving to Manhattan to report for the New York *Herald Tribune.* It proved to be a good fit for Robertson, for if there was no way *Herald Tribune* could match the might of the *New York Times,* it would instead distinguish itself as a readers' newspaper with stylish, high-quality writing.

Robertson joined the paper while the city room was under the leadership of Stanley Walker. Like Robertson, Walker had grown up on a farm, although in Walker's case it was in rural Texas. Walker had attended the University of Texas, interning on a newspaper in Austin, then working for a newspaper in Dallas. A year later, he had headed for New York, working his way through several newspaper and freelance jobs before becoming night editor of the *Herald Tribune* in 1926. By the time Robertson joined the paper's staff, Walker was in his first full year of running the city room.[1]

In 1929 the *Herald Tribune* was doing well, and Walker had the space to fill the city pages with anecdotes about life in Manhattan. A history of the *Herald Tribune,* Richard Kluger's *The Paper,* called Walker's creation "a new style of social journalism that aimed at capturing the temper and feel of the city, its moods and fancies . . . daily helpings of what amounted to urban anthropology." While Walker relied on some veteran newspapermen to help, he mostly called upon the talents of educated newcomers to the profession, luring them in with the attraction of writing for a quality newspaper. Walker liked to hire smart, young men who were not tied to families, able to keep long and flexible hours, old enough to know their way around, but not old enough to be world-weary—and young enough to still feel that reporting in a big city was an adventure. Walker hired these "eager, intelligent, unterrified youngsters" and inspired them to do good work, letting them develop their own styles, insisting that "most of the music in journalism is played by ear."[2]

In the twenty-six-year-old Robertson, Walker would have seen just this sort of reporter—and, perhaps, a little of himself; and as Robertson settled in to his new job chronicling life in Manhattan, Walker took a liking to the copy Robertson turned in. "I have the happy news for you that I am succeeding in my work," Robertson wrote to his father in January 1930. "Yesterday, the boss told me, he would put in for a raise for me next month and that 'the hope of the *Herald Tribune* for me was distinguished.'"[3]

Robertson found a happy journalistic home at the *Herald Tribune,* and he filled his personal journals with anecdotes about the scenes he saw and the characters he met. A friend described Robertson in those years as a reporter who "prowled through the East Side, and lived in Greenwich Village and wrote charming little pieces about ferry boat captains." Robertson's articles sketched out, for instance, the troubles a veteran theater stagehand had seen in his thirty years on the job. One day he would accompany the charismatic African-American spiritual leader Reverend Major Jealous Divine and a group of his followers on a journey around New York; on another, he would walk along with a Ku Klux Klan parade through a rainy Greenwich Village, making notes as he rode with the Kleagle to avoid the downpour, dodging the tomatoes hurled at the parade by angry onlookers.[4]

Years later journalist Helen Kirkpatrick, who worked alongside him on his most famous assignment, would describe Ben Robertson as "basically a tremendously serious man," but one with warmth, intelligence, "a strong sense of the ridiculous, a gurgling sense of humor, and a way of telling even the most banal thing in a fascinating way. He had no self-importance at all."[5]

Robertson's experience reporting in Hawaii prompted the *Herald Tribune* to send him there in 1931 to examine the territory's military installations. In a lengthy examination of the American naval base at Pearl Harbor, Robertson wrote:

> Pearl Harbor is a hard-boiled old trooper really; but she looks like a mother of angels. To know the old girl you must go there at night time during the maneuvers. Then she sheds her flowers and really acts herself. . . . Only then, during that roar and fury, does one realize the magnitude of the destruction which might emanate from that peaceful lagoon. Only then does one sense the power of Pearl Harbor on the world's paper. Even then, however, one cannot connect the village of the noonday with the terror of the dark. The two continue as divorced in memory as Dr. Jekyl [*sic*] does from Mr. Hyde.
>
> Pearl Harbor is essential in our scheme of things; it is intellectually honest; its efficiency, its pace, bring us to a pride in our country's achievement. None the less, the sight of it leaves one with a peculiarly depressed feeling—if only it were not so idyllic in appearance. If only, like Aden, it were on some gaunt,

One of Stanley Walker's "eager, intelligent, unterrified youngsters" at the *Herald Tribune.* Special Collections & Archives, Clemson University Libraries, Clemson, South Carolina.

> rock-ribbed coast; if only, like Gibraltar, there were the glint of iron in its eye; if only it even managed to look like a patch for cabbage. It is no place for orchids.[6]

Walker also gave Robertson opportunities to write about the places he'd been and the stories he'd captured. In 1932, for instance, Robertson wrote about Hawaiians' relationship with the fire goddess Pele. On another occasion, he wrote a character sketch of a cook he had known in Hawaii. Robertson also wrote a piece about the growing movement for Hawaii statehood, which was widely syndicated. He noted that despite concerns about the Japanese ancestry of many Hawaiians, "the Americans of Hawaii are considered there to be as fine, as Nordic and as Saxon in sympathy as are the people of Missouri"; and he repeated a former territorial governor's insistence that the people of Hawaii are good citizens. "About the only thing the territory lacks is independence in name," he wrote. "That, however, is an idealistic thing which always has worried the American people. No group of them for long will accept the privileges of freedom without demanding that they be allowed to accept the obligations and responsibilities. The demand then from Honolulu for statehood may be expected to become increasingly insistent." In another piece, Robertson wrote about Americans in the Dutch East Indies. He found that transient Americans—tourists and sailors—had a fine time and that representatives traveling through on short sales tours ranging from a month to a year managed to find adventure; but that the Americans who were permanently stationed in the East Indies "selling motor cars and gasoline and taking orders for sewing machines and cigarettes," while well-paid and living in grand style, were yet homesick, dissatisfied, and unhappy.[7]

Soon Robertson's talent for character pieces, often written in a warm, personal tone, gained him the attention of Mrs. William Brown Meloney, editor of the *Herald Tribune* Sunday magazine, who encouraged the young reporters to expand their craft. "O, that all editors were as understanding of our genius as Mrs. Meloney!" wrote his Missouri classmate Edgar Snow, who had planned to travel around the world, but who ended up covering China as a Shanghai-based correspondent. "We would—you and I at least—get along so much more rapidly if they were." Robertson completed several articles for Meloney's magazine, many of them drawing on his personal experiences or interests. Among them were profiles of Australian Prime Minister J. H. Scullin; Sir Douglas Mawson, who had led an Australian expedition to the Antarctic; and Robertson's mentor, Walter Williams, who had just been named president of the University of Missouri. "Dean Williams possesses many attitudes of mind markedly akin to those of Mark Twain," Robertson wrote. "Like the great humorist, he is the sort of American who most confounds modern understanding—that citizen who can talk of wagons among the stars without once losing sight of the fact that a hundred copper pennies can make a silver Yankee dollar."[8]

Robertson counted his friendship with Williams as one of his most meaningful and treasured, and he relished any opportunity to visit with his mentor. One day in August 1930 Robertson joined a group of reporters headed out to the liner *Europa* as it approached New York, going aboard to interview notable passengers. In the great ship's lounge, Robertson met up with Williams, "my well-loved friend and former teacher," who with his wife had just completed a tour of Germany. Happy to see his former student, Williams asked, "Well, Ben, how do you like newspaper work?"

"I love it," Robertson said.

"So do I," the dean replied, confessing that as he interviewed German Chancellor Franz von Papen, he was so excited that he fought the urge to cable the story back to America. "I still feel like that," Williams said, "and I haven't been an actual reporter in nearly fifty years."[9]

For Robertson, part of the pleasure he took in reporting was working in a busy newsroom with other young journalists on the way up. The open-minded and easygoing Robertson built friendships that lasted beyond his time at the *Herald Tribune.* One of those friends was John Whitaker, a Tennessean two years

Robertson's junior, not long graduated from Sewanee. Another Sewanee man on the staff, Tom Waring, hailed from a well-known Charleston family; and after a brief period with the *Herald Tribune,* Waring returned to South Carolina to become city editor of the *News and Courier.* Robertson also bonded with another young reporter on the *Herald Tribune* staff, Columbia-educated Robert Neville, who began his journalism career as a fourteen-year-old typesetter in Wyoming. With time Robertson's friendships extended beyond the city room to include members of the Reid family, who owned the paper. And sometimes Robertson found himself explaining the South's idiosyncrasies to some of his colleagues. A Charleston friend of *Herald Tribune* columnist Beverly Smith told her that although alcohol was against the law there, several kinds of homemade liquor were readily available. One day, Smith pulled Robertson aside and asked how much liquor cost in his part of South Carolina.

"Two dollars a gallon," Robertson answered.

"Is it hard to get?"

"You can get it anywhere."

"And how does your part of the state vote on the prohibition laws?"

"Bone dry," Robertson said. "As dry as any section in the country."[10]

For his part, the grandson of a prohibitionist had no problem with visiting speakeasies, or joining in when one of his colleagues said, "I'm going downstairs." Just behind the *Herald Tribune* offices, was 213 West 40th Street, "downstairs" and home of the idiosyncratically named Artist and Writer's Restaurant, popularly known as Bleeck's. A watering hole popular with the *Herald Tribune* staff, the proprietor gave the paper's employees preferential treatment. There, friendships were forged, arguments took place, games were played, wagers were made, and reporters decompressed.[11]

With colleagues he enjoyed and an apartment in Washington Heights—and considering Manhattan's endless array of interesting characters to write about—Ben Robertson's life seemed to have just about everything a young reporter could want. The one thing he didn't have was a romantic relationship. Friends occasionally tweaked Robertson, imagining a young and well-paid New York newspaperman on the town. "How many chorines are you keeping on the surplus?" asked Edgar Snow. "Don't pass up the right girl if she happens along," advised another friend. But no evidence remains that Ben Robertson engaged in a lasting romantic relationship. His personal journals, though long on his thoughts about politics and society and the things he observed, give no indication of any relationships. If anything, his notes indicate a bemused view of romance; on one occasion, he scribbled down anecdotes about scenes he'd witnessed in lobbies and at telephone booths, of young women on the town flirting, of a wife fleeing a marriage. In a letter to a friend discussing a mutual acquaintance's marriage Robertson mused, "I don't know what to think about marriage, either. Friendship seems to be the best and most lasting relationship for a lot of people." That is what Robertson chose instead, building enduring and warm friendships with several female friends. With them, his correspondence displayed a closeness akin to a sibling relationship.[12]

When Mary used Ben's notes from his 1937 sea voyage to complete his novel about the sea, published in 1966 as *The Pilgrim: Voyage 37,* she based protagonist Jack Clemson very closely on her brother. In the novel, Jack turns down his girlfriend's strong desire to get married, choosing instead to go to sea. Though it doesn't destroy their friendship, it ends the romance. Although the episode in *The Pilgrim* is fictionalized, the surviving evidence supports the basic truth behind it. Ben Robertson's yearning to experience the world, to write about what he saw, to have the freedom to go new places when he needed to, and to feed his urge to be on the move, appears to have been far more important to him than marriage. Perhaps if Robertson's life had allowed him to settle in one place, if his work hadn't involved protracted periods far from home and had the call of the next adventure not been so alluring, Robertson might have married and had a family. Instead, Robertson remained unattached, able to go on to the next assignment and the next location without having to leave anyone behind. Memories of losing both his mother and his stepmother may also have haunted him. In any event, the surviving evidence indicates that being single gave Robertson what he most treasured: the freedom to go places.[13]

Travel was important to this man who fed a hundred fascinations, who was genuinely interested in just about anything. Robertson wrote that his hobbies included "birds and sailing ships and the lighthouse, coast and geodetic surveys, the forestry service and national parks and the Indian Bureau." But of all his interests, the strongest was his love of ships and the sea. New York, the great seaport, let him see an endless array of ships and introduced him to men who made their living at sea. One of his friends in New York was Captain Thomas Sheridan, a master mariner with a gift for writing. With Sheridan, Robertson could talk about sailing and learn more about the life of a mariner. And whenever the opportunity arose, he put to sea. In May 1933, Robertson lived out a dream by joining ten other men aboard the *Wander Bird,* a 101-foot, German-built pilot schooner owned by former *Herald Tribune* staffer Warwick Tompkins, for a two-week voyage from Nova Scotia to Gloucester.[14]

But Robertson also saw New York in a time of immense economic depression. Years of economic prosperity came to a close in October 1929 as the stock market plummeted. Confidence in the economy soon fell. In the last two months of 1930, some six hundred banks went out of business. People rapidly lost jobs, homes, and savings.[15] Around Robertson, the signs of hard times were unmistakable. Talking to the owner of a shoe shop off Broadway, he learned that while people once bought nice shoes and had them repaired, they now bought cheap shoes and didn't have them fixed when they wore through the soles. Leaving the shop, Robertson walked past an old woman who told him, "It is a pleasant night." He noticed that her head was wrapped in a peasant's shawl, and that she was playing tunes on a ground organ, busking for small change. She bowed to Robertson when he offered her a dime.[16] One evening Robertson went to a motion picture with Stanley Groth, Robertson's boss from his days in Surabaya. Visiting New York for the first time since the Depression had hit, Groth said he didn't see many signs of hardship. Robertson disagreed, noting that a person "must be here day by day to notice the depression": the crowds everywhere were smaller, seats on the subways easier to get.[17]

In August 1931 Robertson was on a visit to Europe. At Copenhagen, he joined an American freighter headed home from a port call in Leningrad, loaded with Russian timber. One evening he stood watch with a sailor who had left a farm in Montana to earn a living in the merchant marine. The sailor had tried farming, trapping, and being a university student, but found no contentment in any of them. The Depression had left him hopeless; but after his ship's port call in Leningrad, where the American sailors were treated as special guests and were invited to spend the night in the czar's old palace, he was transformed. "The Russians are free," the seaman said. "Whatever I once thought I was, I know, now that I have been to Russia, where I stand in the United States. I am a worker and a worker is a slave. A worker has no more chance in our country than a turnip. I am for revolution." Back in New York, Robertson went to see his tailor on South Street. The tailor asked Robertson if he'd heard about the American sailors who had been to Russia. "What do you think of that?" Robertson replied, "Think? I think that perhaps the Russians are clever." The tailor replied, "That palace tale has spread like magic. A fellow in here the other day from the *President Hoover* told me he had heard it on the Dollar docks in San Francisco."[18]

That December, Robertson profiled "Aunt Molly" Jackson, a folksinger, midwife, and activist from Harlan, Kentucky, who was considered "the coal miners' queen." Jackson had been an advocate for better wages and working conditions for miners. Her work had caught the attention of novelist Theodore Dreiser, who formed a group of prominent intellectuals to address some of the nation's problems and to raise funds to help. Among the group's members were writer John Dos Passos, novelist Sherwood Anderson, and folklorist John Lomax. Members of Dreiser's group traveled to Kentucky to see conditions for themselves, then brought Aunt Molly to New York, where her performances could help raise funds. Robertson met her as she got off the bus and spent time with her as she visited New York. His observations turned into a sympathetic full-page profile in the *Herald Tribune,* and behind the scenes Robertson helped the Dreiser group solicit funds for relief efforts.[19]

As the Depression ground on, other stories of poverty found their way into Robertson's work. In October 1933, Robertson visited the Russian Orthodox Church of Christ the Saviour in Manhattan. Many of its members had lost their jobs, could not find work, and could not support the church. Deep in debt, the church's survival was at stake. Three days after Robertson wrote about the church's plight, a wealthy New York woman promised the church she would pay off its debts.[20]

Privately, Robertson weathered the Depression by remembering the lessons he had learned as a boy, stories of what his forebears had endured. He remembered how his Grandfather Robertson had walked back to South Carolina from a New York prison camp at the end of the Civil War. "I said to myself I need not worry too much if I lost my job—what my grandfather could do in 1865 I could do in 1932. I had the same valley to return to that he had. Both of us had the hills and the fields and home."[21]

In the meantime, Robertson tried to supplement his income with freelance work. But even that could be difficult. Editors, confessing that their publications were facing hard times, apologized for not paying Robertson more for his pieces. And book prospects were scarce. When Robertson wrote a *Sunday Magazine* piece about Australian cattle rancher Sir Sidney Kidman, literary editor George Shively urged Robertson to turn the article into a book. Robertson was reluctant to take the project on without a commitment. Shively understood. "I wouldn't want you to put time and expense in on the project on the supposition that it was a definite commitment, for you understand that we couldn't offer that, particularly in this bad season," he replied.[22]

Instead, Robertson wanted to write a novel about something he knew very well: the life of a newspaper reporter. Shively replied, "I don't know what sort of book we could make with your experiences—not because you lack material but because you have got too much!" Robertson completed a manuscript titled *U.S. Reporter* for Shively, who reviewed it and recommended it for publication. Literary agent Sydney Sanders, praising the book as "entertaining," offered the manuscript to several publishers. Though an editor at Little, Brown and Company recommended the manuscript for publication, the book was never published. And although the fiction editor of *Collier's Magazine* expressed interest in using elements of the manuscript for a series of "short, short" stories, the material from *U.S. Reporter* never made it into print.[23]

Not even the might of the *Herald Tribune* could escape the hard times. A round of pay cuts for top earners in 1932 was followed a year later by an across-the-board pay cut. When the Roosevelt administration attempted to get the newspaper industry to join the National Recovery Act in 1933, the *Herald Tribune*'s general manager, Howard Davis, followed the American Newspaper Publishers Association's philosophy that the newspaper industry should be exempt. When the paper finally acquiesced to the NRA's suggestion of a forty-hour workweek, it did so without hiring any additional help. This meant existing staffers had to work harder for the same amount of pay.[24]

Matters of civil rights also came into play. Lester Walton, a black journalist, had been hired by the *Herald Tribune* after ten years at the *New York World,* but he left the paper after three weeks. A feature writer, Walton had been hired on a space-rate basis and made money only when his pieces ran. Stanley Walker explained to the *Pittsburgh Courier* that the *Herald Tribune* had determined it couldn't devote the space to the articles Walton wrote, and that after that, Walton had quit. The *Courier* brought up that while a connection Walton had to the Tuskegee Institute played a role in his hiring by the *Herald Tribune,* a recent story about the institute's fiftieth anniversary had been written by a "Ben Robertson, Jr." and wanted to know who that was. Walker explained that Robertson was "a young white man from South Carolina who had been on the paper for some time," and added that "the articles had been praised for their fairness and thoroughness." Though Walker praised Walton's work, the *Courier* suspected that managing editor, Armistead Holcombe, "who is said to be from Mobile, Alabama, is said to have opposed Walton."[25]

In 1933, Stanley Walker was on the way out of the city room. His replacement, Lessing Lanham Engelking, was active and demanding where Walker was quietly encouraging. Engelking's volatile, unpredictable nature was at odds with Robertson's gentle style, and "Engel"—who wanted to compete with the *Times*—felt the kinds of local-color stories Walker liked didn't match his vision for the city room. Tom Waring cited Engel as one reason Robertson left the *Herald Tribune.* Engel was "an otherwise fine man who simply did not care for the style of story that Ben could write best," Waring remembered. "He liked things boiled down to the meat, and Ben's chief charm was his handling of irrelevancies which finally added up to an aggregate of importance."[26]

Robertson went to work for the Associated Press in early 1934, initially working in the AP's New York bureau. His first stories were much like those he had filed at the *Herald Tribune,* although sometimes he drew assignments that touched on global matters. He covered an address by Theodore Roosevelt Jr. in which the former governor-general of the Philippines expressed his concerns that a movement toward a "free" Philippines could be dangerous in light of Japan's expansionist activities, and urged the United States to reconsider its policies toward the Philippines.[27]

The developments in the Far East, as the Japanese Empire expanded with the conquest of Manchuria, were never far from Robertson's mind. Edgar Snow, writing from Shanghai, told him of the destruction the Japanese had brought, of women having arms shot off, of families still cooking in the ruins of their homes, of villagers surveying the ashes that were the only remnants of their worldly possessions. "I am prepared to believe the admiralty and military of Japan capable of anything," Snow wrote his friend. "The thrust of militarism is aimed to carve a new continental empire out of Manchuria and China for Japan." Snow considered war between Japan and Russia inevitable, and war between Japan and the United States likely, but believed that "a conflict will be avoided, at least so far as America is concerned, with every possible device, for another ten years."[28]

In the meantime, when eighty-seven Navy ships assembled off New York in May 1934, Robertson was there when President Roosevelt reviewed the fleet. Months after being awed by that spectacle, he was at Asbury Park, New Jersey, covering the horrific fire that ravaged the liner *Morro Castle* just offshore, interviewing survivors of the blaze and covering developments immediately after. Robertson also covered the crash of an airliner in the Catskills that summer. Assignments later in the year let Robertson pursue his interests in music and theater, with stories about the Gershwins and Leopold Stokowski and the Metropolitan Opera House.[29]

Robertson had covered Manhattan for five years. He knew the city and its interesting characters well. But a few hundred miles south, the drama of the New Deal was unfolding. Robertson had caught some of that excitement as he covered the 1932 Democratic National Convention at Madison Square Garden for the *Herald Tribune.* Now he wanted to watch history unfold up close.

CHAPTER 6

Hitting at Windmills

A chill, eight degrees above zero, gripped Washington on the first day of February 1935. Ice clung to the tracks at Union Station and giant clouds of steam billowed from locomotives. A train pulled to a halt, just arrived from New York. Ben Robertson stepped down onto the platform. He stopped for breakfast at a counter, checked in at the Stratford Hotel, then reported to the Associated Press's Washington headquarters at the *Washington Star* building for a meeting with his new boss. For two hours he waited in a depressed funk, wondering what he'd gotten himself into.

Finally summoned, Robertson walked into an office where he saw a long, glass-topped table with a paperweight shaped like a bronze lion. Expecting a harsh reception, he was relieved when his new boss was pleasant to him and asked only two things: come see me if you get dissatisfied, and don't forget you're a reporter. "A strange thing comes over newspapermen coming to Washington," he said. "In spite of hell, in about a year's time, sometimes in less time than that, they are no longer reporters. They're correspondents, they're journalists." Robertson didn't understand. "What is a journalist?"

His editor brought up an example of a reporter assigned to cover the State Department who might decide to write in a way that would please the State Department, not inform the public. "For instance, he won't write a line about the Secretary of State coming to work without a hat because he lost it, but writing reams about a treaty with Poland that nobody in America gives a damn about except the State Department." Richard Rendell, who covered the Justice Department beat, had also offered a similar warning not to forget that he was a reporter. "Reporters in Washington aren't journalists, they are Washington correspondents and a Washington correspondent wouldn't write a line about a murder if Al Capone himself should commit the St. Valentine's massacre at his very feet. Reporting a murder is police work, leg reporting, and they are Washington correspondents —they write about treaties."

After that briefing, Rendell took Robertson on a tour of the places he would soon come to know. They visited the Justice Department's palatial new headquarters to meet the attorney general and solicitor general, then went to the White House for a press conference with President Roosevelt. Already Robertson was seeing Washington as a bizarre world of its own, observing that the Justice Department's ornate new building seemed to have so much wasted space, its interior more confounding than any New York skyscraper. At the White House, Robertson was amazed at how easy it was to walk onto the grounds, pass through a door marked "closed," gain admittance just by saying you were with the press, and end up in proximity to the president. Other aspects bemused him: the obsession with treaties, the easy way lawmakers visited with cabinet officials to get a job for a crony. At the press conference, Robertson noted how aides Marvin McIntyre and Stephen Early smiled at everything the president said. "See how they hang on to his words," Robertson whispered. "They must adore him." Rendell replied, "That's what they're here for. You find adoration all about thrones."[1]

Within a week, Robertson was getting a jaundiced view of Washington in action. He confided to his journal that although he didn't dislike Roosevelt, it made him a little sad to see so many photos of him on walls in Washington. "I know it symbolizes Washington. A few years ago the pictures were all of Hoover. Washington is a tough town, a survival of the fittest, it knows a bandwagon when it sees one."[2]

He soon made the acquaintance of the big names. He met Huey Long, sought by a gaggle of photographers on a train platform. He happened into conversation with newly elected Senator Theodore Bilbo, the outspoken, segregationist former governor of Mississippi—a diminutive man with two diamond rings on his fingers and a diamond stick pin in his coat—who called Washington city a bachelor's paradise, telling Robertson that the South wasn't licked by the Yankees in the Civil War but that "we just wore ourselves out killing Yankees." Bilbo claimed that George Washington had kegs of liquor brought up when he ran for the House of Burgesses—and he repeatedly told Robertson his comments were off-the-record. "Don't quote the Bilbo," the senator said in his trademark third-person style. "Boy, that's off the record." Robertson wrote in his journal, "What strange things politicians say when they're off the record," noting that Bilbo was "a shrewd man, a buffoon of the old order. If this country swings to the demagogues, this man Bilbo will be in the running."[3]

The House of Representatives left Robertson no more cheered. Sitting in the gallery, watching representatives argue for the interests of their individual districts instead of the country's greater good, he found himself appalled at "the ignorance, lack of logic and mere emotionalism of the speeches, appalled at the look on the faces of the men—hardly any showed much thought in their faces . . . from the gallery in the House, one can look down and in a nutshell review America—there are all its prejudices and all its hopes." As representatives raced to the floor "like people on the way to a fire" for a record vote, showing up only because missed votes might be used against them in their reelection efforts, Robertson mused that getting representatives to think about something broader than their own districts "would be as difficult as to change the power of a force in mid-air and suddenly to go off in another direction."[4]

Robertson's disappointment with characters like Bilbo contrasted with his reflections after a long visit in the Capitol's Hall of Vice Presidents. Looking long at a portrait of John C. Calhoun, Robertson wrote that Calhoun's name would grow dimmer in history, for the patrician system he represented had collapsed. "An American to go down in history must represent the masses—not the classes. That is why Franklin D. Roosevelt will be remembered, why Hoover will be forgotten." His disappointment with the way Washington worked, the system he saw working around him, was becoming clear. "Washington is a city of expediency, is with the man with the votes, but it remembers Lincoln, Sherman, Washington in its statues . . . it remembers the men who stood for the people's battles."[5]

Neither did proceedings in the "magnificent tomb" of the Supreme Court encourage him. As Robertson watched the nine justices enter the chamber, he felt "terribly depressed, watching the old judges—they are distressingly healthy in appearance, not much chance of any of the old conservatives dying, there they sat in their robes, like hermits, removed like the President, like priests from the world." Back at the office, revising the files kept on each justice so the AP could quickly generate an obituary should one of them pass away, Robertson silently fulminated about Associate Justice James Clark McReynolds, who had evolved from trustbuster to staunch opponent of the New Deal. The judge "has remained back in 1896," Robertson wrote in his journal, "and the world forty years ago passed him by . . . from his solitude and his monastery he has indeed powerfully flayed the cause of the common man, the moneyed interests have profited by his decisions—he is inclined to the 'divine right to starve' group of Americans." Of the bigoted, ill-tempered McReynolds, Robertson wrote, "Wonder what sad secret there is in his heart. There'll be satisfaction when he dies." Robertson mused that the Court delayed its vacation so that it could decide New Deal–related cases before any of the aged conservative justices died, worried about the judges Roosevelt could nominate as replacements. Robertson called it an example "of court against will of people, retarding the country—anything can be read into constitution—anything has been read into it in past—it's a matter of emotional approach, whether one is born a Hamiltonian or a Jeffersonian, the court today is Hamiltonian, it is old Coolidge and Hoover living on beyond their day."[6]

While in his journals Robertson scorned the New Deal's foes in the legislative and judicial branches, he wrote with appreciation of some of Roosevelt's associates and lieutenants. Not only did he come to like the president, whom he often saw and questioned during sessions in the White House, and not only did he come to know First Lady Eleanor Roosevelt, but Robertson also wrote fondly of Secretary of Labor Frances Perkins. Struck at first by the serious approach she took to her job—"no humor about her, nothing casual—all is competence, a characteristic noted about most women in business, I've found"—he liked her unfussy manner, her willingness to speak candidly and talk off-the-record. Secretary of Agriculture Henry Wallace, friendly and determined, also impressed Robertson as "a pilgrim, a puritan" doing quiet battle against the New Deal's foes. "Wallace deals with the Supreme Court as a farmer does with the weather," Robertson wrote in his journal. "When a freshet comes along and destroys a crop, he doesn't give up and quit, he ploughs the land again and plants something else. A farmer can grow turnips after it is too late for corn."[7]

As Robertson warmed to Roosevelt's people, his views toward opponents of the New Deal grew more acidic. When James S. Beck, a former solicitor general who had argued in the Supreme Court against the Tennessee Valley Authority, died in April 1936, Robertson scorched him in his diary. "My honest feeling was one of satisfaction," he wrote, saying Beck "was not a human being to me, he was an abstraction" who "stood for the scribes and the Pharisees, for the sanctity of money." Robertson compared Beck to the Tories, writing that "the Whigs in my family drove the tories in the family clear out of South Carolina in 1775"; and he complained that Beck constantly looked for precedents in the history of the English Plantagenets, "as though we had no Swedish or Spanish or good Polak [*sic*] background in this country, as though we were not even Irish."[8]

Robertson's views on what it would take to change the country began to show a radicalism. After working on an obituary of Supreme Court justice Pierce Butler, Robertson flayed him in his journal as "corporation minded." He elaborated:

> His life and those of the other judges indicates that a man comes to the Supreme Court of the United States with his political philosophy composed and that he continues to follow that guide, thus the court becomes political—and in times like these it can impede and endanger. It leaves no recourse to labor but violence for by throwing out NRA [the National Recovery Administration, a New Deal program that attempted to establish fair practices and reduce "destructive competition," which the Supreme Court ruled unconstitutional

> in 1935], it leaves no effective lawful way of dealing with industrial trouble out in the cold—so we are responsible, all of us in this country, for deeds of violence in strikes—the only way American labor is going to win shorter hours and higher wages is by violence—the system drives them to it, whether they want violence or not. The court by its rigidity, by its insistence on the letter of the law, just as the Republican Party, can bring this country far nearer revolution than any of the exigencies of the New Deal.[9]

On another day, after watching a debate in the House of Representatives, Robertson wrote "they have little to offer, the needs of the country haven't been considered by them, they wanted to get into congress primarily, what they were to do after getting there was secondary—it still is, as now they're trying to stay here." He mused, "I had rather have cowboys making laws than members of the House of Morgan, for we know what to expect from the Morgans—we tried it in South Carolina, we sent the Calhouns and the Haynes and Cheveses to Congress and we all know where they led us—into a war that was 'a rich man's war and a poor man's fight.'"[10]

That night, in his journal, he grumbled about the carelessness he saw from his perch in the gallery, the antics of congressmen who didn't seem to take seriously their responsibilities to the people they represented. As he drummed the keys of his typewriter, he felt misgivings about his own profession. "Just as they do we fail the people for as much as they are responsible to the people so are we in this country which has entrusted us with its hope for a free press. Nor do we escape the pangs of conscience. We flow in the mould into which we are poured, gather the fluff and carry gossip. We are not allowed to write quietly of quiet things any longer in our papers." Worse, Robertson felt he could not call out what he saw. "We are supposed to tell of what happens in an unbiased way but few of us work for papers that will permit us to make use of ridicule in public places . . . We protect the fools in our solemn, humorless dispatches." Sometimes, if they couldn't tell the truth, they wrote nothing. "Sometimes I think the more ignorant a person is the better is he qualified for reporting," Robertson wrote. "He is not hampered by the qualifications which come with knowledge." The one advantage the reporters had over those they covered, he felt, was "we are the younger men and are less fearful of the future than they are, willing to risk more. We are not as fearful of increased taxation nor of regimentation as they. We are a little more willing in our youth to give up more in our determination that things must be better over here."[11]

Not only did Robertson find himself ahead of the times on economic matters, but he found himself ahead of the times on matters of race. In March 1936

Robertson took two friends to a performance of George Gershwin's *Porgy and Bess,* which featured an African-American cast. Upon learning that the National Theatre, the venue for the performance, was segregated, the cast protested until an agreement was reached to allow blacks to be admitted. During the intermission, two European correspondents asked Robertson what he thought of blacks being there. "I'm very glad," he said. "But I have friends here who differ with me." As Robertson wrote in his journal, those friends insisted "equality had nothing to do with fraternity—which I insist has everything to do with it." Robertson replied that blacks should be given the same rights as any other citizen, and warned that "non-fraternity could be extended to the point I once remember in South Carolina where there was an argument as to whether Negroes possessed souls and to the point in Georgia where the man said he had to either hit a negro or hit a rock so he hit the Negro."[12]

Soon into his Washington stay Robertson was talking with a friend about First Lady Eleanor Roosevelt, who had gone to a Virginia shipyard to christen a new aircraft carrier. They pondered the First Lady's qualms about serving as a warship's ceremonial sponsor while holding strong moral convictions for peace. "Mrs. Roosevelt has to convince herself morally about everything," his friend said. "She can go just so long and she has to hit at a windmill."

"And so do I," Robertson replied.

"Not me," she replied. "I'm no reformer. I saw my mother and my grandmother spend their lives trying to change the world and I saw them get nowhere."[13]

As he had in New York, Robertson found some of his best friendships among his fellow reporters. He accepted an invitation to the National Press Club in June 1935 and befriended many influential journalists. He struck up an especially warm friendship with Ernie Pyle, a national columnist for the Scripps-Howard chain. Pyle, famous for the stories and columns he had written about his travels across America, specialized in writing about the people he had met along the way. Robertson, who also specialized in character-driven journalism, found a kindred spirit in the journalist from Indiana. The two wrote to each other often, and at one point Pyle came to Pickens County to visit Robertson. And while living in Washington, Robertson opened his apartment to his youngest sister Hattie, now a Winthrop graduate enrolled at a Washington secretarial school. He enjoyed showing her the sights of the nation's capital, and sometimes took her to White House receptions and other functions.[14]

While politics constituted his primary beat, Robertson covered other stories out of the Washington bureau. That April, fourteen schoolchildren were killed when a train tore their bus in half in Rockville, Maryland. Robertson was sent out to cover the story and its aftermath. Months later, during the summer break, he filed character sketches such as an account of Navajo leaders visiting Washington. They were most impressed, Robertson reported, by the zoo. "What did you think of Senator Long?" he asked them. "They preserved silence," he reported.[15]

As the *Herald Tribune* had, the AP drew on Robertson's travel experiences and gave him important overseas assignments. In 1935 the wire service assigned him to cover the Second Italo-Abyssinian War, as Italian forces based in Italian Somaliland invaded Ethiopia to bolster an Italian colonial empire in Africa. Robertson went to London and waited for permission to arrive from the Italian government. But in time, it became clear that the Italians were in no hurry to grant Robertson credentials to cover the war in Africa. Instead the AP told Robertson to cover the Second London Naval Disarmament Conference, which began in early December in an effort to impose a five-year limitation on the growth of major nations' combat fleets. The nautical subject matter interested Robertson, and he enjoyed meeting with newspaper people in London. He also liked visiting with fellow Americans who were in England. But London itself did not impress him. In a letter to a friend he dismissed London as "that dismal, gloomy, medieval barbaric city of brussels sprouts."[16]

To Robertson, there seemed a parallel between the England he saw and the Charleston mindset he scorned, and it didn't just have to do with the aristocratic mindset. Just as Robertson complained that the planters in Charleston, whose forbears settled the Lowcountry from England with their wealth already in place, had dragged the upcountry into the Civil War to defend the Lowcountry's economic system, he now felt the British were trying to pull the United States into what should be England's fight in a coming war. "I now believe England is as crass as Germany or Italy but at least you know where Germany and Italy stand—and believe me I KNOW that," he wrote friend Jean Muir.

> "England is more subtle. England says it is the duty of America and Britain to keep the peace of the world when what England means by peace of the world is British prestige. England would turn on us in a minute if it would profit Britain one pound. That is a perfectly diplomatic procedure but I do think the people here should recognize England for what it is—just as I think the people should recognize a lobbyist in Washington for what he is. They are so subtle—they will appeal to us morally, talking peace, as it is there we are most vulnerable—when they have no intention at all of keeping any peace in Europe. I have become a very narrow American—we can do most good in the world by keeping our own peace—at any cost. At least, I think so."[17]

The London Conference dragged on, suffering a major blow when Japan, denied its demand that it be allowed naval parity with the United States and Great Britain, pulled out of the negotiations on January 15. That same day, King George V took ill. Within days word came from Sandringham House that the King's illness "must be regarded with some disquiet." Robertson began covering that story, noting in spite of claims that "everything is quiet here," an oxygen tent had been taken to the monarch's bedside. He watched as groups of people braved the London winter chill, kneeling in prayer outside the gates of Buckingham Palace. And he covered their mourning after the monarch succumbed on January 20. A few nights later Robertson stood in the rain, watching a long line of people standing outside St. Stephens Hall to file past the King's coffin and pay their final respects. At 4 A.M., the police announced no one else would be allowed in, and the doors were closed. As Robertson watched the people obediently disperse, he felt "enraged by their attitude. I couldn't understand that quality of acceptance in the British," he later wrote, and felt it suggested "the meekness of sheep."[18]

Before returning to the United States, Robertson managed a visit to Denmark where the endlessly curious author wanted to visit Kronborg Castle, the legendary castle at Elsinore where Shakespeare's Hamlet lived. A friend in a Copenhagen tavern told Robertson that Americans and Englishmen visiting the castle seemed to become "moonstruck" when they saw it for the first time: "You know very well that Hamlet was a mythical figure, yet I have seen some of your most learned men and women walk about Elsinore as though they were tramping hallowed ground." Robertson explained that to Americans, it didn't matter that Hamlet had never lived; it was enough that Shakespeare said he had, and that the Bard had said Elsinore was his home. When Robertson passed through the gates and arches at Elsinore and beheld the castle before him, he was as moonstruck as his Danish friend had predicted. "No flight of the British or American mind could ever imagine a more perfect place for Hamlet to have seen the ghost of his father than the platform before this castle," Robertson wrote. "Elsinore is as Shakespeare's readers would have it; it is one of those rare places which prove finer in reality than in contemplation."[19]

In February, Robertson returned to the United States in a stormy crossing on the American liner *Washington.* As Robertson returned to the nation's capital, another presidential election was drawing close. In July 1936, when the Democratic convention was held in Philadelphia, the White House reporters accompanied Roosevelt there aboard his train. The sight of thousands of people lining the route and waving to the President, combined with watching Roosevelt give his acceptance speech before one hundred thousand people at Franklin Field, infused Robertson, a quiet supporter of the New Deal, with what he called "a great feeling of great moment."[20]

But moments like that had become the exception. When he had reported to Washington in February 1935, Robertson had felt depressed as he waited to meet his editor for the first time. It had been an omen. Whatever excitement he felt about getting to Washington had quickly dissolved as he observed the theatrics in the nation's capital, as he saw the shortcomings and foibles of bureaucrats, as he saw lawmakers and judges he felt had been there too long and were out of touch with what Americans needed. As much as he loved wandering around Washington's memorials and monuments, and even though he admired certain officials in Washington, it had been a frustrating two years. His private journals overflowed with his disappointments, his belief in Roosevelt and the New Deal, his anger with those who stood in the way of meaningful reform in favor of self-interest and an ossified system, and his praise of organized labor as a check on corporations.

Hoping a respite might heal his outlook, Robertson applied for a few months' leave so he could write a book. The Associated Press denied the request. Fed up, Robertson left the AP in September 1936 and headed back to Pickens County. "I'm shooting the works," he wrote to former *Herald Tribune* colleague John Whitaker. "I quit . . . I couldn't get leave and the AP is no career and I never intended staying with them that long anyhow—I wanted to get to Washington and I got what I wanted to from them." That he quit the AP was no surprise to those who knew him. "I could hardly imagine your staying in Washington much longer," wrote his friend Don Wharton at *Scribner's Magazine.*[21]

But to Edgar Snow, Robertson wrote of not only exhaustion but disillusionment, and hinted that what he had witnessed in the halls of power made him want to take a stand. He confessed he had had an idea of what he was getting into, but "I wanted to get to Washington and it seemed like the only way." Once there, he had found himself disgusted by "the dessicated, gutless way of fence riding between the few Democrat publishers and the thousands of Republican publishers." His letter read:

> I have been in and out of Washington for two years, a wonderful time in a wonderful place, and it certainly taught me where my social sympathies lie—not that I've become a wild howling hack for reform but I did see the lobbyists at work, day after day, the same mugs appearing before committee after committee, unreasonable, opposing with all their great power, every single progressive measure—regardless—and also I sat in the Supreme Court

> through these last two sessions and, my friend, that changes one. I used to pray that McReynolds, Van Devanter, Butler or Sutherland would die—but it is one of the most distressing sights in the United States today—the perfect health of those fossils.
>
> I even thought that democracy as an institution was at stake in this last campaign—if the people had elected Landon when the issues that were at stake were the issues of that campaign—drawn so closely as they were—if the people had elected Landon then it was time to consider the dictatorships. God, nobody was more surprised—I had no idea the people were so fine, so well informed. I believe some genius guides the people—that even Andrew Jacksons can be trusted.[22]

The crystallization of Robertson's values would in time lead him to consider political office himself. First, he felt he had to tell a story that had lingered in his head for too long.

CHAPTER 7

A Vague, Confused Plan

Robertson had long dreamed of writing a book, and on occasion had talked about it with friends in the publishing world. Leaving the journalism profession may have been an extreme act, but it gave him the time he needed. He planned to take a year off, sustain himself through freelance work, and then return to New York and resume his newspaper career. But inside, Robertson doubted himself. A few months before, in a spaghetti restaurant on Connecticut Avenue, Robertson confided to a couple of friends that he wanted to write a book but didn't feel he had the ability. Now that he had the time, his self-doubt intensified. "Back to South Carolina after thirteen years, appalled at what I've cut out to do," he wrote in his journal. "Now that the time actually to begin has arrived—it is to be lonely work and is so uncertain."[1]

The quiet life in Clemson was a stark contrast to the bustle of Washington and New York. Robertson wasn't sure what to make of the sudden stillness. "There is a quiet timelessness to time here," he wrote. "The days go by, there is difficulty telling either day of week or month." And seeing what had become of places he knew well appalled him. "Shocked at ugliness of Pickens," he wrote. "Glaring town, no shade trees." Though the roads were now paved, the town seemed to have deteriorated in the ten years he had been away. It was no longer the place he remembered. He saw many people standing idly around. As he explored the town, a crippled beggar approached Robertson and asked him to drive him around.[2]

Feeling lost in a place that once had been so familiar, Robertson retreated to his father's house in Clemson and tried to begin the task for which he had sacrificed his Associated Press job. He tried to set aside his unease and misgivings; but he had to admit even to friends that his vision of such a future was less than perfect. To Edgar Snow, he confided that he had been "keeping to a kind of vague, confused plan."[3]

On his mind was the vision that had lingered since those long days on his cot in Surabaya, stricken with illness, reading Walt Whitman and thinking of that long procession of history. Since then, Robertson had wanted to write about the people he came from and the pioneer spirit that drove them. From September 1936 to January 1937 Robertson worked on a manuscript he titled *Land of Hope and Glory*. It was the saga of an old South Carolina family named the Caldwells, "a family that is old in an old state," as they settled in the South and later moved westward across the North American continent, people who "have always gone in each generation to settle the West—lonely, searching people, never at rest." Robertson wrote "with all the pure passion" he could muster, but he was not sure if he had succeeded.[4]

The basis for Robertson's epic was his own family line. Although he maintained that no actual figures from his family's past were characters in the book, he did use as inspiration the pioneers of his own family. Many real names appeared in the book, and those who were renamed were thinly veiled composites of his ancestors; anyone who knew Robertson's lineage could easily recognize many characters' real-life counterparts. Even the home that was the central point of the story had the name Forest Mansion, the same name the Clayton family home had borne. He also used "old letters at our house and old legends and on my own lonely reflections when far from home." Robertson even drew on his own childhood experiences: the stories told on the family's front porch, the long days working in the fields of the family farm, the afternoons exploring the wilds of the upcountry with Wright Bryan and other friends. Through the devices of literature he could resurrect beloved relatives, now gone, who had inspired him as a child. He could also conjure family members he had never known, but whose stories formed so much of the family's lore.[5]

The sprawling narrative not only told the story of the Caldwells over two centuries, but in it Robertson also examined the evolution of the South, its people, and its economy. While celebrating his region's heritage, Robertson wrote of its shortcomings: the refusal to diversify crops, the tendency to cling to land past the point of reason. His distrust of the Lowcountry mindset informed a sordid chapter set during a trip to Charleston, depicting the port city as a cradle of temptation. Another chapter, depicting the opening of a cotton mill, contained Robertson's unease about what the industrial mindset would do to a people accustomed to the rhythms of an agricultural economy, the belief handed down from his family that working in a mill after years tending land was tantamount to imprisonment, that industry exploited the common man to enrich the industrialist.

Although the concept for the story had been in his head for years, and even though Robertson felt especially close to the material, he still found the writing process difficult. His friend Harry Ashmore remembered, "He would sit at the big round dining room table and hammer away at his typewriter until his eyes began to hurt, then he would go out and walk around and talk to Doc McCullom and John Lane and Bo Williams, or he would sit on his porch and listen to the night sounds and think about the roots that bound him to his valley."[6]

From all these hours of relentless typing, aching eyes, and wandering conversations came a massive manuscript that boggled his agent, George Sanders. The early critiques passed along by Sanders—noting that the genealogy of the book's characters was confusing—left Robertson feeling discouraged and frustrated. Those criticisms compounded Robertson's self-doubt about the manuscript. By January 1937, he wanted to get his mind off the project. He was also feeling restless; having seen the world and lived in big cities, going for long walks and talking with friends wasn't enough. Robertson felt confined to Clemson. He needed to find other horizons.[7]

A week in Charleston visiting friends, relatives, and former colleagues left Robertson feeling better about the book. Encouraging words from his friends also renewed his hopes, and he returned to Clemson and started incorporating some of Sanders's suggestions. But Robertson still felt annoyed by the constraints of the literary world, especially since he didn't like revising his work once it was down on the page; he wanted to keep going. "If the characters get confused in genealogy then it is up to me to make it evident that I don't give a damn or not whether they get mixed up or don't," he wrote a friend. "I'll have to superimpose on the whole thing a feeling of the procession through time." In the end, Robertson created a lengthy Caldwell family tree to guide readers through the narrative.[8]

In between sessions at his typewriter, Robertson wrote to his friends, caught up on reading, and tried to enjoy the quiet pace of life at his father's house. He particularly enjoyed listening to the conversations among the black servants who helped around the home. On January 20, as President Roosevelt took the oath for his second term, the Robertsons listened to the inauguration ceremonies as they were broadcast on radio. A reporter stated that seven hundred people were coming to lunch at the White House. "Gracious God," said Mary, the household's servant. "How they going to serve all them folks? Nobody but Jesus could feed all them people." Robertson, whose admiration of Roosevelt had grown during his time at the White House, was amused, and wrote to a friend that Mary had grasped the "enormity of Him in the White House."[9]

Robertson also used the lull to inquire about something that had piqued his curiosity. An admirer of the books of Thomas Wolfe, whose style inspired his own work, Robertson had learned that Wolfe's middle name was Clayton—a name that figured in the Robertson family tree. He wrote to Wolfe to ask if they shared a common ancestor. Wolfe did not know the answer and politely referred

Robertson to his mother, Julia Wolfe, for an answer. Robertson scribbled "It doesn't matter" at the bottom of Wolfe's response and filed the correspondence away.[10]

Robertson completed his rewrite of the manuscript and sent it back to Sanders, who would farm it out to several publishing houses. But as Robertson was finishing up those revisions, the Ohio River Valley was under siege from torrential rainfall. It began to overflow its banks in mid-January, and cities began to drown. Martial law was declared in some areas. Tens of thousands were left homeless. The federal government sent resources to assist. Relief organizations, including the Red Cross, moved in to help those in need. For Robertson, it was an opportunity to put his professional abilities to work, to help people, and to get out of Pickens County.

In late January, Robertson went to Memphis to assist the Red Cross with news releases. This job put him on the scene observing boat captains, watching volunteers at work, talking to victims, viewing the damage for himself—seeing a disaster that made no distinction between blacks or whites, rich or poor. In refugee camps, he noted the candy and kites available to amuse the displaced. He witnessed their patience and recorded their belief they were being punished by the will of God. He wrote that many of them were poor and ignorant, that pellagra and venereal disease were often in evidence. The medical workers were glad to have a chance to give dried brewer's yeast to those suffering from pellagra, and Salvarsan vaccinations to treat those afflicted with syphilis. The conditions Robertson saw appalled him. "People of Mississippi refusing to face facts . . . don't want change . . . want things stay . . . don't say themselves they responsible . . . so ignorant, unable read, some came write letters for them, hard, hungry look . . . but friendly." Robertson wrote that he would "often think why we brag about American standard of living . . . wouldn't see such people in Norway nor in Sweden."[11]

In Memphis, Robertson saw the effects of what he called "the peonage system," with many farmers not making money on their farms. "So many in such debt, having work out time, practically in slavery," he wrote. He noted that when the owners of large farms tried to get the Red Cross to give them money to care for their workers, the Red Cross saw through those requests and turned them down. "Care for all and any persons as come and need." He watched as a Movietone cameraman filmed two mules being rescued from the raging river, only to watch one mule roll over and drown. When a group of refugees arrived—112 refugees and one corpse—they had the corpse held until the press could arrive so that a picture could be taken for use in fundraising efforts. "Person died in good cause," Robertson wrote. "Not everyone fortunate in their dying."[12]

Robertson watched refugees stream in carrying what was left of their lives: clothes, dogs, banjos, hams, and radios. One man in an attic came out with his radio because he had been listening to news reports about the flood. Into Memphis, Robertson noted a long procession: old cars, herds of cattle, chickens, hogs, the surreal scenes of the Coast Guard floating down the Mississippi River. Arriving to help were Army officers, along with newspapermen to record the scene. "Whole country concentrating on Memphis," he wrote. But not even disaster, suffering, and death could call a halt to casual racism. It offended him. "Stories hear every flood . . . niggers in attic not going leave until the water is higher or the liquor is lower," he wrote.[13]

Back home to Clemson on February 13, stirred by the devastation he had witnessed, Robertson needed time to work through his emotions after helping with the disaster relief efforts. After working on some articles for the Associated Press and handling some freelance articles, he went back to work on the book. It was difficult work, and Robertson's self-doubt made it more so. On the last day of March, eyes aching after spending the previous day at the typewriter, Robertson went for a walk to rest his eyes and mind. Wandering through the countryside near his father's home, he thought about the questions of his life. Back at the house, he wrote his way through his doubts in his journal. "Can I endure—am I composed—am I at peace—try to be simple, alive." A few days later, the gloom had not let up. Walking home, he thought of how he felt "bored, despondent . . . unable read much, typing unk—always feel bad when typing." The task before him, and the confinement to Pickens County, had overwhelmed him.[14]

Now Robertson thought in earnest about another element of his "vague, confused" plan. The novel about his Southern ancestry had been one ambition. But even before his return to South Carolina, Robertson had started planning a second book, similar in theme but different in subject. This book, he wrote his old *Herald Tribune* colleague John Whitaker, would address the "lonely, restless searching" of Americans by studying "the simplest of the American professional wanderers, the sailors."[15]

Robertson's interest in the sea had persisted since his days covering the port in Charleston. He had taken many voyages on passenger liners and freighters whenever he could. And in New York, Robertson's presence in the world's largest seaport had given him numerous opportunities to see all kinds of ships and know distinguished mariners, including Giles Stedman, Harry Manning, Frederick Fender, and his friend Tom Sheridan.[16]

Robertson had been planning a long sea voyage since before he left New York. But, Robertson felt, he had to have a purpose. "I can't just go any more for the sake of going," he wrote. After he joined the AP, Robertson wanted to go to sea in order to write about the sailor's life. In June 1935 he bounced the idea off Captain Sheridan, who liked the idea. "I do not think that this particular phase of modern life, pertaining to the way men make their living today on the sea, has been touched deeply by any writer," Sheridan wrote.[17]

But even with Sheridan's help, Robertson had a difficult time finding a shipping line that would let him sail along. Few freighters permitted passengers, as the only passenger facilities most of those ships had was a single cabin meant for agents or consuls, and new maritime regulations had made it more difficult for passengers to be carried aboard freighters. His best chance, it would turn out, would be to go to sea as a working sailor. Even as late as January 1937, Robertson still had no idea just which line he would sail with, or which route he would take. One possibility would take him to Singapore, where he could visit his friend Edgar Snow. Another route would take him to the familiar shores of Australia. In late April, he scrawled in his journal, "May—left for Australia. Gone until September." They were the words of a man being released from confinement. He was out of exile, off to Philadelphia to sign on as a member of a ship's crew.[18]

The *City of Rayville* was an unglamorous, hard-working ship. One of several freighters in the American Pioneer Lines fleet, the 401-foot, 5,800-ton ship earned its keep hauling cargo from the East Coast to ports in the Far East. Having plied the seas since 1921, its most frequent routes took the ship to ports in Australia, a nondescript ship doing the kind of work that gets no attention, hauling livestock and wool and timber and wheat and whatever staples of civilization needed to be moved over the sea. One manifest from a year earlier included 3,400 tons of heavy equipment for a Ford automobile factory near Brisbane, and 36 pedigreed beef cattle destined for Sydney. The *City of Rayville* had occasionally taken on passengers, but it was far from a luxury liner. It was a working ship. But Ben Robertson had no interest in sailing as a tourist. He wanted to work alongside professional seamen, hoping to understand what drew them to leave everything behind and chase a variant of the same pioneering spirit that had intrigued him for years.

With 4,400 tons of cargo and 37 crewmen aboard, Captain A. P. Cronin guided the *City of Rayville* out of Philadelphia on May 26. They reached the Panama Canal on June 8 and then spent several weeks crossing the Pacific, with pleasant weather providing calm seas. With a top speed of 11 knots, the *City of Rayville* gave Robertson plenty of time to gather material. In between his duties chipping rust and applying paint, Robertson took notes on life at sea, got to know the ship's crew, and fought the homesickness that mingled with his adventure and excitement.

The ship arrived in Brisbane on July 6. A series of port calls followed: Sydney three days later, Melbourne on the 15th, Adelaide on the 20th, and one more call at Sydney on the 30th. The visit to Adelaide gave Robertson a chance to visit the city he had briefly covered while reporting for the *News-Limited* nearly a decade before.

The voyage home began in early August. Along the way the *City of Rayville* anchored briefly off Pitcairn Island, famous as the site where mutineers from the HMS *Bounty* settled. Several islanders rowed out to the *City of Rayville* and came aboard, eager to trade trinkets and souvenirs with the ship's crew. After another transit of the Panama Canal in early September, the ship stopped in Kingston, Jamaica, to deliver some cargo.

On September 13, the *City of Rayville* arrived in New York. Robertson signed off from the crew, taking home notebooks full of material and a completed outline for the book. But he'd have to put the project aside for a while. His first novel was about to become a reality.[19]

CHAPTER 8

A Literary Gale

While Robertson was at sea, copies of the revised manuscript for *Land of Hope and Glory* had been evaluated by several prominent publishing houses. The story that Robertson had woven from these letters and memories was unlike most stories of the founding of America. Rather than presenting his forebears in the sainted light most writers preferred, his book portrayed them as passionate, hard-living people with episodes of lust, drinking, and murder alongside tales of exploration and adventure.

Land of Hope and Glory tells the story of the Caldwell family as it makes its way from Pennsylvania and Virginia, finally to settle in the upstate of South Carolina. The patriarch, Silas Caldwell, aspires to build a great house from which members of his family would go out into the world. Using his grandfather's admonition, words that later appeared almost verbatim in *Red Hills and Cotton,* Robertson has Silas tell his family, "Never sell a foot of the land—never mortgage an acre, no matter what . . . nothing in the world can ever budge us if we hold on to the land—we'll be above everything."[1]

Although Silas does not live to build the great house, his son Carter does, and he names it Forest Mansion. From this home, stories unfold. Carter's brother, Stephen John, becomes a hermit. His sister Narcissa has an affair with a traveling clock salesman and is murdered by her husband. Carter fathers a child during an affair with a slave woman. The family members drink, feud, cheat, commit murder, survive the hardships of the Civil War—and then face a changing economic system that drives down crop prices and brings textile mills and industrialization. They watch tenant farmers trade their free but penniless agrarian existence for jobs in the textile mills, where they are guaranteed a wage but live by a clock and work within a factory's windowless confines.

The book closes with the story of another Stephen John, a modern-day descendant of Silas who leaves South Carolina, earns a Harvard degree, and becomes a successful attorney in Manhattan. As the book concludes, Stephen John looks to the future and puts Forest Mansion up for sale. But he keeps one link to the past, and the mansion's weather vane, which Silas made by hand, becomes the centerpiece of a gallery exhibit in Manhattan.[2]

The story itself was an epic. Robertson's means of telling it, however, were rough. As talented as he was as a journalist, his inexperience with writing fiction hampered his tale. Descriptions of scenes and characters did not flow in a manner that might engage the reader; instead, they became inventories of fine details that slowed the story and taxed the reader's attention: "He made his living peddling the fine wooden clocks of Connecticut, wonderful time-pieces with engraved and silvered brass dials. They were driven by weights. Some of them with chimes told the day of the month, the moon's age and seconds."[3]

Other times, Robertson's prose meandered as he struggled to express the emotions he felt about the South, what it meant to live there, what it meant to want to wander while also wanting to remain rooted: "Brooding home in the south! It was a sorrowing land these children loved, moody and often melancholy, and these children reared within its hollows reflected its somber, ecclesiastical, wild power."[4]

Robertson's decision to tell his family's story through fiction brought the need to invent scenes and scenarios, many of which came across as contrived and thus detracted from the story's power. Scenes of sex and violence, of which there were several, veered into the gratuitous, distracting, and sordid: "The boys held Stephen John by his arms and legs, stripping him of his clothing and then they tied him to a post in the center of the big bare room. The woman who had been picking her teeth removed most of her clothing and without any show of mirth began moving about Stephen John. In a hard voice, she began singing a song."[5]

Robertson could have corrected the errors of a first-time novelist had he allowed others to critique his draft, or had he sought more feedback from George Sanders. But *Land of Hope and Glory* was too personal a project, its telling too dear for him to tell in any other way but his own; and arguably not helping matters was the rapid way Robertson wrote. His friend Jeanne Gadsden, who served as typist, editorial consultant, and confidant for all of his book projects, remembered that Robertson "did his best work at top speed—at white heat, literally." In a back room of his father's house, with the temperature at ninety degrees, Robertson would pound out pages—up to seven thousand words a day—in all lower-case, a habit from years of rapidly typing stories to be sent via wire service. It was not a writing style that lent itself to reflection, as Gadsden recalled. "Ben never read the completed manuscripts. He couldn't bear to look at them. Once he was through he was through, and left it to the proof readers to pick up the mistakes I made. No one else read the manuscripts of the last books before they were published. Some of his friends read the first ones, but Ben found that too varied criticism was apt to confuse him, although he was quick to take a suggestion if he agreed with it."[6]

In spite of Sanders's misgivings, the manuscript went out to several top publishers. None were interested. Harper replied that although "the conception of the story is unusual and its possibilities very real," its pace varied between being too fast and too slow, the text was "somewhat overwritten," and that the book suffered from "a sense of shapelessness." Farrar and Rinehart passed on the book, citing its "looseness" and "adjectival" style. "If this book had come off," associate editor William Sloane wrote, "it would have been a magnificent thing, but we don't quite feel that it does." Stackpole replied that although *Land of Hope and Glory* contained "excellent material," the writing was "either ham or overripe. . . . Somebody might take him patiently in hand and make something out of it more sound than the American Dream," its editors responded, "but it would be a terrific job." Scribners sent only a note saying it could not publish the book.[7]

If Robertson had felt discouraged by his agent's evaluation of the original draft, the publishers' comments about the revised version made him feel worse. His words, he wrote to a friend, "have been so battered and I am concerned about them all. I almost have an edition of typed chewed copies." The editors' comments almost seemed personal, particularly since the book's subject was so close to his heart, and he refused to make the changes the publishers demanded. Telling the story his own way mattered more. "I said I would type them and not change a thing, for if I started changing words I would start thinking about them," he wrote, "and I haven't time to think about them right now. After all, it is 'wrote' now. I can recite them."[8]

Frustrated in his attempts to get a publisher to print *Land of Hope and Glory* as he wanted it done, inspiration struck during a visit to a trusted friend. One afternoon Robertson went to see John Lane, who taught English at Clemson and had provided guidance on the novel's first draft. As evening fell, they sat on Lane's front porch and discussed the rejection notices that had troubled Robertson. As they talked, Robertson remembered a suggestion another friend had made. "Hellfire, we'll publish it ourselves," he told Lane. They persuaded Robertson's cousin B. O. "Bo" Williams, a Clemson sociology professor, to join in. With $500 in capital, the three formed the Cottonfield Publishers. "We figured the money it took to bring out this book was equal to the price of four mules or nineteen bales of eight-cent cotton," Robertson explained. The new publishing company planned to have the book, now titled *Travelers' Rest,* printed by the R. L. Bryan Company of Columbia. In November 1937, Robertson sent the book's text, a check for the printing costs, and a request that the imprint read "Cottonfield Publishers."[9]

With Dr. John Lane, Clemson professor and trusted friend. Special Collections & Archives, Clemson University Libraries, Clemson, South Carolina.

Over the winter, the Bryan company refused the job. Robertson claimed the printer did not review the copy before sending it out for typesetting, and upon examining the proofs for the first time "they sent for their lawyer and they called me on the long-distance telephone to say they would be liable to a year in the Carolina jail if they printed such a book." Instead, the Southern book would have a Northern printer, J. J. Little and Ives of New York. On the end flaps of the book's dark green dust jacket, Robertson had Little and Ives print comments from the publishers' rejection notices. The author, going it alone, was having the last laugh.[10]

After his voyage aboard the *City of Rayville,* Robertson had planned to return to New York and find another job. Sitting in Clemson had left him feeling confined, and he'd hoped the *City of Rayville* adventure and the writing of *Travelers' Rest* would give him a chance "to do what I wanted to do and have had a hell of a good time at it—and what more can you ask."[11]

Instead, the last day of November 1937 found Robertson in his study at Clemson, listening to music on the radio, preparing to turn his sea experiences into a book, again anxious about the task ahead. "Tomorrow I begin work on the seamen," he wrote. "A sort of hopeless, helpless feeling. But I believe in what I have to tell, I believe I can tell it."[12]

As Robertson began turning his journals into a manuscript, his friend Burnet Maybank, who had been mayor of Charleston since 1931, was planning a run for governor. Robertson volunteered to do some public relations writing for Maybank's campaign. Then in February, Robertson's friend Theodore Vaughn decided to run against incumbent Democrat Ellison "Cotton Ed" Smith for the United States Senate. Robertson, who felt the race-baiting Smith was an embarrassment to South Carolina, was excited by the prospect of Vaughn as a Senator. At thirty-five, Robertson and Vaughn were the same age, and both were graduates of Clemson. They shared an upbringing in the cotton culture; as Robertson had grown up on a cotton farm to become a globetrotting journalist, Vaughn had gone from working in a cotton mill to working in farm organizations. His work in those organizations interested him in sociology, and at the time he was working on a doctoral degree from Columbia University.

Now Vaughn wanted to challenge "Cotton Ed," an opponent of civil rights who used his oratorical skills and his Senate seniority to his advantage. At the 1936 Democratic Convention, when a black minister gave the invocation, Smith walked out. His account of the incident, told with relish at his campaign stops, was vintage Cotton Ed, saying that when a "slew-footed, blue-gummed, kinky-headed Senegambian started praying," Smith walked out, "and as I walked, it seemed to me that old John Calhoun leaned down from his mansion in the sky and whispered, 'You did right, Ed.'" Smith also opposed raising wages for workers in the South, fearing that paying Southern workers as much as workers in New England were getting would destroy the South's key economic strength, cheap labor. "Why don't some of these people call in God and tell Him that He must stop this thing of making one section more advantageous than another?" To Robertson, Smith's blatant racism and antiquated economic views symbolized so much that was wrong with the South, an ugly and stubborn mindset that kept the region from achieving its true potential. Privately, Robertson admitted his friend didn't have a chance against the powerful Smith. But he nevertheless decided to help Vaughn with his campaign.[13]

Robertson's participation in the Maybank and Vaughn campaigns let him channel the frustration he felt after his two years in Washington, his firsthand experiences with the proponents of the New Deal and his frustrations watching its opponents in action and seeing the real-life effects of poverty while working with the Red Cross along the flooded Ohio River. He had come home from those experiences weary with how little progress he saw in America. He wanted to do something about it. But as long as he was employed by a press organization, he had to remain a neutral observer. Publicly, little trace of his feelings was in his articles, but in private his correspondence and journals recorded his anger and disappointment, his appreciation of leaders such as United Mine Workers leader John L. Lewis—and his frustrations with the Supreme Court and other entities holding back reform. Now on his own, he could turn his frustrations into actions that could make a difference. He could work on behalf of candidates promoting progressive ideas. He could also speak for the causes he believed in. Robertson's transformation from journalist to advocate, and his possible trajectory from advocate to politician, was well in progress. In some of his writings, there are traces of the loving yet critical view of the South at the center of *Red Hills and Cotton.*

One of Robertson's earliest public political statements came in November 1937, as Senator James F. Byrnes of South Carolina filibustered an anti-lynching bill introduced by Senator Robert Wagner of New York. Just back from his sea voyage, Robertson was invited to speak before the Anderson Kiwanis Club, and he chose the occasion to deliver a speech in favor of the bill. Robertson was a reluctant public speaker. "You've been learning the rhumba—I've been learning to speak in public," he wrote to friend Dorothy Spalding that January, a night before he was to lecture to fifteen hundred students at Clemson. "It is just as odd, believe me . . . I'll about die tomorrow night about eight o'clock but I'm going to do it."[14]

Robertson had since made some peace with speaking, and that night in November he took the dais and delivered a clear message of support for civil rights. "The time has come for us publicly to re-examine and re-state our opinion on lynching," he told the crowd. Robertson acknowledged that the principal objection to the anti-lynching bill was that it would make lynching a federal crime rather than a state matter, thus inflaming suspicions dating back to Reconstruction that "the north is trying to put something over on us once more." However, Robertson argued that such opposition made it seem that the South was condoning lynching when, in truth, it did not. "The time has come for the South to support the bill—for political reasons, if for no other," he said. Robertson delivered a similar address to a gathering in Seneca. And even if he never fully warmed up to public speaking, he still felt a sense of achievement. "I have learned what I wanted to learn," he wrote. "To be able to speak in public well enough for the uses I will make of that—which will be much. But every citizen ought to be able to speak."[15]

Robertson employed a clever means of getting his progressive message across. In his heart, he believed anti-lynching legislation should be passed, believing blacks were entitled to the same civil rights as any other American. After all, he had known blacks not only as workers, but as friends, all his life. But he knew that to sell such a message to a conservative audience, he had to appeal to its anti-federalist sentiments. It was a tactic he would employ many times, most notably in his most acclaimed work.[16]

A month later, Robertson wrote to his cousin Bo Williams. Calling his work with a group seeking federal anti-lynching legislation "truly important," Robertson provided not only help with using the media, but a potent personal point of view. "Let me urge all of you to make your proceedings as dramatic as possible—even be sensational," he counseled. "It is entirely legitimate in this day and age. In fact, it is necessary." Robertson added, "It seems to me that one of the South's problems is mental—it lacks curiosity, it is polite, people don't say what they think for fear of disagreeing with someone other person. Somehow the South's mind must be stirred, it must will itself to change, curiosity must be aroused. . . . When the South is criticized in Congress, in the North, why must every Southerner jump at once to defend the South? Why does every Southerner assume that the South needs defending? . . . The South is a great force in the nation, it is itself, it need not be so sensitive. Such super-sensitivity indicates a feeling of inferiority, of being vulnerable. Why not admit the facts publicly? Admit if the attack is true that it is true."[17]

While Robertson worked on his friends' political campaigns, his first book made its debut. *Travelers' Rest* appeared in early May 1938. Its appearance resulted in polite, but scant, press attention. "Ben Robertson knows how to tell a story and his book is proof of it," stated a brief piece buried in the *Charleston News and Courier,* a former Robertson employer, prior to the book's release. A lengthy review, published nine days later in the same newspaper, stated that the Caldwells' doings "should interest anyone in South Carolina who can read—and a lot of folk outside the state, too." Delving into the book's origins and its author's eclectic background, the review stated, "Like the Caldwells, Robertson has been a doer rather than a sitter."[18]

But brief and polite notices didn't sell books. Rejected by the big publishers, denied the publicity and sales assistance a big publisher could have provided, and out the cost of having five hundred books printed, Robertson needed to get his book noticed and profitable. After some thinking, he and some friends in the press decided to gin up a little controversy. Not only would it let the news services carry the freight, but in the process Robertson could tweak some of the same sensitive, defensive Southern philosophies he criticized. Although it was not openly stated at the time, Robertson's friend Harry Ashmore, who worked for the Greenville *News* when the *Travelers' Rest* controversy happened, later wrote that "a good part of it [was] slyly stirred up by Ben's newspaper friends."[19]

The book had been out for less than a month and had drawn only spotty attention when Robertson's friend George Chaplin, the twenty-four-year-old city editor of the Greenville *News,* asked Mrs. John Logan Marshall, State Regent of the Daughters of the American Revolution, if she had read the book and what her thoughts were on it. Marshall's response made headlines the next day.

"A literary war broke out today across the South," stated an Associated Press story on June 13, as Mrs. Marshall responded that "the Red cotton hills of South Carolina, scene of the book, had suffered an 'inexplicable tragedy.'" She stated, "I am tired of reading so many bad things our people have done. I want to hear about some of the good things once more. So I protest the appearance of *Travelers' Rest.*" She called upon the wife of Governor Olin M. Johnston to state "if she thinks *Travelers' Rest* is the sort of book she would give to her son to read."[20]

Mrs. Johnston's agreement the following day delighted Chaplin and Robertson. "I have great respect for Mrs. Marshall's judgment and I feel that she is well worthy of reading after," the governor's wife said. "I don't know what is in the book, but if it reflects in any way on South Carolina I will resent it. I resent anyone's reflecting on our state. We may be poor, but we are very proud."[21]

Robertson responded with a broadside of his own: "The settlers of this country didn't wear powdered wigs or lace ruffles," he said in an Associated Press story. "I put them in buckskins so they would feel at home. You can't expect the niceties of society when you are carving an empire out of a forest. They're my people and I don't think telling the truth about them hurts."[22]

Robertson also prepared a lengthy statement in anticipation of Mrs. Johnston's public damnation of *Travelers' Rest.* "South Carolina is home to me, just as it is to them," his statement read, "and although I am liable to attack on some things where personal opinion is concerned, I insist I am invulnerable when it comes to the subject of my love for the upcountry cotton country as my country. I did not write to be read aloud. I wrote to be read in private." He added, "I wonder what Mrs. Marshall and Mrs. Johnston would say of the Book of Ecclesiastes and of the Song of Solomon."[23]

Friends and relatives weighed in. Robertson's father offered to send Mrs. Marshall a copy of *Uncle Tom's Cabin* to add to her summer reading. Clemson professor Alester G. Holmes wrote a supportive review of *Travelers' Rest* distributed by the Associated Press on June 13. "Reality is in Robertson's book in its sordidness and beauty, but the book is nonetheless idealistic in its portrayal of the hopes and longings of American life," Holmes wrote.[24]

While Robertson made public protest of Marshall's statement, privately he was elated with the outburst Chaplin provoked. "I think it has all been wonderful and I thank you and Harry for the way you have handled things," he wrote

Chaplin from Clemson. "We certainly have enjoyed it over here." Robertson offered to pay for telegrams to the *New York Times* and the *Herald Tribune,* and suggested Chaplin mail copies of the stories to *Time.* "Maybe they'd run something," Robertson mused.[25]

Chaplin promptly fired off a letter to *Time,* writing of "a literary gale" sweeping the state. "It occurred to me that perhaps *Time* would be interested in carrying something on the word war, which broke out when Greenville newspapermen asked the state regent of the Daughters of the American Revolution, Mrs. John Logan Marshall, for her reaction to the book," he wrote.[26]

In the meantime, Robertson and Chaplin developed further angles. "I can get you one more story," Robertson wrote, informing Chaplin of an upcoming family reunion. "I can get you an old mountain clan story—blood runs thicker than water and I know now they'll all be for me. They may think the book is hell but a Robertson is a Robertson."[27]

Chaplin agreed to the reunion story, which ran the following week. "The upstate Robertsons rallied defiantly today behind a kinsman whose Carolina book precipitated the state's worst literary uproar since the Peter Moody rumpus," it read. "Meeting on Conneross Creek, 65 members of the Robertson, McKinney and Armstrong families voiced their approval of month-old 'Travelers Rest,' which drew strong comment last week from the state DAR regent. . . . The book by Ben Robertson, Clemson college graduate and writer-traveler for the last 15 years, became an early topic of conversation: 'One of the kinfolks wrote it and that's all I want to know,' boomed Jim Alex Robertson, one of the clan's older leaders. . . . Sixty-five relatives added their verbal support of the author and the book." Newspapers also ran a photograph of "Generalissimo Robertson" showing off "fortifications"—in reality, a mound of dirt—around his Clemson home. It was there, said the caption, against anyone who might turn to violence to protest *Travelers' Rest.*[28]

Chaplin suggested to Robertson several other ways to draw attention to the book, including attempts at getting local Baptist Associations to issue denunciatory resolutions, and other ideas to draw the attention of potential publishers. "I can't think of any that doesn't carry a jail term or a tarring for you," he wrote. Chaplin even suggested planting hecklers at "Cotton Ed" Smith's campaign rallies who would shout, "You sound like a fellow in that book, *Traveler's Rest*!"[29]

The campaign finally got attention in the north. New York *Herald Tribune* columnist George Tucker interviewed Robertson in his nationally syndicated "Man About Manhattan" column on June 18. "It has let loose a lot of skeletons," Robertson told Tucker. "Folks have been coming to me to say they have the same kind of stories in their Carolina background." The author even confessed that "some of the papers have asked me to write reviews for them, so I guess that is the strangest break any writer ever got. I have been very modest, just saying it was a fine book and they ought to buy it." Tucker told his readers that *Travelers' Rest* was "the Illiad [*sic*] of pioneers who planted the corn and fought off 'the painted death,' as the Indian scalping parties are called."[30]

The controversy spawned more serious, and less charitable, examinations in book review sections. *Herald Tribune* reviewer Fred T. Marsh stated that Robertson's storytelling was "sketchy" and contained "considerable to complain about," but had "a quality here, too, a freshness and a poetry at times; it is a clean-cut tale." Others were not even that kind. "Mr. Robertson has gathered material enough for two or three books but he seems to be sadly lacking in the power of selection and organization," stated G. O. Mudge in the *Raleigh Observer.* "Taken as a whole, the writing is of a character that will hardly do credit to a high school senior."[31]

Although reports on Mrs. Marshall's reaction to the book had been carried nationwide by the Associated Press, no amount of press attention compared to the July 4, 1938, *Time* article on *Travelers' Rest.* "Southern literary tempers still have a big pinch of gunpowder in them," began *Time*'s stylish treatment, based largely on the information supplied by Chaplin:

> Latest Southerner to get scorched is 35-year-old Ben Robertson of Clemson, S.C., whose novel about his ancestors brought on himself the wrath of old settlers, neighbors and the D.A.R.
>
> An honest, spotty book, *Travelers' Rest* traces the violent history of an old Southern family through their fights with nature, the neighbors and each other, shows old pioneers with their buckskins off and their coonskin caps hanging from the wrong hatracks, wenching, gambling, stealing, murdering. What bothered old settlers was that Author Robertson attributed these activities to prominent people readily identified as his ancestors—Indian scouts, Senators, wealthy planters, Civil War heroes. When neighbors complained, "You've really slung mud over us all," when a regent of the State D.A.R. jumped to the attack, the Robertson family called a reunion at near-by Chauga Creek and with clan spirit outweighing pride in their distinguished ancestors, defended the book and outspoken Descendant Ben.[32]

The *Time* article brought a moment of high-level interest. Warner Brothers requested a copy of *Travelers' Rest* for examination so "we may determine its possibility as a talking picture subject." Robertson also submitted the manuscript to Macmillan, hoping the book's sudden notoriety would translate into interest from a major publisher.[33]

Instead, slowly, the book faded into obscurity. Odd reviews still popped up, less focused on the controversy than the book's merit as a work of literature. "It is too ambitious" to capture the Caldwells' story in one volume, the *Atlanta Constitution*'s Ole Lexau wrote. "This novel contains purple passages aplenty; also examples of stark beauty, rare in their intensity—also, alas, passages decidedly overwritten. It fails—if it does fail—because it has attempted the impossible."[34]

One last protest came in September, when seventy-eight-year-old "Uncle Charlie" McJunkin, a retired printer from Greenville's newspapers, the *News* and *Piedmont,* burned a gasoline-soaked copy of Robertson's book. "Why, I can remember nearly everything that young upstart wrote about," McJunkin said as he watched the pages go up, "and I can say the people of South Carolina have been libeled. . . . It ain't no use showing up all the human weaknesses of our forefathers. I'd rather have our children worship those men as the heroes they undoubtedly were. How can they have any faith in a hero when people like Ben Robertson show him running around in his underwear?"[35]

Scattered (and likely staged) protests like McJunkin's notwithstanding, the controversy had passed like a summer storm. Governor Johnston's wife never issued a direct opinion on *Travelers' Rest.* Later that year, when she released a list of books she deemed fit for South Carolina schoolchildren to read, she explained the omission of *Travelers' Rest* by saying she did not feel it would be appropriate to include on her list.[36]

Thus *Travelers' Rest* became an obscure entry in the Southern literary canon, overshadowed by Robertson's later, and better, works. As a work of literature, its moments of brilliance were overwhelmed by its many excesses. But for Ben Robertson, *Travelers' Rest* had served its purpose. It had satisfied his need to tell the story he had yearned to write for years. The controversy he and his newspaper friends generated had let him tweak the state's cultural establishment. The writing and publishing process had taught him much, and the simple fact the story was between hard covers gave him satisfaction. Although *Travelers' Rest* was raw and unrefined, its underlying themes would someday emerge in a much better, and more enduring, work.

CHAPTER 9

A New South

In May, Theo Vaughn abandoned his long-shot run for the Senate. "Cotton Ed," the incumbent senator who often claimed to be acting in the traditions of Robert E. Lee and Wade Hampton, vanquished his remaining opponents and won the Democratic primary. In a solidly Democratic South Carolina, that assured his reelection.[1]

With the campaigns in full swing, Robertson went to work covering the fall elections for the *Anderson Independent.* As the candidates—eight running for governor (including Burnet Maybank, for whom Robertson had done some work behind the scenes), and several running for the House of Representatives—traveled the state courting support from voters, Robertson followed and reported on the proceedings. Reporting for a small daily newspaper might have seemed like a letdown for any other reporter who had, only years before, been putting questions to the President in the Oval Office or capturing vignettes of life in Manhattan. But for Robertson, a born storyteller who loved capturing color and detail, the chance to cover home-state politics for a paper close to his hometown not only kept him busy but let him have some fun. Writing in his distinctive style full of character details, Robertson's tales of the 1938 campaign form some of the most entertaining accounts of South Carolina politics of the period. After covering a stump meeting in Newberry that August, Robertson wrote:

> Blackmon, the automobile salesman, a young man in a green suit, introduced himself as a man paying his own way, as a man running because he thought the state ought to have a good man for the governor. "Burnet Maybank's middle name is Rhett," he shouted. He reminded the people that a man named Rhett—R. Goodwyn Rhett—had been president of the People's State Bank. "That man is a kinsman of Mr. Maybank, he added, "and that man, so I am told, took the stump for Maybank when he ran for the mayor

> of Charleston. If that is so . . . if Maybank used the name of Rhett when he was running for mayor why is he ashamed to use it now?"
>
> Blackmon said his name was Dewitt Talmadge Blackmon and he was not ashamed of any part of it.
>
> Easterlin, the Spartanburg man, told of being called two years ago by the Almighty to fight alcohol—he pronounced it "alky-hol" and labeled it "the arch-enemy of the human race whether called wine, beer, liquor, white mule or white lightning."
>
> He seldom spoke of being a candidate for governor; more often he spoke of "making this campaign against the evil." He said if elected governor "liquor would never touch his lips."[2]

Later that same month Robertson was back in London for an article he was writing for the *Saturday Evening Post.* There he observed the relationship between the people of Great Britain and King George VI. "The King represents British security and freedom—the England that for 900 years has never been invaded," Robertson wrote, characterizing Buckingham Palace as "a sort of fulltime Williamsburg, Virginia, with a vast number of ladies and gentlemen who stand around in Elizabethan costumes and keep up an elaborate palace ritual." But within Robertson's observations were signs his feelings about the British were changing: "Their Majesties are trying, with the best intentions in the world, to fill the role the British have created for their constitutional monarchs. Their Majesties are long and strong on duty, and when thousands of their subjects were prepared to flee London during the German crisis, they, as King and Queen, came at once to Buckingham from the security of Scotland. Their subjects wrote letters to the papers about this act of their sovereigns, and in these letters King George and Queen Elizabeth saw themselves referred to, for the first time in their reign, not as The King and Queen, but as 'Our King and Queen.'"[3]

Robertson's views of the European situation changed further while sailing home aboard the French liner *Normandie.* One day, he overheard a discussion about British Prime Minister Neville Chamberlain's decision to cede the Sudetenland to Hitler. One of the ship's officers replied, "Well, that means we'll have one more year of peace, and I can use another year." As Robertson realized how close war was, his perspective changed. "I realized then that our lives during war mean nothing at all, and all our plans are nothing," he wrote after the war began. "Only the war matters."[4]

Back in the United States, Robertson quickly made plans for a new article that would let him return to sea, checking with his maritime contacts about catching a Standard Oil Company tanker from Charleston to Aruba so he could report on the booming oil industry in the Dutch West Indies. Tom Waring, whose brother-in-law had worked on a construction job in Aruba, told Robertson that many Charlestonians had worked there at one time or another. With some help, Robertson arranged to leave for the island in March 1939.[5]

Always happy to help his alma mater, Robertson accepted an invitation to speak at Clemson. Student Arthur Williams, later to become a physician, was walking home with friend and future journalist Earl Mazo after hearing Robertson speak about covering the king and queen of England. "It is hard to believe," Williams said, "that Ben was educated in this isolated school, goes out and talks to the world's important people and comes back here reminiscing about them like a country bumpkin who was fortunate to get to see the world's leaders."

"I don't see anything unusual about that," Mazo replied. "He's a man who knows exactly who he is, part of a great big family that possesses the sun and lets China use it part-time. He couldn't be anything but what he is."[6]

The week before Robertson sailed for Aruba, he and Bo Williams drove to Columbia for a meeting of the South Caroliniana Society. Burnet Maybank, who had won his race for governor, invited them to visit his office at the State House while they were in town. As Robertson sat in the governor's office, he couldn't help feeling impressed with how Maybank had carried out his new duties. "Quietly, he has begun where his predecessor, Olin Johnston, so different in every respect from Burnet, left off. Olin railed, called out the troops, threatened, attacked . . . got nowhere. Here Burnet in office six weeks has had to start on, quietly, calmly, constitutionally."[7]

Maybank invited Robertson and Williams to the governor's mansion that evening for dinner. As they had coffee and macaroons after dinner, the three discussed the South's status in America. Maybank began talking about Huey Long. As governor, "the Kingfish" had put Louisiana deep into debt to pay for badly needed improvements in public roads and education, and had fought corporations he believed took advantage of the state's people. He parlayed his popularity into election to the United States Senate. Long attacked the New Deal as being inadequate to fix the nation's economic problems, proposed a radical "Share Our Wealth" plan for income redistribution, and veered into demagoguery. Before he was assassinated in 1935, some had feared Long held the potential to become a dictator.

As Charleston's mayor, Maybank had stated that Long would not be welcome in the city should he visit. But as governor, he privately confessed, "I think the

South would have got far more from the nation if Huey Long had lived. Huey got things done." The admission startled Robertson. "Aren't you afraid of the ultimate implication of Huey?" he asked. Maybank replied, "Not for the South."[8]

A week later Robertson was aboard a ship bound for Aruba, headed for a small colony of Americans working in the oil industry. Young, well-educated, male engineers were sent to Aruba on two-year contracts with oil companies. There, the single men competed for the attentions of the small number of single American women on Aruba, whom the men outnumbered twenty to one. In the *Saturday Evening Post,* Robertson described this modern-day paradise as a place with "no depression and no unemployment," where workers lived in nice, stuccoed houses and had their every need met by the oil company. "The company has a retirement plan for their old age, and, as the oil business gets bigger every year, they have faith in the security of the future," he wrote. Their main worries, Robertson noted, concerned "how they are going to get the money Germany owes them and what would happen if sometime a warship would appear and drop just one shell among the storage tanks."[9]

In May, Robertson repaid a debt to his mentors at Missouri by agreeing to speak during Journalism Week. From St. Louis, Robertson traveled to Columbia in a chauffeured limousine with *Cosmopolitan* editor Frances Whiting and fellow newspaperman Homer Croy. As they sped along through the spring rain, they talked about the writing trade. For Robertson, it was an enjoyable visit to a campus he hadn't seen in ten years. Frank Martin, who had supervised the *Daily Missourian* when Robertson was a student, was now the journalism school's dean. That night, Martin had the distinguished guests over for dinner, where they discussed Missouri politics and the influence of Kansas City political boss Thomas Pendergast.[10]

While Missouri politics were the main topic of conversation during dinner, those of his home state had been on Robertson's mind. Robertson believed South Carolina's devotion to the Democratic Party was becoming a hindrance. Although he was a devoted Democrat, Robertson felt the party took the South for granted and needed a viable opposition to keep it responsive to the people. Robertson complained to friends and family that "we as good Democrats have got to organize a Republican opposition in the South," saying the party's leaders "are not going to pay the least attention to us in national politics until we do have not only a real opposition but a threatening one."[11]

In February he had told a meeting of the United Daughters of the Confederacy that if the women of the South announced they would vote against the Democratic presidential nominee in 1940, it would force both Washington and the national party to listen more carefully to the South. Such a move, he maintained, would "change the South from a defensive to an offensive unit." On his way home from the Missouri gathering, he amplified this case in a speech before the Advertising Club of Atlanta. "I believe the time has come for us to think about the price we are paying for staying a one-party section of a two-party country," Robertson said. "American politics is based on making trades. It is based on good horse-swapping and the Democratic South has nothing to swap. Do we want to remain in the position of a man who goes to a horse-swapping convention without a horse?"[12]

After the address, while Robertson chatted with an *Atlanta Journal* reporter, "a child-like figure breezed over, effortlessly, as though flying," and struck up a conversation with him. It was Margaret Mitchell, author of the best-selling *Gone with the Wind.* Robertson characterized her as "just in her element, with all Atlanta people about . . . she is Lindberghlike." As they made small talk, Robertson thought of how some of his Atlanta friends believed Mitchell had suffered with the sudden success of *Gone with the Wind.*[13]

A few weeks later Robertson, long an enthusiast of folk singing who had decried the lack of interest in preserving this form of folklore for future generations, made a permanent contribution to the cause. Robertson's friend John Lomax, a folklorist who had been fascinated with folk songs since his childhood in Texas, was working with the Library of Congress to record and collect folk songs from around the country. The project, which began in 1933 as a Works Progress Administration program, ultimately collected more than ten thousand folk song recordings for the Library of Congress.

In 1939, Lomax and his wife Ruby set out on a recording expedition through Texas, Louisiana, Arkansas, Mississippi, Alabama, Georgia, South Carolina, and Virginia. Robertson had mailed the Lomaxes a flyer about an upcoming group singing in Toccoa Falls, Georgia, and offered to take them over so they could make some recordings at the event. On Friday, June 10, the Lomaxes drove to Clemson from Murrells Inlet, arriving at the Robertson home that evening. In their field notes they wrote, "The home has a very fine library and there were evidences around of Mr. Robertson's activities as a writer."

On their first full day the Lomaxes recorded two quartets that Robertson invited over. The following day, Robertson, the Lomaxes, and a student reporter from Clemson drove to Anderson, where they visited a radio broadcast by one of the Toccoa festival's organizers. Then Robertson stopped at the Anderson County Convict Camp and asked to have a small group of the black prisoners sing for the project. But Robertson and the Lomaxes were horrified to find all eighty prisoners fastened by ankle chains onto a single larger chain. In order for a small group to sing for them, all eighty prisoners had to come outside the tent. In group singing, Lomax couldn't move the microphone closer. When a singer said he could get no closer to the microphone, all the others on the chain had to shuffle their leg chains along the big chain until the singer was in microphone range.

John Lomax was moved by how the prisoners handled this indignity with a good nature. And he was appalled by what he later called "the hard fate shown by these black boys as they slowly dragged themselves about with their legs manacled to that long chain." Though as a folklorist Lomax was familiar with the term "chain gang," and though Lomax had often defended the South against charges of brutal treatment of its prisoners, it was the first time he had actually seen a group of prisoners chained together. Robertson said he had never seen such a thing either. As upset about the prisoners' treatment as were the Lomaxes, he urged them to write Governor Maybank about it, and Robertson himself wrote letters to express his own protest. After lunch, the foursome drove to Toccoa Falls for the Georgia-Carolina Singing Festival. About twenty thousand people from three states had gathered for the festival, where the Lomaxes gleaned more recordings for the Library of Congress.[14]

That evening, Robertson wanted to take the Lomaxes to a traditional service at a rural Negro church, and they set out for the Little Hope Baptist Church. As clouds loomed overhead, the group stopped to talk with some of the congregation's members, who told them the service would be held at the nearby schoolhouse instead. The fifty or so in attendance, in a dimly-lit schoolhouse that was not their usual venue, seemed uncertain as the service began. Trying to beat the approaching storm, the Lomaxes set up their equipment and began to record. Soon all in attendance found their song, giving the Lomaxes "several lined hymns and one very pretty cradle song" before they stopped. By then the rain was pouring. Robertson raced outside, backed his car up as close to the schoolhouse door as he could, and the deacons helped the Lomaxes load their equipment into the car. While Robertson eased the car along the slick clay roads that led home, John Lomax thought of all those in attendance, wondering what their fine Sunday clothes would look like after having to walk home through rain and mud. "They are a very patient, fine-spirited people," the Lomaxes wrote in their field notes.[15]

That summer, Ben Robertson visited the College of Charleston to deliver an address on the condition of the South. Those in the audience no doubt expected a warm, gentle tribute to their native region. What they got was something else. In his remarks Robertson distilled all he had seen and felt in a lifetime's experience and a decade of reporting, the stagnation he felt in Washington, the poverty and suffering he had seen everywhere from Pickens County to the flooded Ohio River valley, the countless conversations with Bo Williams about education and poverty, the anger he felt over Southern politicians who relied on racism to stay in power and who refused to act against lynching. It was, by far, Robertson's boldest political statement yet, a counterpart to how the *Travelers' Rest* controversy had tweaked genteel sensibilities the year before.

Robertson told his audience that he had "come down here to the city of the aristocrats and talk to you about the Upcountry that I belong to—the country of the poor whites." In outlining his vision of the "three Souths" he encountered, Robertson used literary analogies. One South was that of Thomas Wolfe and William Faulkner, where the emphasis was on suffering. Robertson asked why Southerners had such a fascination with suffering, blaming it on the entrenched politicians who refused to provide civil rights to all, and the poor economic conditions of the South:

> We pass along the Southern country roads on a Sunday night and we hear the black people singing "I'm troubled in my soul" and we hear the white people singing "I'm weary and heavy-laden" and we say the melodies are beautiful but the words are so sad. We feel sad when we see so many thousand acres of Southern land washing away and it makes us feel sad to see so many of the old homes deserted. We see the tenant farmer and his wife and three children counting their money in the fall after they have sold the cotton crop. They have $250 to live on for the next year. We hear a man singing "Eight cent cotton and forty cent meat, how in the world can the poor man eat?" We see a fourth of the tenant farmers packing everything they have in a wagon and moving on to another farm. Every autumn they will move on somewhere else, hoping to find something better somewhere.[16]

The second South, characterized by Wolfe in *Look Homeward, Angel,* had never stopped mourning the Lost Cause. This was a quality of the South that Robertson had known from his earliest days, as he had listened to his family members tell stories of the Civil War, the subtext of defeat ever apparent. He asked the audience to imagine a beautiful, proud, but poor lady who spent her days in a rocking chair, weeping. A man stopped to ask what the matter was. "Uncle Joe is dead," she cried. The man tried to comfort her by asking if Uncle Joe had lived in that house; the lady responded in the negative. "He didn't live here but my mother told me about him." After several moments of questioning, the man asked when Uncle Joe died. "He died at Gettysburg," she wept. Robertson explained:

> We have let Uncle Joe become our symbol. We know more about Uncle Joe and feel a lot sadder about him than we do about our own brother John who was killed by the Germans at St. Mihiel. We grieve over the Gettysburg peach orchard more than we do over the poverty of the tenants or the erosion of our soil. We mourn over the Civil War so much that we have come to live our Southern lives at third hand—rather than have adventures of our own, we live over what our mother said about her brother.
>
> Why exactly do we mourn? Well, who is Uncle Joe? He stands for a way of life and when he was killed, that way of living was taken from us. . . . We wanted to live in a rural country, and we had an industrial America forced on us. We are lost Jeffersonians in Alexander Hamilton's land.[17]

The third South that Robertson described was that of Ellen Glasgow, the Virginia writer whose novels spoke of a South whose people discarded the social and economic norms of yesteryear. It was the South of leaders like Burnet Maybank, people of vision who helped working-class Southerners solve their problems. "Those are the real Southerners, and if anybody in the South is entitled to look back to glory, Miss Glasgow's Southerners are the ones. The South of their fathers was a real glory. But it was not Uncle Joe's South."

Robertson urged his audience to become more interested in events outside the South—"You can travel a week through the South without hearing anything more than casual references to situations in Europe," he warned—and to sacrifice some leisure in order to solve the South's problems. "I believe the South has already gone too far in its casualness," he said, before encouraging a new ethic:

> Let's organize our days better and work harder, let's realize that we are in an industrial world and, while keeping all we can of farm life, make the most of the world we are obliged to live in. Let's realize that we are agricultural and that our natural resources, other than ourselves and our land, are few. All we have is water power and some coal and iron. What we must combat is exploitation. Let's try to become kinder-hearted, let's try to develop a Southern passion for social justice, let's open our eyes to human suffering. And the next time anybody mentions Gettysburg, let's get up and go plant a pine tree or pile rocks in a gully. It won't change the South, but it will change us, and before long we'll find we are gathering an entire new world for our books.[18]

And echoing Governor Maybank's surprising words from their conversation months before, Robertson dropped a bombshell. "What we need in the South is a new leader," he said. "What we need is a man with the heart and mind of Jefferson and the tactics of Huey Long."[19]

Robertson's appeals for social progress and help for the downtrodden were aired in venues large and small. Speaking to a group at Clemson, he criticized those who cited a verse from the eleventh chapter of Deuteronomy as proof the Bible justified the world's poor: "For the poor shall never cease out of the land." Robertson said if those people would continue reading that verse, they would find the words, "Therefore, I command thee, saying, thou shalt open thine hand wide unto thy brother, to thy poor, and to thy needy in the land." The real meaning, Robertson said, was that suffering needed to be relieved; the verse's true meaning was one of progress.[20]

His efforts to help those in need continued: writing to a South Carolina congressman to get help for the Catawba Indians, writing to Governor Maybank about propagating soybeans as a crop in South Carolina, and even quietly extending loans to college students. But the chance meeting from his Atlanta visit was about to echo in one of the most bizarre moments of Robertson's journalism career.[21]

After Margaret Mitchell had breezed over to him after his Atlanta speech, Robertson had wondered if she really had suffered after the success of *Gone with the Wind.* Now that the novel was becoming a motion picture, Robertson began a feature about her for the *Saturday Evening Post.* He had no problems getting Mitchell's friends from Atlanta and elsewhere to contribute to the story. Mitchell herself was another matter. Robertson found her not only reluctant to cooperate, but a very contradictory figure who simultaneously loved and loathed her newfound fame.

In a letter to his editor at the *Post,* Martin Sommers, Robertson wrote his findings about "Scarlett O'Mitchell, the Lady who says No." Robertson was bemused. "All of MM friends are puzzled by the quality of mind which seems to force her to lay down rules and formulas. She sticks to them but then goes all the way round to do almost the same thing in another way. . . . She will not autograph a book but she will write a three page letter telling why she can't autograph it and sign her name to the letter. . . . To Atlanta, Peggy is a strange combination of a simple girl and the great world author who is too busy for a moment's time—there is all the mail waiting and there is all the pressure and all the telephone calls. Yet she will stand on the street and talk half an hour and ask you to come on home for supper—take pot luck which may include turnip greens and cornbread. . . . She is a mixture of incongruities as one friend said 'She is Shirley Temple and Mae West and Dr. Jekyll and Mrs. Marsh.'"[22]

Sommers believed Mitchell's behavior was a normal reaction to sudden fame, but encouraged him to gather the information and write the article, then submit it to Mitchell "saying that you've done it regardless; she might, in such a circumstance, open up and really give."[23]

Robertson took his editor's advice and wrote the piece, then submitted it to Mitchell for her comment with a courteous, almost apologetic letter. "The *Post* has told me to go ahead anyhow and write a story about you," he wrote. "I am sorry to have to do this . . . I want to do as serious a story as I can, a friendly and sympathetic one, too, that will not only be about you but will also be about a current aspect of the United States—how fame has given you no time as an author to write, but has caused you to give up all your time to attending to the business that has developed because of your writing. Which shouldn't be. I want to show that you have been a victim of fame in much the same way that Lindbergh has, only you have not become bitter." Robertson, in an unusual ethic for a journalist, offered to "change anything you say and send it in, changed as you wish it."[24]

Mitchell responded with a five-page letter objecting to the article. "I want you to believe that I am trying to save both of us from something that is dangerous and embarrassing," she wrote. "It will injure me if a superficial, erroneous article is published about me, and it will hurt your reputation and standing if you are the writer of it, and I just cannot see how this article could be anything other than that." Mitchell stated she was willing to write to the editors at the *Post* to have the story killed.[25]

Robertson felt stung. "Boy, oh boy, I stepped in the where angels don't tread," he wrote to his friend Jack Alexander at the *New Yorker.* "That Margaret Mitchell idea sounded fine to me, so I said I'd have a try at it and I walked in. What an experience! She is the kind who keeps things from being printed about her by yelling she'll be damaged and will have to see her lawyer and she's written me a letter as long as *Gone with the Wind* calling me no gentleman and a betrayer of great authors in the homes of their intimate friends. . . . She won't talk but her friends will talk their heads off. She can take up a simple little statement like Margaret Mitchell is 34 years old and write a treatise on it as long as the Battle of Atlanta scene and make you think in the end no one is ever thirty-four and that there really is no Margaret Mitchell and that anyhow she will be slandered and have to file suit. Nuts."[26]

To other friends Robertson expressed his bafflement. "I have been in Atlanta wrangling with Miss Jesus Christ Margaret Mitchell," he wrote to Bob Neville, a *Herald Tribune* friend now working as *Time*'s foreign news editor. "There wouldn't be any free press in the US if everybody acted like J.C. How do you like this for her attitude—the world premiere of *Gone with the Wind* is to be in Atlanta and the stars are coming but she doesn't want reporters or photographers present. And she was a newspaper woman herself." In the end, the article never progressed beyond the draft stage.[27]

At the end of August, Robertson was in New York to finish up an article for the *Post.* While there, he saw a friend off on the German liner *Columbus* as it prepared to sail for Europe. As they talked, his friend noticed the ship's crew acting in haste, wanting to get the ship underway as quickly as possible. "They've heard something," his friend said. "I don't know what it is, but I can tell by the way they are all hurrying about."[28]

Three friends reunite in Palm Springs, California. Robertson (at right) with Robert Neville, a colleague from the New York *Herald Tribune.* Between them is Merle Sproul, onetime hostess at Honolulu's Moana Hotel. Special Collections & Archives, Clemson University Libraries, Clemson, South Carolina.

On September 1, they found out. Germany had invaded Poland, and Europe was at war. The crew of the *Columbus* had been scrambling to get the ship out of New York before it could be seized.

Robertson, just back from New York, spent the day listening to radio news reports. "Now that the war has come at last I find I am not as appalled as I was this time last September," he wrote. That morning, Robertson wrote to the Secretary of War and offered his services as a war correspondent should the United States enter the hostilities.[29]

Inside, he chewed over his feelings about what was to come, feeling Europe was in danger but balancing that against his impressions from London years earlier. "This war begins with us in this country divided in mind," he wrote. "It ought to be and it ought not to be."

> And we know very well where our sympathies lie. We are for France and England. I say to myself that I ought to be neutral, that this country ought to be neutral, that there is no hope for permanent peace in Europe, that war is their pattern and that we can do the world a service by staying out, by saving ourselves. I say they didn't pay us for the last war and they insulted us and called us Uncle Shylock and I say our forefathers came to this country to turn their backs on Europe. I remember every time I ever got on a train in Waterloo Station for Southampton how I felt that I was getting away from Europe, that I was going home and that an ocean separated us from Europe. And then when I heard the French had captured the *Bremen,* I was delighted. It was only rumor and I was sorry to hear it. I stayed up last night trying to hear what I hoped I would hear—that the British had bombed Berlin. For I think a little terror would do the Germans good. . . .
>
> Why shouldn't President Roosevelt dig out one of President Wilson's old notes and send it again. We are back again where we were then except that we have radio and airplanes and a new crop of boys. And we have had three revolutions—the Italian, German and Russian revolutions. And what will we face at the end of this war—revolution. I have said many times that the British Empire could not come through another great world war, win or lose, it would see its ruling caste go down and perhaps the crown would go with it. Being an American Democrat, I am against the British snobbery but I can't say I am ready to see the Empire go . . .
>
> Can Britain come through, granting it will win? Can we come through? Are we not buying our way off? What is the New Deal but buying? We are not solving the problem of distribution in our civilization; we are not willing to divide the work, to give leisure to the masses. It all is part of a great world

> movement and Hitler is merely a symptom. The status of the tenant farmer here is a part of it and the strikes in the mill are a part of it. It is involved and far reaching and its base is economic. . . .
>
> We should not enter this war. But will we?[30]

Around the world—in Europe and in the Far East—war winds were stirring. Against this backdrop, Robertson flew to Honolulu in January 1940 to report on American defenses and potential American bases across the Pacific, spending a month in Hawaii to survey the situation there. While there, his old editor at the *Star-Bulletin* persuaded him to write a feature on the Ewa Plantation Company's golden jubilee celebration. "It was an American show," he wrote, "a native Hawaii demonstration of the mechanical genius of the United States. More than that, it was a reminder to those of us who know the facts that Hawaii discovered long before certain other parts of the United States that the best way to get along is to cooperate."[31]

Robertson flew on to Guam from Honolulu, making stops at Pan American World Airways' seaplane bases on Midway Island and Wake Island. At Guam, Robertson looked into the American presence there, where the United States took care of twenty-one thousand of the island's residents. Although Robertson noted many good things the United States was doing for the people of Guam, such as vaccination and education programs, he lamented the island's poor economy. He didn't like that the United States refused to open the island up for trade, or that the American government didn't fortify the island, work that would also provide employment for the natives. The people of Guam hoped Congress would extend the Federal Homestead Act to the island, a measure that would provide them some help.

A decade before, Robertson had written of Hawaii, Australia, and Java in quaint, colonial terms that, as did many stories of that day, made the people of those places sound like happy and exotic curiosities overseen by benevolent nations. But now a more mature, more seasoned Robertson saw Guam as a place whose residents were being shortchanged by a distant, indifferent government. Robertson wrote his findings in an article, "What Are We Doing in Guam?," which was later published in the *American.* Privately, he became a proponent of federal aid for the people of Guam. From Guam, Robertson went on to visit China, Japan, and the Philippines. He sailed for home aboard a Norwegian freighter, leaving Manila in late February and arriving in Los Angeles on March 21.[32]

Years later, Robertson's sister, Mary, looked through her brother's notes from the Pacific trip. In them, she found detailed listings of American defenses in the Pacific, surveys of Guam and Midway and the Philippines and other strategically-important locations, and information about the Japanese presence nearby. On one piece of paper, Robertson had scribbled "maybe enlist 'mc' to work undercover." In addition, she found a radiogram from the State Department authorizing a four-month extension of his passport to visit ports in Asia, and directing him to surrender it to the State Department when he returned. After these discoveries, Mary wrote to Wright Bryan that she was convinced Ben was working as an agent for the State Department when he took the Pacific tour—a relationship, she insisted, that continued through his subsequent assignments.[33]

The voice that had once merely described people, places, and events had grown more discerning, more analytical, and more opinionated. And, with the world consumed by war, a job was coming Robertson's way that required just such a voice.

CHAPTER 10

"My God, what a war!"

Ralph Ingersoll hadn't set out to become a newspaper publisher. Now, he was one. His career had started at the *New York Journal-American,* but he had quit after determining that the paper's owner, William Randolph Hearst, was a "lying charlatan." Ingersoll became a writer at the *New Yorker,* using his high-placed social contacts to feed his new creation, a column called "Talk of the Town."[1]

Ingersoll's success at the *New Yorker* got the attention of publisher and fellow Yale alumnus Henry Luce, who had launched the weekly news magazine *Time* in 1927. Luce hired Ingersoll in 1929 and put him in charge of reviving the struggling *Fortune* magazine. Ingersoll rebuilt the ailing magazine with dispatch, bringing in the likes of writer James Agee and photographer Margaret Bourke-White. The success of the restyled *Fortune* prompted Ingersoll to propose a new publication, a weekly picture magazine that illustrated the news and life itself through distinctive photography. Luce put Ingersoll to work on the project, which premiered in 1936 as *Life.*

After *Life*'s debut, Ingersoll answered a summons to Luce's office, hoping to hear praise and encouragement from his boss. Instead, Luce told him *Life* was no longer his to manage. Even after Ingersoll's long hours and intense effort on the project, Luce worried that Ingersoll's ambitions exceeded what the company could bear, and he feared being held personally responsible if overoptimistic management bankrupted the entire company. Instead, *Life* would be turned over to a more cautious lieutenant, Roy Larsen.

Stunned, Ingersoll learned not only that the magazine he'd created was being taken from him, but that his new job would require him to support that lost project. *Time* would help support *Life* by providing personnel, resources, and money. It was now Ingersoll's job, Luce said, to "take over *Time* and see that it goes on making the money I'll need to spend on *Life.*" Coolly concealing his disappointment, Ingersoll decided that when *Life* was profitable, or when five years had passed, he would leave Luce's organization. As he left the meeting, Ingersoll silently vowed to "never again lose myself in the creation of a publication that belonged to someone else—even Harry Luce."[2]

As Ingersoll set about reorganizing *Time,* hiring new writers and trying to change writing styles and editorial outlooks that had been lampooned, he also started thinking about a way to reform the American newspaper. While on vacation, Ingersoll dictated a sixty-one-page prospectus for "a daily newsmagazine" that used quality writing and photography, elements he had used to turn around *Fortune* and develop *Life.* And the newspaper itself, to be aimed at the lower middle-class, would seek "truth and the idea of a better mankind."[3]

Back in New York, as his techniques as the publisher of *Time* made the money needed to make *Life* a success, Ingersoll discussed the newspaper concept with Luce. At first, the magnate showed interest in the concept, and it seemed Luce might not only lead Ingersoll to investors but might contribute a little funding himself. Unfortunately, the relationship between the two men was turning sour. They disagreed politically and philosophically, with Luce's increasing Republicanism clashing with Ingersoll's more liberal views. Luce disliked Ingersoll's use of "scientific principle" in the management of *Time.* And on a personality level, the two men just were not compatible. In 1939, Ingersoll received a telegram telling him *Life* was profitable; and making good on his pledge to quit when the magazine was in the black, he left Luce's empire. With that, he could begin work on the new "daily newsmagazine."[4]

At the time, there were eight major daily newspapers in the New York metropolitan area. Ingersoll's would be distinctive. It would combine top-quality writing and photography with Ingersoll's political commitments to the New Deal, to antifascism, and to excellence in journalism. The newspaper would give editorial freedom to its reporters, letting them report and interpret events according to their own perceptions and informed judgments.[5]

By early 1940, Ingersoll's ambitious idea was becoming reality, and it had help from President Franklin Roosevelt. The president, who had decided to run for a third term in office, had taken a beating from conservative papers such as the Chicago *Daily Tribune.* Ingersoll, a supporter of the president, had notified Roosevelt of his plan. The president liked the idea of a new, liberal daily newspaper. Through direct and indirect persuasion, Roosevelt helped Ingersoll get the $1.5 million he needed to start the newspaper, money that came from an array of contributors that included advertising executive Chester Bowles, chewing gum magnate William Wrigley, and department store heir Marshall Field III.

The new paper, which debuted on Tuesday, June 18, 1940, was named *PM.* It was a stylish five-cent tabloid with beautiful printing and typesetting, high-quality photography, and also an activist point of view. Ingersoll embraced interpretation in his paper's editorial policy; the new paper would seek to represent "truth," not "objectivity." Rejecting that a reporter could be "impartial," Ingersoll stated: "We are against people who push other people around, just for the fun of pushing, whether they live in this country or abroad. We are against fraud and deceit and greed and cruelty and we seek to expose their practitioners. We are for people who are kindly and courageous and honest. We respect intelligence, and accomplishment, openmindedness, religious tolerance. We do not believe all mankind's problems are soluble in any existing order, certainly not our own, and we propose to applaud those who seek constructively to improve the way men live together. We are American and we prefer democracy to any other form of government."[6]

Ingersoll built his staff from three major sources: experts who had little professional background, journalists who were newly trained in "new" journalism of the sort practiced in *Time,* and established professionals from the wire services and major newspapers. One of Ingersoll's first hires from his lieutenants at *Time* was Robert Neville, as foreign affairs editor. Neville, knowing his department needed good writers, thought of his friend Ben Robertson, with whom he'd worked at the *Herald Tribune.* Robertson was intelligent, progressive, well-traveled, and had a distinctive style—a great fit for *PM*'s foreign desk.[7]

Back in Clemson, Robertson was toying with translating his progressive politics into a run for office. His eyes on the South Carolina Third District seat in the House of Representatives, Robertson queried his newspaper friends about his chances against incumbent Butler Hare, a conservative Democrat who supported poll taxes and opposed Roosevelt's union-friendly Fair Employment Practices Commission. Greenville editor George Chaplin told Robertson he "would make a fine race for Congress . . . you'd either win by a big margin or get hell beat out of you." Earl Mazo, a recent Clemson graduate hired by Chaplin, told Robertson, "The consensus is that with your knowledge of publicity, and your liberalism, you'd beat hell out of John Taylor, but they're not so sure about Butler Hare. They all say that they want you to run."[8]

While Robertson pondered his political prospects, an offer arrived from *PM.* Ingersoll's editorial policy, which placed emphasis on humanity, was a good match to Robertson's style. He'd get to work with Bob Neville. Ingersoll promised Robertson leeway in his interpretation of events as he saw them. Robertson dropped his immediate political plans and went back to New York.[9]

Halfway around the world, the England that Robertson had visited only two years before was in peril. Germany had overrun Poland, and France had fallen after a forty-day collapse that culminated with the surrender of Paris and the French retreat to North Africa. The British had been forced off the continent, having managed to avoid total defeat with a hasty, miraculous retreat across the English Channel back to Dunkirk. The small, island nation was standing alone against the mighty German menace. Across the channel the Germans were making plans for the invasion of Britain. Ben Robertson set out for Britain in June 1940, with his first assignment for *PM:* to report from London on British preparations for a German invasion from occupied France.[10]

Robertson flew from New York on a Pan American flying boat. Among his fellow passengers was correspondent Whitelaw Reid, of the family that owned the *Herald Tribune;* the paper was sending Reid to cover Britain as it prepared for war. As the Clipper flew through the June night, Robertson tried to sleep. But too much was on his mind—his worries that England would soon be invaded, his worries about what could happen to him there, his feelings about Europe dating to the Wilson era of "bitterness and disillusion and to isolation and peace"—and for as much as he loved traveling by train or ship, Robertson wasn't a happy flier. He tried to sleep but couldn't. Every few minutes he looked out his cabin's small window at the moon and clouds outside. A storm bounced the airplane around and rain knocked at the window. Robertson strapped himself into his seat and, in time, drifted into sleep.[11]

The Clipper continued its journey, stopping at Horta the next morning for fuel. Then it was off for the last leg, to neutral Lisbon. As Robertson and Reid disembarked in the Portuguese port city, they saw its residents trying hard to appear happy and normal, and local officials presented the two journalists with invitations to an exhibition about the city's history. But the tension beneath was unmistakable. The city teemed with refugees from the conquered cities of Europe, all of them trying to arrange passage across the Atlantic, but few likely to make it. Robertson thought of frightened rabbits chased by hounds and hunters, and he wondered if Portugal would be the killing field.[12]

After appointments with ticket agents, consuls, air attaches, ambassadors—the first taste of the red tape that was ahead—Robertson and Reid finally flew out. The Dutch plane, which had been flown to England when Holland fell, had a half-Dutch, half-British crew. Half its cabin was taken up with extra fuel and emergency supplies. "We had a feeling of all or nothing when we took off that morning for England," Robertson remembered. The pilots zigzagged through the sky, using clouds for concealment. Inside the frigid cabin, the passengers tried to sleep through the bumpy ride. Soon the British shore unfolded beneath them, and the airliner landed in a field amidst camouflaged airplanes.[13]

Where Robertson had expected frenzy, he instead found airmen going about their duties with calm and cheer. Out the corner of his eye, he saw a serviceman tending the roses that grew nearby. An RAF man apologized for the delays in clearing customs, as the field had only recently become a port of entry and they were new at customs duties. To pass the time, servicemen brought out cups and a big pot of tea. Robertson, certain this sort of casualness signaled impending defeat, could only think to himself, "My God, what a war!"[14]

That afternoon, on a train to London, the country didn't seem at war. Aside from seeing many people in uniform and supplies laid in at the stations, Robertson saw a beautiful country in summer. The train was fast and comfortable, the passengers calm.[15] Underneath, the preparations went on. At the Hotel Waldorf his chambermaid instructed him on getting a gas mask. Seeing heavy blackout curtains on his room's windows made him realize how he had taken light and air for granted in a room. After dinner, Robertson looked out over a blacked-out London; the city he once knew seemed forbidding and appalling. Back in his room, his mind raced through a thousand worries—what if the staff didn't alert him of an air raid? Would he sleep through the air-raid sirens? Worried, he asked a porter in the hallway. The man smiled, knowing Robertson was scared but not telling him he knew, and told him not to worry. "The siren's as loud as destruction itself." Robertson went back in his room, gathered the things he'd need in an emergency, then lay in the dark listening to the sounds of London. Soon he was asleep.[16]

The next morning as Robertson was typing, his chambermaid, Maude Hall, came in. She was full of questions about Americans' attitudes toward Britain. Robertson assured her that America was sympathetic to the British cause. Out tumbled her thoughts, her fears, her hopes, the first of many times Robertson would encounter British people wanting encouragement from Americans.[17]

Off through a city preparing for battle Robertson made his rounds, registering with the police, meeting the censor. On a walking tour of the city, Robertson watched soldiers string barbed wire and put up barricades. He saw members of the Home Guard drilling on rooftops, and held back tears, imagining if this had been his home town. In Westminster Abbey, Robertson watched as among the kneeling was a soldier with a rifle on his shoulder. "The sight of this man took me home, and in a single flashing thought I was closer to Massachusetts than I had ever been before. I knew for the first time what it really meant to be a Pilgrim—I understood what it meant to take up a rifle and make your way to church."[18]

This and a hundred other scenes made Robertson reconsider his judgment from the previous day. This was a country that was going to stand. Robertson, who thought he was supposed to be "a hard-boiled tough American newspaperman," instead found himself admiring the country's determination. "I never for a moment after that morning ever doubted that the British would stand."[19]

The next day, Robertson registered as a war correspondent and had his first meeting with U.S. Ambassador Joseph P. Kennedy. It was the beginning of a complicated relationship. Robertson would find Kennedy a valuable personal friend who helped in countless ways. But the ambassador's positions on the war itself would soon baffle Robertson and his fellow correspondents. Something else that caused Robertson no end of frustration was that the brand-new *PM* was not known of in Britain. During his first month Robertson found himself repeatedly having to explain that *PM* was the real name of an actual newspaper that had real subscribers. To the amusement of Vincent Sheean, a veteran correspondent now working for CBS, Robertson "sputtered like a college freshman when he had to deal with repeated incidents of this kind." Only when Robertson's *PM* dispatches were reprinted in the British papers, with attribution, did the problem ease up.[20]

In the days and weeks thereafter, Robertson chronicled a city and a country preparing for war: the good cheer of Londoners as they maintained routine, the citizenry training to shoot and to fight fires, the Shakespeare quotes posted in windows, the air-raid notices in pews in Westminster Abbey, the tombs of monarchs covered in sandbags. He watched the procession of women and children at the railway station, coming in from Kent to take trains to safer areas, and was moved by the occasional sight of a lone child carrying a gas mask, a doll, and a small bag. On a trip to Dover, Robertson looked across the Channel at Nazi-held Calais, twenty miles away, while the coastal town resolutely went on with life. A housewife told him, "I've sharpened up my kitchen knife. Just let a parachutist put foot on my doorstep."[21]

On a train to Plymouth one sloppy day, Robertson felt the train slow up; they couldn't outrun an air raid, but slowing down gave them time to react if the track ahead was damaged. Overhead they heard the drone of aircraft engines. A lieutenant commander in the compartment, who worked aboard ocean liners in peacetime, told Robertson of his ship being bombed 266 times in seventeen days off Norway, of dozens of bombs that fell and the one that finally hit. As the droning aircraft neared, the officer said, "We only have to go once." As the train sped back up, Robertson pondered those words and eventually adopted them for his own mindset. "You acquire perspective in times of great danger, you think very much of yourself and of the importance of your life," he later wrote. "Freedom becomes the thing that counts—freedom is more important than you."[22]

Robertson found Plymouth busy—shipyards working around the clock, the city's entrances guarded, air raid shelters under construction, the people in fighting spirit. That afternoon he walked to the Mayflower dock to think for a while, wondering why the world could not live in peace, thinking about America and Great Britain, concluding that in England he was closer to America than he had ever been. "I found myself thinking of the Puritans and Pilgrims, of Daniel Boone and the pioneers of the west. You do not stand alone in war, you become a figure in time—you live in the river," he later wrote. "Peace must be fought for. That is the only kind of peace worth having."[23]

In Plymouth, Robertson stayed with Lord Astor, the Lord Mayor of Plymouth, and his wife Nancy Astor. A woman of Virginian ancestry who had cousins who lived near Charleston, and possessed of a sharp wit, Lady Astor and Robertson intrigued one another from the start, when she stared at him and said, "Oh, yes, you're the young man who wrote in the *Saturday Evening Post* that I have spindly legs."[24]

Vincent Sheean wrote that Robertson's "unshakable South Carolina accent . . . endeared him to Lady Astor's heart." One of Robertson's fellow reporters, Helen Kirkpatrick, a correspondent for the Chicago *Daily News* who had been in London since the start of the war, recalled that Robertson and Lady Astor had "wonderful conversations. . . . They were comparing this war with the Civil War, which of course neither of them had lived through." Their friendship grew so close that, as Kirkpatrick wrote Robertson while he was home a year later, Astor confided to her, "I've missed Ben far more than I ever miss Ronny when he goes away." And of Lady Astor, Robertson wrote she "is one of the meanest, nicest people I know. I have forgiven her for once thinking the thing to do was to appease Hitler."[25]

That first night in Plymouth, at a dinner with the Astors and several civil and military officials, they talked about the days after the fall of Paris, an hour of despair followed by resolve, knowing they were alone and drawing courage from being alone. After dinner, Lady Astor and Robertson sat alone and talked about many things. Robertson found himself struck by how different Lady Astor was without an audience—in public brittle and mocking, but in private talking simply and listening closely.

In his room, Robertson went to bed expecting sirens to wake him at any time; but storms prevented an air attack, so Robertson had a peaceful night of sleep. The next day, Lady Astor took him out to see the bombed houses and to meet locals. Robertson saw her arrange for a French boy in the hospital to be reunited with his brother, watched as she held the hand of a ninety-year-old woman wounded by shrapnel, telling her, "We must keep up our courage, Mother." In the eyes of those whose neighbors had been killed or injured, Robertson saw fury. As Robertson got on the train that evening, the sirens went off. Through the darkness the train rolled on to London, and as the guns pounded outside Robertson realized he was now part of this war.[26]

The hard view of England that Robertson had in 1935 was now gone. Seeing "the plain common people of England . . . doing everything in their power now to win this war" had changed him. In Plymouth, Robertson attended a church service that, he wrote his father, "seemed to me like something out of Colonial times in Massachusetts, like the Pilgrims at church—there the congregation listening to the preacher and some of the soldiers had their rifles along with them and some of the officers had pistols in their belts."[27]

In the British he began to see in them the qualities he learned to admire as a child—faith, courage, bravery, determination—the same qualities that had helped his ancestors carve a life out of the red hills he loved were now helping a brave, island nation defend itself against a dangerous and threatening onslaught. In a way, he was among his kinsmen. He wrote as much to his newspaper friends in Greenville, invoking the name of a favorite ancestor. "Some of the Californians think England at the present is like Alcatraz but to me it is more like Daniel Boone's stockade in Kentucky. The Indians are around and the people are in the fort and the door has been slammed shut. . . . There is a fine new burst of vigor and of democracy in this country that would do the people good at home to know about. The plain common people of England are doing everything in their power now to win this war."[28]

To Lord and Lady Astor, Robertson wrote, "It was inspiring and encouraging to find Plymouth so filled with spirit and I shall never forget the woman who said Plymouth was going to beat the beliving [*sic*] daylights out of them blarsted [*sic*] Europeans. . . . More and more, I am glad I can be here at this time—this is the finest and noblest England I have ever seen. . . . The times of action are the real times to live in. The times when causes rise up and living becomes universal, rather than personal. I think it is a great privilege to be living now for we know that the world is going to depend on how we stand and on what we do.[29]

As privileged as he may have felt to be there, however, Robertson chafed under the constraints of British censorship. Mail leaving England was inspected, and all news stories had to pass muster with government censors. Robertson expressed his frustration in subtle ways—to his newspaper friends in Greenville, he mentioned visiting "one of those towns that you read about in the 'southeast of England.'"[30] But to Lord and Lady Astor, Robertson was more candid. "I am ready to take my stand with England," he wrote, "and if the people of the United States could see what I am seeing I know all of them would too—so why can't we turn loose on the people at home? I believe in sending back the truth, as uncensored as possible. What a newsreel it would make—showing an air-raid, the sirens sounding—that alone would chill them, the people going to cover, the scene in the shelter, the all-clear, and the town resuming its normal affairs, saying they'll beat them Europeans."[31]

In London the weeks of July passed, the pleasant summer weather contrasting with fear of imminent invasion. Trenches and fortifications continued to be built, and units continued to drill. It seemed everyone had a belief about when the invasion was coming. Robertson's chambermaid brought in an astrological chart, insisting that Hitler followed astrology and that signs pointed to an invasion soon. The old doorman speculated, "Nobody knows when they're coming except Hitler, and he's got to wait until he dreams." Robertson, seeing the preparations, was again reminded of Daniel Boone, and felt he was in a frontier town. They knew they were alone. One afternoon, Robertson watched the last train head for the last American ship to leave Britain, having a feeling of burning a bridge, the helpless feeling of knowing not even his own government could help him if things went wrong.[32]

In the weeks of waiting, in between his rounds of the officials, Robertson continued quiet advocacy for matters back in the United States. Still bothered by what he had seen in Guam, Robertson wrote to Senators Millard Tydings and Henry Cabot Lodge about Guam's need for a breakwater, for a tuberculosis hospital, and for the same support the United States gave the Philippines. "The people are only a minority group—only 21,000—but they do deserve the attention that any other 21,000 Americans get," he wrote.[33]

Robertson watched the proceedings of Parliament, saw Churchill speak in a Commons that reminded Robertson of a Presbyterian synod, the great man commanding the scene, the timing of his remarks as perfect as a sermon in a Negro church back home, "marvels of feeling and beauty." And Robertson heard the British speculate on why France had fallen so quickly. One told Robertson that the final hours of France must have been like lifting a stone off damp ground. "The stone was lifted and suddenly all kinds of small white spineless creatures began an incredible activity."[34]

As the tension built, some British families were sending their children to the United States to wait out the war. Robertson learned that a friend at the *London Daily Express* wanted to send her ten-year-old nephew, Leslie Phillips, to the United States. Robertson arranged for the boy to live with Jeanne Gadsden in Summerville, and he had provided money to help her with Leslie's living expenses. Through the war, Gadsden wrote Robertson long letters about her experiences caring for Leslie. "I can't tell you what wonders he has done for me," Gadsden wrote. "Leslie has been responsive and wonderful material to work on."[35] As it turned out, the young boy had escaped from England just in time.

CHAPTER 11

London Is Burning

That summer Robertson set off for Dover with Ray Sprigle of the Pittsburgh *Post-Gazette.* They sat silently in a third-class car, afraid to speak for fear of being suspected as aliens. Sprigle wore a cowboy hat and affected a tough attitude. But as the train pulled out, Sprigle lit his corncob pipe. He started talking to Robertson about finding a couple of seven-year-old girls from a working-class family to send to America, where they could spend the war in safety with his own seven-year-old daughter. Four soldiers nearby listened to the colorful Sprigle talk to the quiet Robertson. "Are you an American?" one asked. Sprigle said he was. The soldiers opened up, telling of the battles at Narvik and the horrors of war. Robertson realized that he didn't have to worry about talking to strangers in England, and that the English didn't look at Americans as aliens.[1]

At Dover, free to visit wherever they wished, Robertson and Sprigle stood on the beach. They could see France, twenty miles across the channel. Robertson felt he was on the edge of a volcano that could blow any second. As they talked to a soldier who had seen a bombing at Dover, a feeling of unease spread. The two reporters soon hurried off toward the rail station, stopping in at a nearby pub. The barmaid told them that business was good, there was plenty of food, and though the vulnerable had been sent away, the rest were staying. "If we must go, we must go," she told them. "The way I feel is if the bomb has 'Mary Swift' on it, there is nothing I can do about it. My time has come."[2]

Though official American support was not coming, a little piece of America arrived in late July when a regiment of 150 Americans who had enlisted in Canadian service arrived. It was led by P. J. Duignan, a deputy sheriff who brought his star badge so he could legally arrest Hitler in the name of the state of Illinois. Duignan's posse included an Arkansas possum hunter, coal miners from Pennsylvania, a Distinguished Service Medal winner from World War I, and at least one member fleeing "love trouble." They had brought baseball bats and banjos. They seemed eager to join the fight. Robertson was struck by their lightheartedness and color, of how one spoke of "a sneaking feeling we'd like to help." But he also knew that beneath the bravado was the uncertainty and sadness of having left America behind, and the knowledge they might have to pay with their lives. And they knew he knew their worry.[3]

The following day, the Royal Air Force arranged for Robertson and nine other reporters to visit a bomber unit at a nearby airfield. Driven out in limousines, the reporters had sherry with the group commander and dinner with the flyers. At one end of the dining hall, Robertson noted the pilots for that night's mission sitting cheerful but subdued, wanting to be left alone. When the time came, they climbed into trucks and headed for their planes. As the twin-engine Wellingtons roared into the night sky, Robertson's knees felt shaky and he felt unease in his stomach, remembering how he felt flying from Portugal to England only weeks before. He hadn't wanted to be shot down, and he had ten years on these pilots, but off they went to be shot at over enemy territory, like modern-day crusaders. In the flight room, they listened to a ground controller called "Father" direct them on their mission.

The long hours passed, the airfield silent while the planes were away. In the officers' mess, they drank beer and smoked and talked to airmen. Soon the Americans began talking less about the British and more about themselves. The tension too much, Bill Stoneman of the Chicago *Daily News* said, "Let's don't talk any more." Soon the word came that the planes were coming back, and the reporters crowded into the operations room to listen in over the radio. At four the planes came back. The young pilots changed their clothes and washed up, had breakfast by candlelight, and talked about where they had been and the resistance they faced bombing airfields on a rough night over the Rhineland.[4]

Early in August Helen Kirkpatrick had a feeling something big was happening. She told Robertson he should get to Dover immediately. With David Bruce of the American Red Cross, Bob Casey of the Chicago *Daily News,* Vincent Sheean, and another reporter in tow, Robertson headed back to Dover. Ambassador Kennedy, finding out the reporters were headed for the war zone and feeling personally responsible for them, warned them not to take unnecessary risks.[5]

The next morning, after a tour of the shelters in the Dover cliffs, the reporters went out to Shakespeare Cliff. The morning was quiet. Seagulls soared overhead, bees buzzed, hundreds of white butterflies flitted through the air, wheat waved in the wind. To Robertson it was as calm as a summer day in Montana or Missouri.[6]

Then the drone of engines began. The Luftwaffe approached from France. Soon British fighters roared up to join the battle. The Germans began firing on Dover's barrage balloons. Antiaircraft fire from Dover opened up. Soon the battle was over and all was quiet again. An hour later the sirens sounded and a raid occurred. Robertson and his colleagues could never adjust to how quickly those moments of death could mingle with the moments of life. "Under the warm summer sun and the bright blue sea beyond, with the butterflies fluttering about and the gulls making heathenish noises, it is impossible to feel that this is actually bitter war going on overhead," Kirkpatrick wrote.[7]

For much of August Robertson and his fellow reporters watched the battles over Dover, working out of the Grand Hotel, watching battles by day and writing stories by night, grabbing a few moments of relaxation at a local pub, getting what rest they could. Sometimes they had to return to London to attend to business, or to file stories on the many occasions when the military had commandeered Dover's telephone and telegraph lines. The battles became almost routine, with the Germans flying over five times a day as if on a schedule. "You could lie on your back, with glasses, and look up and there was the whole damn air battle!" said Drew Middleton, covering the war for the *New York Times.* Kirkpatrick recalled that watching the air skirmishes above Dover "became quite a thing to do" until the British mined the cliff when the danger of invasion became imminent.[8]

Those days on the cliffs did more than provide facts for stories; they built friendships. Robertson found a kindred spirit in David Bruce, who frequently joined them. Bruce had been an industrialist and politician in Virginia until the war broke out; sensing that the United States would soon be involved in the war, he had gotten appointed chief representative of the American Red Cross in London. Robertson the Carolinian and Bruce the Virginian struck up a friendship based on their regional similarities, spending hours talking about Confederate generals, the Civil War, and about improving race relations. As Bruce's leading biographer wrote, Robertson and Bruce "had that easy way of open-minded white southerners, inexplicable to outsiders, of talking unselfconsciously in the same breath about Confederate generals and the need to improve race relations." This relationship took on added significance when Bruce became a top aide to General William J. Donovan in the formation of the Office of Strategic Services the following year; although only fragmentary evidence of Robertson's involvement remains, it is likely he helped feed intelligence to the Allies during the war.[9]

On a personal level, Robertson's greatest reward was the friendship he built with Ed Murrow of CBS. In many ways, Murrow was the broadcast counterpart of Robertson. Both had been born in the Carolinas; both came from rural agricultural backgrounds; both had sought higher education and left their hometowns to see the world and do great things. Even their philosophies toward journalism were similar. As Robertson used tiny observations and fine details to build a scene, so did Murrow employ what he came to call the "little picture" approach, letting the details of a situation tell a greater story.[10]

Robertson and Murrow sat on the cliff, smoking cigarettes, watching the action thousands of feet overhead, and swapping stories. Robertson spoke of cotton harvests and train rides and tales of the Civil War, while Murrow reminisced about working in logging camps in Washington State. One day, Murrow confided to Robertson that he wished he had never gone to college for a "half-baked education" and that he could still be a lumberjack in Washington State. "There was a satisfaction about that life," Murrow told Robertson. "I've never known that kind of satisfaction since." The trust they built was deep. Robertson was an occasional guest correspondent on Murrow's CBS broadcasts, and Murrow sometimes wrote for *PM* when Robertson was busy.[11]

Robertson's *PM* stories described the daily battles in detail, spoke of British resolve and provided encouraging words. He found himself believing that England could hold on. But in Robertson's mind, something more personal and profound was happening as they lay on the cliff and watched knights of the air joust high above. "Those were wonderful days in every way—they changed me as an individual," he later wrote. "I lost my sense of personal fear because I saw that what happened to me did not matter. We counted as individuals only as we took our place in the procession of history. It was not we who counted, it was what we stood for. And I knew now for what I was standing—I was for freedom. It was as simple as that. I realized the good that often can come from death. We were where we were and we had what we had because a whole line of our people had been willing to die. I understood Valley Forge and Gettysburg at Dover, and I found it lifted a tremendous weight off your spirit to find yourself willing to give up your life if you have to—I discovered Saint Matthew's meaning about losing a life to find it. I don't see now why I ever again should be afraid."[12]

Robertson chronicled what he saw and sent it back to *PM*. On occasion, he would run afoul of British censors. In one story, he wrote that for every seven German planes shot down, the Royal Air Force lost three. "It was, we all thought, a grand story and a fine tribute to the RAF," Quentin Reynolds wrote. But the censor ordered the mention of British losses stricken. Robertson, whom Reynolds called "a tenacious young man," went to the censor's supervisor, then to the supervisor's boss, and on up the chain of command to the top. "The story was eventually sent, but it took Robertson thirteen hours to have it released," Reynolds wrote.[13]

Near the end of August, they got word that sirens were sounding in London. They left for the capital city.[14]

On Labor Day 1940, as Robertson and some of his fellow correspondents drove along the Thames to London, he thought about how the roads would have been crowded with holiday traffic only a year before. Now, the roads were deserted. The homes that had been lovingly tended a year before were neglected, grass lawns growing high, flower beds growing wild. At every long stretch of road, they found themselves anxious when there were no trees or ditches to provide cover in the event of an air raid. During a stop in Ramsgate to survey bombed areas, Robertson noted that the townspeople were not so concerned about the damage as they were grateful that the people had escaped. Robertson again thought about back home that day—about thousands of motorists on the Henry Hudson Parkway, a beach at Coney Island that was not strewn with barbed wire—and tried to process the juxtaposition.[15]

Back in London there was a sense that people knew a battle was about to begin. But Robertson didn't note fear. "There was faith and there was courage and there was a noble humility I had never known before in any British city. It was as though the people felt themselves in the sight of God." The city was at peace with itself. It was ready.[16]

Robertson and his fellow correspondents braced for the bombing campaigns they believed were imminent. They could not know that across the channel the Luftwaffe was almost ready for the campaign, but delays were pushing back the start of the air war. "The bombing has been put off and put off for six weeks," he wrote Wilton Hall, an editor back in Anderson, telling him of the rampant rumors of when the Germans might bomb and invade. "The English say they wish Hitler would get on with it and quit messing around. . . . nobody knows in England, I don't suppose—I don't suppose they even know in Germany, only Hitler and he will have to dream the day."[17]

On the afternoon of September 7, Robertson, Murrow, and Sheean borrowed a convertible and drove to the countryside across the Thames. It was a bright and clear Saturday, and they had a feeling there would be a battle to watch. Murrow and Sheean, who enjoyed arguing politics with each other, bickered playfully as they drove, with Robertson joining in from time to time. The three had reserved rooms at a riverside inn for the night. Along the way, they stopped at a farm, filled their air-raid helmets with apples, paid the farmer for them, and then drove to the riverside. The three men plopped down in a haystack in a field and looked back toward London as they talked and joked.

Late in the afternoon the familiar sound of sirens and guns began. British fighters roared aloft to meet a colossal wave of German bombers and fighters. The correspondents ran to a ditch, soon joined by a boy and girl on a bicycle and the occupants of a quickly-abandoned bus. Nearby, shrapnel fell to the ground. The British fighters broke off to refuel. While the fighters were away, two waves of German bombers flew in perfect formation and loosed their bombs on

London. A fourth wave of bombers flew high overhead and the men took cover, worried those planes would target a nearby airfield. As Ed Murrow took cover behind the haystack, Vincent Sheean lay down in the ditch, memories of covering the Spanish Civil War suddenly flooding his mind. "This is just like Spain!" he yelled over the drone of the German engines.[18]

After the raid the men went to a pub and talked to the proprietress, who was worried about the city. Then they went back to the haystack and watched the hellish fires over London, smoke rising to the North Sea. More planes flew over. Searchlight beams crossed the sky. Guns boomed and shrapnel fell. The city glowed red with flame. Stunned and sickened by a scene out of Revelations, a thousand years of human effort destroyed in thirty seconds, a numb Robertson kept saying "London is burning, London is burning." The night grew cold and windy, and the men drove to their hotel, sleeping in their clothes as the distant sounds of guns and bombs disrupted the night. The scenes haunted their sleep—Vincent Sheean dreamed that the Germans were landing in New Orleans and had taken St. Louis.

Bad weather the next morning meant the men could probably get to London without the risk of an imminent raid, so they drove back to the devastated city. The city that had been peaceful and quiet the day before was now pocked with destruction and fire. At the Waldorf, Maude came in Robertson's room and wept because the bombing had destroyed the home of a nearby neighbor, and because the Germans were bombing the East End, where poor working people lived. She let out a wail. "Oh, this is a horrible kind of war."[19]

To everyone, according to Robertson, the first raid seemed like the end of civilization. But there was more to come. That night, Robertson tried to sleep in his fifth-floor room. Instead, he found himself looking out the window of his darkened room, listening to the whistle of bombs, occasionally diving for shelter in his bathroom, and counting the hours until dawn. Red-eyed and tired, he bathed and dressed for breakfast, finding everyone else just as tired but carrying on with life.[20]

When Robertson went out to survey the city, he found tremendous damage; but he also saw the people of London digging through rubble, repairing utility lines, and cleaning up last night's damage. They knew another raid was coming, and they wanted to be ready. They began to tell stories of what they had gone through, so many that soon it became difficult to get people to listen. London was becoming a community, the classes united in their struggle against the bombings. Robertson considered the mercilessness of the war, knew that life in London in those times was chance, that death could be near. Eric Sevareid of

The London correspondent for *PM.* Special Collections & Archives, Clemson University Libraries, Clemson, South Carolina.

CBS told Robertson of starting out for somewhere, but being delayed, only to find out that if he'd been on time he would have been killed.[21]

As each night brought a new raid and new destruction, Robertson saw the people taking it and moving ahead. They were not terrorized. "Suddenly six million people came to realize that human character could stand up to anything if it had to." On the 10th, he wrote, "The people this morning are saying to one another in surprise that the third night was not as bad as the second and the second not as bad as the first." By the 12th, Robertson sat in the dining room of the Dorchester Hotel as a guest of Diana Cooper, watching guests continue eating and an orchestra happily playing along as bombs fell. Outside, an incendiary fell in the street, quickly extinguished by firemen. At midnight, the orchestra played "God Save The King" and everyone stood up. As the last notes played, a big gun blasted outside, and everyone laughed. Robertson started back for the Waldorf, unfazed by the clamor of the battle nearby, but unsettled by the unexpected sound of an owl hooting. Startled, he ran back to the Dorchester and spent the night on a sofa in David Bruce's room.[22]

London settled in for the siege, and Robertson saw new courage in its people. "Six million people who had humdrum lives now learned what it was like to live for civilization," he wrote. They felt a duty in going about their daily lives, showing up for work no matter how fierce the fighting had been the night before, the shopkeeper's purpose as vital to the war effort as anyone else. Churchill ordered antiaircraft guns into London, and soon the sound of the guns and falling shrapnel "was a wonderful sound—it gave the city new courage." And the British maintained their sense of humor. After the first week of raids Robertson went to see Gary Cooper's new film *The Westerner.* The audience roared with gales of laughter during the gunfights; after weeks of sustained raids, the pop of six-guns seemed funny compared to the thunder of bombs.[23]

Robertson wondered how New York would handle such a siege, concluding that the city would be ready by the time a raid happened, and that Americans would summon the same resolve that Washington's men and Lee's men displayed in the past. But inside, Robertson dealt with his own worries. In bed at night, he would listen to the drone of German planes and wonder if a pilot pushing a button would mean him living or dying. The amateur student of architecture wondered how the bombing campaign would influence the design of future buildings and cities.[24]

Robertson went out one night with Helen Kirkpatrick and Bob Post of the *New York Times* to watch the fire brigades at work. Near a police station, the bombing had started a fire. A bomb whistled down and policemen ducked inside the station, some of them pushing the correspondents to the floor for safety. A block away, the bomb landed. Just as quickly, the firemen went back to work. Inside the station, Robertson watched a policeman calmly answer the phone: "Very sorry, madam, we can't come at the moment. We're quite busy just now." After the fire was out, the reporters sat in a car with the chauffeur, talking. They heard more bombs coming. The reporters braced, but the chauffeur didn't react at all. "I got used to bombs like those during the first night on the docks. They're either going to get you or they aren't."[25]

Sometimes between raids Robertson walked through London, believing that even in ruins the old buildings looked magnificent in the same way the Acropolis or Colosseum looked. One day, after St. Paul's Cathedral had been hit, he saw people standing at a railing and looking up at a hole that had been blown in the ceiling. "I realized then that they meant what they said when they told you it would be better to see London in ruins than to save it as the French had saved Paris," he reflected. "Notre Dame to these Londoners was a dead monument—a dead church in a humiliated city."[26]

Robertson's reports from London pleased his superiors back in New York, none more so than Ralph Ingersoll. "As you may have gathered from my editorials, I think your pieces are swell," Ingersoll cabled from New York. Robert Neville reassured Robertson's father, "Ben is really doing fine and is taking the London bombings in stride. The office here is more than pleased with his work." Neville also promised, "Realizing that people can't live forever in a city which is having continuous bombings, I think we shall be bringing Ben home before many more weeks have passed."[27]

Neville's words could not have been more clairvoyant. As the fall months came and the days grew shorter Robertson came to dread the coming of dark, knowing it meant nighttime bombing raids would last that much longer. Meanwhile, the people prepared, reminding Robertson of a ship's crew battening down against a coming storm. He visited the shelters, appalled by the conditions. In some shelters, fourteen thousand Londoners endured: bodies so close to each other, the tight space, the lack of privacy, the hard cement floors that shelter-goers had to sleep on. But through it all, they maintained their decency and kindness. Robertson was heartened to find that a Londoner could put his or her name on a piece of paper reserving an area, and the request would more often than not be honored.[28]

Robertson took an early October tour of the Midlands' industrial cities with Helen Kirkpatrick and the BBC's Erika Mann, cheered to find morale and resolve strong in Birmingham, Manchester, and Liverpool, workers cooperating with the government, production not bent in the least by routine bombings. After touring factories, Robertson and the two women went to see the last half of *Gone with the Wind.* As the movie went on, an air raid started. "We weren't sure whether the sound was on the screen or outside," Kirkpatrick recalled with a laugh. An announcer said that anyone who wanted to go could, but the movie would continue. After the movie, they came out of the theater with fires burning outside, a real-life echo of the scenes they had just seen of Atlanta in flames. "It was quite a combination of the real and film life," Kirkpatrick remembered.[29]

In Liverpool, Robertson visited with the consul general of the United States. His wife and daughter had left for the United States in July, and since then the consul general had passed the long evenings by peeling apples and putting up jelly. As they had lunch, Robertson learned about the case of Harvey Hiott. The twenty-year-old Hiott had signed on as a sailor aboard a Danish freighter in San Francisco, hoping to catch a ride back to Charleston. Instead, the ship ended up in Liverpool after a long journey. There, Hiott went ashore and asked the consul general what he should do; and the consul general advised him to jump ship. However, the British had commandeered the Danish merchant fleet. When Hiott could not present papers, he was arrested as a deserter. Under the Neutrality Act, Hiott could leave only on an American ship, but the last American ship had left England four months before. Hiott was being held in a prison that was often bombed during the German raids.

Robertson and Kirkpatrick visited Hiott, bringing him some warm clothes and some fruit and candy, and promising to get him released. When they returned to London, they contacted Ambassador Kennedy and pled Hiott's case. Kennedy contacted Home Secretary Herbert Morrison, and five hours later Hiott was out of prison. Although he could not yet return home, Hiott was taken to the country farm of an American family in Surrey, where he would be safe from the bombing.[30]

In mid-October Robertson rode the train to Scotland, a night train full of soldiers who sang during the trip. Robertson found Glasgow heavily bombed, but with shipyards working at full capacity and the people with spirits up. Though Robertson found "a very small minority group among workers who do not support war as wholeheartedly and as unreservedly as the rest of Britain," he noted that "the great majority is working hammer and tongs to win the struggle."[31]

The war continued to change London and disrupt lives, including Robertson's. Covent Garden, just behind Robertson's hotel room, had been bombed, which had cut off the water to the Waldorf. Robertson had to bathe at the Savoy Hotel, and soon moved there. Ed Murrow told Robertson that for old time's sake, he'd gone to the haystack where they watched London burn the month before. The little pub they had stopped at that afternoon was now a hole in the ground. London, Robertson noted, reminded him of Louisville and Cincinnati and Memphis in the midst of the Ohio River flood.[32]

The stress of life in wartime, the press of constant deadlines, and a lack of sleep had worn down Robertson's nerves and resistance. Tired, and fighting a cold, Robertson dragged himself into Helen Kirkpatrick's office one day. "I've had it," he declared. "How do you feel?" Kirkpatrick said she hadn't slept well, either. "Well, let's get out of here," Robertson said. "Let's go to Cliveden." Robertson phoned the Astors, who were in Plymouth. Lady Astor said, "Oh, you go on down and tell Arthur to take care of you." The two reporters drove there that afternoon; there, an hour outside London, they had "a nice, peaceful night by ourselves in this huge house." Robertson collapsed on the bed into a deep sleep, only to suddenly wake up in the middle of the floor, jolted awake by the sound of the clock striking the hour.[33]

A refreshed Robertson returned to London, soon hosting Ralph Ingersoll, who had come to London to see the war for himself. Robertson stayed busy showing the publisher around as he gathered information for a series of articles. Ingersoll seemed fascinated by the night raids and appalled by the situation in the shelters. To Robertson, these things had long been a fact of life. Watching Ingersoll's reaction reminded Robertson how much he and his colleagues in London no longer really noticed. Upon his return Ingersoll wired Robertson's father, "He is well, busy and happy and asked me to wire you to this effect and send you his love."[34]

On November 5, Robertson and his fellow correspondents stayed up through the night waiting for the results of the 1940 presidential election. A Roosevelt defeat, they feared, would jeopardize American help for Britain. Though Robertson felt confident that Roosevelt remained "the people's candidate," the reporters sweated through the night, an air raid taking place outside, glumly listening as early reports gave the advantage to Republican Wendell Willkie. At six the next morning, the word came that Roosevelt was ahead in four key states. "We knew everything then was okay," Robertson wrote to friends at the *Greenville Piedmont.*[35]

As he breathed easier with Roosevelt's re-election, Robertson was headed to survey conditions in Ireland. When war had broken out in 1939, Irish Prime Minister Eamon de Valera had announced that his country would seek to stay out of the war. De Valera promised that Ireland would not be used as "a base for attacking Britain." His government also had to deal with the Irish Republican Army, which had mounted a terror campaign against the British since 1939 and which would see an obvious opportunity if England fell. Along with all this was controversy over seaports that had been returned to Irish control in 1938 with an informal understanding they would be made available to the British in the event of war. The British now wanted the ports back, but the Irish refused.[36]

Robertson's visit was complicated by the need to coordinate the visit among embassies and comply with neutrality laws, and only as a working journalist could Robertson get permission to visit Ireland. His clearance finally granted, Robertson flew up on a Saturday in mid-November, arriving at his hotel just in time for tea. He watched his waitress set out seventeen pats of butter, twenty-one lumps of sugar, four sandwiches, a plate of buttered bread, buttered muffins, a pot of coffee, a pitcher of milk, and six pastries stuffed with whipped cream. It was a spread unlike anything Robertson had seen in wartime England, where food was rationed. As a hungry Robertson wolfed down treats that now seemed so exotic, the waitress asked, "Are things really that bad in London?"[37]

That evening, Robertson went out with Wally and Peggy Carroll of the United Press and Ed Angly of the *Herald Tribune.* As the sun ebbed, they watched the street lights wink on. They counted all the lights, wondering how much in fines that would cost in London. At the hotel, they ate unrationed steak and potatoes with butter, followed by rich desserts; they went to a show and saw girls in stylish, long dresses. It all seemed strange after so much time in a besieged England, and Robertson found himself worrying about how London was. To him, Dublin was like leaving behind the gloom of war for the airiness and freedom of peace—but at the same time, it was like "the vacuum which exists in the center of the hurricane." War was one hour away by air and submarines were three miles off the coast.[38]

As Robertson talked to the Irish about the war, he came to believe that although the Irish felt for the British, "I formed the conclusion that they were going to keep their sovereignty even if they lost the last shred of it," he wrote. "They were quite willing to accept the protection of the British empire," but that was as far as they intended to go. "If England lost the war, they knew that Germany would swallow up Eire anyhow, and if England won, then Eire would go right on being Eire, without having been bombed. Ireland had become one of those countries that expect to ask and to receive."[39]

Robertson was not alone in his criticism. Helen Kirkpatrick had learned from Minister David Gray that German submarines were surfacing near uninhabited regions off the west coast of Ireland to recharge their batteries, and that the Germans had set up a wireless station to relay intelligence picked up from Britain. Kirkpatrick also reported that while Northern Ireland was blacked out along with the rest of the isles, Southern Ireland was ablaze with lights at night. This made it simple for the Germans to triangulate from the south of France to Ireland to fix on targets in Britain. Robertson shared his findings with political acquaintances back home, hoping they could help influence the Irish.[40]

While in Dublin, Robertson found out that Coventry had been hit, and he left on the next available flight. After a quick stop in London, Robertson and Whitelaw Reid took the train to Coventry. Walking the last few miles toward the bombed city, Robertson had the feeling of "walking into a trap."[41]

Robertson and Reid saw before them the aftermath of a raid the Germans code-named "Moonlight Sonata." Although the city had been hit several times before in smaller raids, Moonlight Sonata had dropped more than 500 tons of high-explosive bombs and more than 30,000 incendiaries on Coventry, an all-night raid meant to knock out the city's industrial contributions to the war effort. A third of Coventry's buildings were destroyed or seriously damaged, 568 people were estimated to have been killed, and more than 1,200 were seriously injured.[42]

As Robertson toured the devastation, he found that though the people of Coventry were shaken, they had the same resolve he had seen in London. "We inspected the factories and it was then that we knew that Germany had not whipped this city. We realized, too, that the German blitz had not broken the spirit of the Coventry people. The people were very tired and very sad, and momentarily they were discouraged. They would say to you: 'When will it end? What is it to come to?' But there was not the slightest indication that they intended to give up. They accepted their trouble as a challenge and there was even a fierce pride about the way they told you that Coventry could take it the same as London." That night they returned convinced that fire bombs could not defeat England.[43]

By this time Robertson was so accustomed to the bombing raids—sometimes heavy, sometimes light—that he often tuned out the sound of the guns and the bombs. One night in his Savoy room he was typing away when the sound of a bomb got his attention as it usually didn't. He dove for the bathroom floor, mouth open, fingers in ears. A blast seemed to pick up the giant hotel and set it down. A bomb had drilled through five of the hotel's floors. In the hallway, Robertson learned that two roof spotters had been killed. A group of men and women, several drinks into the evening, left the elevator laughing. Frank, the floor's very proper waiter, looked on in disgust. "Those silly bastards think it's funny," he growled to Robertson. "I liked Frank after that explosion," Robertson remembered. "We became friends."[44]

As the year ended, Ingersoll sent orders for Robertson to come home, wanting him to see what he could do to help the British get aid from the United States. As much as America tried to forestall direct involvement in the global conflict, it was becoming harder to avoid. On November 8, as Robertson had awaited clearance to visit Ireland, the *City of Rayville,* the freighter on which he had sailed three years before while researching his book about life at sea, struck a German mine off Australia and sank, killing a crewman. An American ship had been sunk, and with it, American blood had been spilled.[45]

In his last weeks in London, as he waited for official clearance, Robertson wrote a series about what he had observed watching London's women in the midst of the war, nominating six—Queen Elizabeth; the wife of General Martin Scanlon; reporters Helen Kirkpatrick and Hilde Marchant; his chambermaid, Maude; and the woman who scrubbed the floors at the Waldorf—as the bravest he had seen. But when the story appeared in London, several women he left out told him the list was inadequate. "I certainly put my foot in it," he cabled back to *PM.* He met up with Ernie Pyle, just arriving for his first visit to wartime London;

and Robertson told him tales of what he had endured. Among the veteran correspondents, Pyle wrote, "I feel like a mental child beside them. Yet almost without exception they are friendly and helpful. And I discovered that among them almost nobody stands higher than my one old friend in London, Ben Robertson of *PM*." Pyle wrote that Robertson "told me his entire outlook on life has changed. He feels that nothing can hurt him now. He feels that never again can he be afraid of anything."[46]

As the holidays approached, Robertson also spent time up close with Prime Minister Churchill. He wrote in *PM* of Churchill's remarks that watching *Gone with the Wind* had left him "reduced to a pulp, that he hadn't a bone left in his body; he said thank God he could get back to his own war." Robertson witnessed Churchill and a group of friends listening to the Southernaires sing American Negro spirituals and gather around a piano to sing "When That Midnight Chu-Chu Leaves For Alabam."[47]

Meanwhile, Robertson tried to get passage to Lisbon for the trip home. Unable to sail home from Britain, he had to fly to Lisbon to get to a ship or flight back to the United States. His reservation for a December 18 flight had been canceled when the new British Ambassador to Portugal took over the plane. The day before clearance finally came, Lady Astor took Robertson to lunch. When the check came, Lady Astor grabbed it away from Robertson, took a glance, then placed the check back on the table. "Oh, it's only a pound," she said. "I thought it would be at least five pounds and I was going to pay it myself. I know nobody from South Carolina has that much money."[48]

Finally, Robertson boarded the train to the same airfield where he'd arrived in June. While the train ride in June had been very proper, with little conversation, now Robertson heard people on the train talking with each other regardless of class or status. As the train pulled away from the station, the sirens sounded, and the lights went out.

On Christmas Eve, Robertson flew with fellow reporters Quentin Reynolds, Merrill Mueller, and three officials to Lisbon. They spent the evening in a hotel bar, drinking egg nogs and listening to a London broadcast by the Archbishop of York: "To endure pain, of body or of mind, for a great cause out of our love for me has a nobility far surpassing in value any kind of comfort."[49]

Four days later, Robertson boarded the liner *Exeter* for New York. His berth would be a mattress on the lounge's floor; but after sleeping in a shelter with 171 others, and after the pounding of bombs, it didn't matter. "I had heard a Queen snoring and I had heard a cabinet minister snort in his sleep. Where I slept was merely relative." And even the plentiful lights and butter and sugar aboard the

American ship didn't impress Robertson, not after the bravery he had seen over the previous six months in a nation under attack. "In the depth of the English blackout I had seen the stars."[50]

As the sun slipped below the horizon, the *Exeter* steamed out of Lisbon. Ben Robertson was headed home.

CHAPTER 12

"What are we going to do about it?"

Ben Robertson walked the streets of New York the evening of January 7, the glow of streetlamps making him feel he was in another world. People weren't scurrying home, trying to beat the next raid. Store windows spoke of plentiful bounties, of being able to buy a thick steak for one meal that would have been two weeks' ration in London. The city was calm, its offerings abundant. As he walked along through the night, Robertson lit a cigarette and marveled for a moment that he could do that without getting arrested.

PM, happy to have its star reporter home, made the most of it. The afternoon Robertson arrived, a photographer captured him happily devouring a spoonful of ice cream. The photo ran the next day alongside an article Robertson quickly composed about how it felt to be home after the hell of London under siege, of the wonder and strangeness he felt in New York. "You can walk and you can stay at home and do nothing if you want to," he wrote. "There is no compulsion. You find it makes you very happy and at the same time very sad to get home again from London."[1]

Robertson had little time to rest. Almost immediately he began distilling his experiences into a series for *PM,* due to begin in a week's time. On top of that, before Ambassador Kennedy delivered a radio address on January 18, Ingersoll pulled Robertson aside for an extended interview about Kennedy. While stenographers jotted down their words for publication in the following day's edition, Robertson and Ingersoll discussed the varying statements Kennedy made to the British and to the Americans, and the ambassador's ambivalent feelings about Britain's chances in the war. Robertson said that Kennedy often avoided the bombings in London by staying in the country, and once said "I can't make head or tail out of what this war's all about. If you can find out why the British are standing up against the Nazis you are a better man than I am." Correspondents had tried to decipher the ambassador's attitudes, but Robertson finally concluded Kennedy's business sense governed his feelings about the war. "He was a confirmed pessimist and would sell anything short," Robertson said. "He told us one day, 'This war's raising hell with my business.'"[2]

On January 20, Robertson's stories of London in wartime began in *PM.* Free from British censorship, he could be candid in detail and assessment. He wrote of the strength of the British people, of watching Churchill lead a nation at war, of how a bombing raid felt, of the gruesome aftermath of German raids. He described the heroism of Coventry and his disappointment with the Irish. He wrote of a class system giving way to unity in a common cause. He wrote of the British attitude that they could win against the Axis. And in his final piece, he delivered a piece of advocacy:

> The British think, too, that this war will be the last war in which the U.S.A. will be privileged, as it always has been, to sit back and pick and choose. Wars after this will be thrust upon America as they have been thrust for centuries upon Great Britain. America, they think, will become enveloped along with the rest of the world in the airplane era.
>
> Britain's war aims are evolutionary, rather than revolutionary, and they say they will turn to the formation of a better world when the war is over. Meanwhile, they must win the war.
>
> From what I have observed in England, I would say that if war aims are to be stated we must state them. We know how to fight wars with propaganda better than the British do. We know how to take up the 14 points and make them take the place of cannon. It is we who know the force of slogans. The Whig has always counterbalanced the Tory.[3]

With his obligations to *PM* temporarily fulfilled, Robertson managed to get back to Clemson; but it was anything but a restful return. A steady stream of visitors descended on the Robertson home, asking the same questions about the war and Britain's prospects. Harry Ashmore, a young Greenville journalist, watched Robertson deal with endless questions, "pacing the floor smoking cigarettes chain-fashion, eating 10-cent lemon drops from a big silver bowl . . . manages to answer everybody, lacing up his statements with a flow of intimate anecdotes about the great and the near-great who are fighting Britain's battle against the Germans." The only time it was quiet at the house, Ashmore noted, was at night, when Robertson was off fulfilling one of the countless speaking requests that he received.[4]

And there was another project. In between obligations, Robertson sat at his father's kitchen table with a portable typewriter, turning his notes, recollections, and previous dispatches from London into a book he called *I Believe in England,* which he quickly sold to the Knopf publishing house. Knopf, which had recently published William L. Shirer's bestselling *Berlin Diary,* saw Robertson's book as an inspiring counterpart to Shirer's dark tale of wartime Germany. Robertson pounded out groups of pages at a time at the kitchen table, then had Jeanne Gadsden retype them and send them in groups of fifty pages to Knopf. Editor Bernard Smith wrote Robertson, "This is swell stuff, and gets increasingly powerful as it goes on."[5]

Lectures and speaking engagements beckoned in the meantime. In a Greenville speech Robertson advocated for American involvement. "The war will be long unless the British themselves can get in position to attack the Axis, which they can do only by obtaining the necessary equipment from the United States," he said. "Britain is nobly fighting her own battle, but it is America's battle too. The United States would be in an intolerable position in event of a German victory." Robertson repeated his criticisms of Joseph Kennedy, saying the ambassador "wants to leave each of his numerous children a million dollars when he dies, and this to him is more important than the future of the rest of the United States."[6]

At the University of Georgia, Robertson spoke about the war in Manchuria. Among those in attendance was Koji Ariyoshi, a former Hawaiian coffee farmer who remembered Robertson from his *Star-Bulletin* days. Ariyoshi shared news of the encounter with the *Star-Bulletin,* which later carried the text of Robertson's speech. At Clemson, he addressed a group of young writers, urging them to read the works of authors such as Sarah Orne Jewett, Sherwood Anderson, Willa Cather, Thomas Wolfe, Nathaniel Hawthorne, and Walt Whitman so they could understand "the greatest theme in American literature, the great theme that is trying to express ourselves to ourselves." And back home, there was just enough time for a Robertson family reunion, with the family's own war correspondent telling stories of what he had experienced in a country under siege.[7]

In a flicker, the respite was over. Robertson was off to Bermuda on February 22, to catch a ship to Lisbon. In Bermuda, he noted signs of things to come. A detachment of American Marines had arrived, and Robertson perceived sadness among the locals, fearing what establishment of an American base in wartime would do to their culture. Aboard the liner *Excambion,* Robertson met passengers who had left the free world to return to conquered countries where their families were trapped. The tension built the closer the ship got to Lisbon, as emergency drills prepared passengers for the possibility of attack from sea or air, and Robertson and his fellow passengers pondered their chances of becoming a personal footnote to history.

Robertson spent his days in Lisbon trying to get clearance to fly to London, and evenings at the Estoril Hotel talking about the war with the other Americans who were stuck in Lisbon—diplomats, attaches, journalists, and businessmen. In the evenings their discussions boiled over into violent arguments that Robertson said "did every one immense good. Some of us were called better Englishmen than Americans and we called the others pro-Nazis." But when emotions had been expended, they found themselves in agreement that America had yet to gauge the full power of the German menace, that "this war was America's war and we knew which side was our side."[8]

Seventeen days after leaving New York, Robertson finally arrived in England, with spring about to begin and the nation preparing for the next stage of battle. He steeled his nerves for the return of nightly bombing, convincing himself that the stakes of winning the war meant more than his own life. Some in the traveling party suggested staying in a safer city for the night instead of going on to London, but an American diplomatic aide would have none of it. "Coming to England is like going to work in Yellowstone Park," he told them. "If you're going to work at Yellowstone, you've got to accept the fact that sooner or later you're bound to meet a grizzly bear."[9]

In London, Robertson returned to the Savoy Hotel. It seemed nothing had changed. The doorman recognized Robertson as he approached. "You are getting back just in time for it," he said. Old acquaintances provided news: the waiter at his table had become a father, a bellboy had joined the RAF and was on leave. He reacquainted himself with the shortages and simple rations of wartime, finding a dish developed by a Savoy chef "the most elaborate way ever invented for cooking two potatoes, two carrots and a parsnip."[10]

As Robertson toured London he found it as busy as Manhattan had been. The people had adapted to the ruins around them. As the people of the East End went about their daily business—as housewives in markets bought bread and vegetables, as buses droned past—workers knocked down damaged buildings and stacked salvaged materials, no one giving any of the signs of destruction a second look. The city was battered, but it was very much alive, and as determined as it had been when Robertson left for home.[11]

British spirits had also been buoyed by American military hardware extended under the Lend-Lease Act, with a supply of tanks, aircraft and fifty obsolete destroyers transferred for British use. Although the British knew they would be hit again in the spring, they also knew British planes would soon begin bombing targets in Germany, including Berlin itself. A speech by President Roosevelt on March 15, making plain the importance of American support to Britain under

Lend-Lease, further cheered the British. "There is tremendous rejoicing," Robertson reported. "Publicly and in private I have heard Britons saying today they were glad the President had begun to talk about American participation in the peace, because without American participation there could be no world peace."[12]

On March 17, Lady Astor told Robertson she believed Plymouth would soon be bombed. She was headed there; it was her home, and if the city was going to be on trial, she wanted to be there with it. "Why don't you too come to Plymouth?" she asked him. "Why not see what an English city looks like that knows it is going to get it?"

Robertson took an overnight train to Plymouth and had breakfast with Lady Astor's nephew. Robertson and Lady Astor spent the day touring the town, talking with various people, going to a movie. The next day they went to the train station to greet the royal train, as King George VI and Queen Elizabeth visited Plymouth for an inspection of the city's civil defense forces. Robertson watched as the head of nurses smiled and talked with the queen. At Lady Astor's house, the royal couple had tea and sandwiches. The king spoke of how moved he had been by President Roosevelt's speech. The queen looked out the windows toward the sea and said the view seemed so quiet and restful. An hour later, the king and queen were on the train back to London.

Three hours after the king and queen had departed, Robertson, Lady Astor, and her nephew were around the dinner table having coffee. The sirens went off and the guns began to pound. Something felt different this time. Quickly Lady Astor made sure the tubs were filled with water, that sand and shovels were ready. Then they went on the porch to watch fire bombs and high explosives rain down on Plymouth.[13]

The Astors' servant, Rose Harrison, put on her tin helmet. She looked around for Lady Astor, only to see her standing in the middle of the street with Robertson, watching the raid. Over the noise of the bombs and guns, Rose kept yelling for the two of them to come inside. In response Lady Astor grumbled, "Shut up, Rose!"

Finally ordered inside by an air-raid warden, Lady Astor and Robertson came through the door. As they entered the hallway, they heard the whistle of falling bombs and threw themselves to the floor. The explosion blew the glass out of the front door. Another blast blew out the window through which the Queen had gazed at a peaceful sea hours before.

Down they went to the basement shelter, with Lady Astor resolutely reciting from Psalms. In the basement, as Rose picked the glass shards from her lady's hair, Lady Astor spoke warmly of Rose, of how they had "worked together" for thirteen years. "Rose is the only woman who will put up with me, and I'm the only woman who will put up with Rose." Rose said, "Mr. Robertson, her ladyship is the kind of woman who takes a lot of understanding. It took me nearly three years." Lady Astor laughed. "There, Rose, you have the advantage of me. I've never got to understand you."[14]

Arthur Bushell, the Astors' butler, told them an incendiary had fallen on the roof. Lady Astor shouted, "Come on, everybody," and they scrambled upstairs to extinguish the bomb. At one point, Lady Astor looked out the window at the fiery destruction outside. "Isn't it beautiful?" Robertson heard her say. "No wonder Nero burned Rome." Her eyes welled up. "My dear, beautiful city. There goes 30 years of our lives . . . it doesn't matter. We have built Plymouth on a rock."

The raids lasted until midnight. Lady Astor wanted to go survey the damage, but the others persuaded her to wait. At dawn, she was making the rounds of rest centers and hospitals. The nurse who had spoken with the queen the day before now wept as she told Lady Astor that a bomb had killed several expectant mothers, babies and nurses. Robertson surveyed bombed ambulances, parents whose children had been killed, families torn asunder by the devastation.

Robertson had planned to return to London that day, but Lady Astor persuaded him to stay another night. Again, at the dinner hour, the raid began. To Robertson the second raid seemed more horrible than the previous night's. As Robertson left for the train station the next day, Lady Astor told him, "It's hell, and we know it's hell, but don't think it's going to break our spirit. Nothing in God's world matters now but beating Hitler."[15]

The terror of bombing raids, and the thought of forty million people having to cope with the possibility of death over the previous six months, prompted Robertson to think while he was in Plymouth. Don Minifie of the *Herald Tribune* asked Robertson if he'd ever given up all hope of living. "No," Robertson said. Minifie recounted how he felt when he was captured by the Fascists in Spain. "You pass into a phase beyond fear," he said. "You know a period of complete quiet. You accept death as it approaches."[16]

To Ed Murrow, Robertson's stories of Plymouth's devastation meant something disheartening. He showed Robertson a summary of American news sent over to the Ministry of Information, in which American commentators had little to say about the heavy raids of the previous week. "You know what this means," Murrow said. "It means we have written so much about the bravery and courage of the British that the folks at home are beginning to take air raids for granted. The newness of an air raid has worn off for the folks at home."[17]

As it happened, Robertson was about to inform an audience back home—including a readership far beyond *PM*'s reach—about the horrors of air raids, and the strength of a nation under siege. On March 31, Knopf informed him that his book, now titled *I Saw England,* was being published. Not only that, but *Reader's Digest* wanted to run a six-thousand-word version in its May issue. Jarrolds Publishers quickly made an offer for a British edition.[18]

I Saw England, in which Robertson combined his *PM* dispatches with new writing to form a chronicle of his experiences during the Blitz, emerged to a warm reception from critics. John Cournos of the *New York Times* called it "a stimulating, and in some ways, inspiring book, one not to be missed." Frank Kelley of the *Herald Tribune* wrote that Robertson, "one of the finest reporters of his young generation, has turned in an enthralling account of the England he has seen at war . . . In the depth of the blackout Ben Robertson had seen the stars. He has written beautifully about it." *Foreign Affairs* called it "an excellent piece of reporting."[19]

As Robertson's advocacy made its way into bookstores and magazines back home, he continued touring the island fortress and the machines of its defenses. As he visited an aircraft factory in early April, he noted with pride that the Spitfires that defended British skies were built with machinery made in America. In London, he watched the signs of spring pop up among the ruins. Watching flowers bloom in parks and wild ducks swim in St. James's Park, he thought of bombed houses and destroyed families and ruined landmarks, wondered about people he had known the year before and what had become of them, and wondered what would be hit next.[20]

To Robertson, the clock was ticking. America had to get involved. "This war has now become a matter of food and ships," he wrote in an April 9 piece. "England's need from across the sea is a steadily rising curve and the outcome of everything will depend on when the British curve bisects the rising American curve that represents supply. Over here you feel an urgency about everything, you feel a battle going on against time, you now find yourself thinking constantly in terms of convoy."[21]

A ten-day tour of eight blitzed port cities strengthened Robertson's beliefs. In a series for *PM* Robertson wrote of the pounding these cities took, stories of destroyed shelters, of families destroyed in houses collapsed by bomb damage. "You want to cry when you visit these British cities," he wrote. "What would you think if you saw a decent plain working man searching in a pile of rubble for a finger or a foot of his wife and four children? What would you think if you saw a soldier with a piece of fur collar and a strip of brown dress—all that he could find of a girl he was going to marry?" Meanwhile factories continued to work, ports stayed busy, and the citizens' resolve stayed strong.[22]

Robertson wrote his father from Plymouth that the city was recovering nicely, adding, "It is sad to see so much destruction. The temper of the war is changing, as it does, I suppose, in all wars—the bitterness naturally increases. You actually are glad now to hear that Berlin has been hit. You hope it has been hard hit."[23]

Back in London, Robertson returned to find that more enemy action had hurt people at the hotel, that Don Minifie had been injured, that a guest of the hotel had disappeared in a recent raid. In his room, Robertson went through his mail. In the pile was a New York newspaper. As Britain dealt with death and devastation, Robertson read of a New York distracted with society news, with spring fashions, with advertisements for four-star food and fun, with columns about skating at Lake Placid. Robertson felt disgust at how Americans seemed to play on while the world burned, and he fumed as he composed his concluding article on the seaport tour.[24] In cables back to *PM,* Robertson was unrestrained. Sometimes these cables were reprinted in the paper. One read, "When I visit these British cities and see them struck down again and again and always rising for another count, my conclusion is we ought to be in this war."[25]

On April 25, *PM* fully devoted itself to the cause of American involvement in the war. It was Ralph Ingersoll's crusade. Under a campaign titled "What Are We Going to Do about It?," Ingersoll dedicated the paper's editorial stance toward the defense of Britain and the involvement of America in the war. As part of the editorial, Ingersoll reprinted a cable from Robertson: "Our military officials over here feel the situation is much graver than reports from home would indicate our people realize. Our military officials naturally cannot speak publicly and somehow we feel that some political reason is holding President Roosevelt from speaking—American journalists in London feel that. As we see the situation developing, our opinion is that we are doing exactly what every other nation has been doing right along—one by one the democratic nations stand alone and fight alone. The feeling among journalists and among a number at the embassy is we have declared ourselves, we have aligned ourselves, and it would seem the time has now come when we ought to assume responsibility. Everything seems desperately urgent. Action is needed much more than public speeches."[26]

The campaign provided an excellent opening for Robertson's piece the next day, in which he described sentiments he had heard from the British. "The British public now understands that time is everything in this present race, they know they are unable to match the Germans in equipment and they know that their only hope is America," he wrote, warning that while the British were seeing a lot of patriotic orations, they weren't seeing much in the way of substance, and they were worried. "They see a lot of first class bandages, some tea wagons and some ambulances. Desperately, the British are now saying that if only the Americans would send over planes, England would not need those hearse carts." Even though the Americans were sending planes and other hardware, the public was not perceiving that aid was arriving. Meanwhile, pro-isolationist voices such as Charles Lindbergh and Senator Burton Wheeler made American sentiments seem cloudy. "What the British people think is that both American and British political leaders ought to stop talking so much about being the defenders of democracy and get to work as two first-class business partners who have great assets to protect. People over here would like to know definitely how long they really must hang on and exactly what America is going to do, when and where."[27]

Over the coming days Robertson continued the point, suggesting that American inaction could be a morale booster for Hitler that would imperil America in the long run, but that if American ships helped in the Atlantic it could open new ways for the British to defeat the Germans. On April 30, Robertson told readers, "It seems that not only the day but the hour has arrived when folks at home have to either put up or shut up." He wrote, "We either fight with England within the next few weeks or we get ready to fight alone, or we give in without fighting to our Lindberghs and the form of American policy which they desire. We feel the world is closing in over here and our conclusion is that the America that hesitates is lost." Other stories examined stricter rationing in London to head off the possibility of shortages, of the need for more ships to counter the tonnage losses the British merchant fleet was enduring, and dire consequences for America unless it came to British help. "We believe from all we have seen that unless America takes a hand and wins this war against Germany the time will come as certain as the setting of the sun when 4000-pound bombs will drop on the White House and in Times Square in New York. Of one thing we can be sure and it is that aerodynamics are not static. They are moving faster than any other force in the world today."[28]

Robertson's advocacy fit in with the *PM* ethos—and he was hardly alone. The more his colleagues saw, the more they found ways to incorporate calls for action into their own broadcasts and dispatches. Robertson's friend Edward R. Murrow told listeners, "This is not a personal plea to send American boys to die in the skies above Britain. Those remarks have not been been stimulated by an official source. I've been impelled to make them . . . because I've seen the faces of men who've come back from Dunkirk, Norway and Greece, asking bitterly, "Where are our planes?"[29]

Robertson's colleague Helen Kirkpatrick likewise felt the need to alert a complacent America. As she remembered:

> Our feelings that many of us had about the necessity for the United States, or the inevitability of the United States, coming into the war and writing to my family, and I said, "Bill [bureau chief Bill Stoneman] and I went last night to the right person to persuade them that the time had arrived for a frank appeal to the United States to come in at once. The outcome, if it comes off, will be known to you long before this reaches you." Well, obviously, it didn't.
>
> I think we must have gone to [John] Winant, the [U.S.] Ambassador. And I said, "Don't believe people when they tell you the United States can't do anything or give help in time. The Germans are trying hard to convince Americans of that and it should be combatted. You know that I feel strongly, not only because of my ties here, but as I told every audience, because it matters vitally to the United States. I gather from reports coming back that that is beginning to dawn on people." Most of us felt quite strongly that it was important.[30]

Robertson, Murrow, and their contemporaries helped reporters become observers who could impart their information with analysis, thereby conveying something greater than a mere account of events. And in their way, Murrow and Robertson and Kirkpatrick, among others, made it possible for future generations of reporters to use not only their eyes, but their minds and hearts, as reporting tools, and to spur an audience into action.[31]

As Murrow's colleague Eric Sevareid maintained, reporters and editors should not treat both sides equally when they know "one side is utterly wrong and even lies . . . After all, what is our training for? What are our experience and judgment and brains for? There is no magic instrument to tell you where to draw the line. You have to put it up to your professional soul."[32]

In May, Robertson became interested in a neglected part of the war story, and wrote to Lord Beaverbrook about the possibility of traveling on one of the British flying patrol boats to Iceland. He wrote that he wanted "to write about all that exposed part of the world on the flank of the United States. I think it is important to write about that part of the world at this particular time." Although an intriguing topic, no surviving evidence indicates Robertson made the trip to Iceland to report this story.[33]

Robertson also expressed his admiration for Winston Churchill in a "simple, frank" note before the Prime Minister traveled to the United States that month. "I think you are a great man with a wonderful gift for forceful and colorful expression," he wrote, "and you have a way with you that is going to appeal to the people in the United States. I'm just one person but I think you are going to have a first-class chance to tell your people at home how immediate and urgent everything is. I think they need telling and in plainer words than anybody has yet told them. The time to be polite and thanking is past, I think, and I hope you sock them in the eye. Good luck and great success."[34]

Ralph Ingersoll wrote from *PM*'s Brooklyn headquarters with news on how the paper was doing, and he expressed his hope that American forces would soon be taking part in the war, that American naval patrols would begin firing on German submarines and planes "damn, damn soon." Ingersoll mused about taking a quick, two-week trip to revisit London, but only if he could come over with a bomber crew instead of waiting for a Clipper for Lisbon. "I understand some oaf gave bomber writing privileges to a Hearst correspondent and there was a kick back on it," Ingersoll griped. "I do not know what said oaf expected to have happen—giving credentials to a paper which is anti-Administration, anti-British and anti-interventionist." Ingersoll asked Robertson to see what he could find out about arranging such a trip.[35]

On May 10, a feeling swept London that a raid was coming. That night, as Robertson hurried to the Underground, he looked up and beheld "a most horrible full moon shining—so full and terrible that we had little doubt the Germans would soon be over." Back at his hotel, he lay down and read for a while. All at once, sirens sounded, guns went off, and bombs fell. Knowing a hard night was ahead, Robertson went to the shelter with Quentin Reynolds, Ed Beattie of the United Press, and Larry Rue of the Chicago *Tribune.* Robertson stewed over how, as an American, he could do nothing to help England. The night was terrible, he remembered, and he felt they lived on simply because their time had not come. At one point they went outside for a look at a scene that was depressingly familiar: flames roaring against a night sky, the sound of walls crashing down, the furious heat and crackle of fire. Sometime during the night a middle-aged Englishman suddenly began making rude comments to Robertson and threatened to knock his block off.

"Knock ahead," Robertson replied.

"I don't know who you are, but you should certainly know who I am," the man responded.

"I know all I care to know about you," Robertson growled. "It's that you have no manners."

As dawn broke Robertson and two other reporters put on their tin helmets and explored streets full of shattered glass and rubble, of people evacuating shattered homes. A woman on a horse rode down one of London's main streets.

Flames roared the length of the tower of an eight-hundred-year-old church. Inside another church, fires lit up its stained-glass windows.

As the all-clear sounded, Robertson noticed the fire and smoke "setting off a sky of purest early morning blue." Back at the Savoy, Robertson collapsed on his bed. Four hours later, emerging from sleep, he heard organ notes from a small chapel outside his window. Inside the little church, the voices of its congregation raised the lyrics of a hymn Robertson recognized from back home: "The Church's one foundation / Is Jesus Christ her Lord."[36]

Again, London dug its way out, the skills accumulated over nine months of war helping its people move rubble, make repairs, and prepare for the next raid. Robertson visited the bombed-out House of Commons, where days before he had watched Prime Minister Churchill and former Prime Minister David Lloyd George spar over the war effort. Now Commons was a gutted ruin that seemed "as old as the Coliseum." But the House set up in a temporary meeting space, prepared to carry on as usual. "The House had brought its entire ritual with it across London, nothing had been lost in transit, not even the House's sense of humor."[37]

After President Roosevelt declared an "unlimited national emergency" in a May 27 speech and said that the United States would do everything it could to protect its land and ships on the sea, Robertson cabled several editors around the country to urge support for England. "We must do more immediately," he wired.[38]

CHAPTER 13

The Advocate

As spring went on and more bombings happened, Robertson continued to chronicle what he saw around him and continued to advocate for American involvement. He chronicled the proceedings of British politics, visited an RAF night-fighter unit as it prepared to take on German bombers, and paid a return visit to Dover, noting that while explosions still rocked Dover a year later, they were now from British bombs falling on France. Comparing his experiences from 1940 to those of the present moment—with more guns and more planes ready to defend England—Robertson got the impression that "the front line of England is entirely ready for anything the Germans can begin."[1]

With the war well underway, Robertson was finding less and less to write about. He felt an obligation to stay in London—"the American newspapermen feel they have a sort of public duty to stay on so long as we still are not actually fighting in the war; we must keep feeding facts to those who are for England," he wrote.[2]

During the summer lull his mind turned back home, to the Third Congressional District seat held by Butler Hare. "You may not believe this," he had told Harry Ashmore in January, "but I want to come back to South Carolina and run for Congress." From London, Robertson wrote to Burnet Maybank, *Greenville News* publisher Roger C. Peace, and Senator James F. Byrnes for their advice. "The reporting side of newspaper work keeps a man sitting on the fence, seeing both sides," he wrote Byrnes, "and I have now reached the point where I want to get down off the fence and pitch in and do what I actually can to get things done. I have a lot of energy and ambition and I have learned something about fighting—also this war has had a maturing and sobering effect on me."[3]

Robertson quickly made arrangements to come home. Before leaving London, he visited H. G. Wells, who was "writing 'a couple of books or so,'" who characterized himself as "an old, irascible, dying man." Lady Astor took Robertson to visit George Bernard Shaw and his wife. Robertson wrote that Shaw called himself a "dodo" and was "able now to write only a couple hours a day."[4]

Back in Lisbon, Robertson watched the American troopship *West Point,* just converted from the new luxury liner *America,* ease into the harbor. Off the ship came dozens of German passengers back from New York, dressed in fashionable clothing, bringing with them piles of luggage and luxuries from America. "They looked clean and dressed and refreshed," Robertson wrote in *PM.* "The Germans looked like cruise-ship passengers docking in the luxury days of peace." He contrasted those refreshed Germans with the harried Americans desperate to get out of Europe. Most of them had endured hardship at the hands of German soldiers who had delayed their transit to Lisbon; these Americans found relief only after the U.S. government informed Berlin that no German would be allowed to disembark in Lisbon until every American was safely in Portugal.[5]

The *West Point* was headed back to New York with a cross-section of humanity fleeing the horrors in Europe: common people alongside consuls general, businessmen and dignitaries, and survivors of bombings, torpedo attacks, air raids, and captivity. One of them was Richard C. Hottelet of the United Press, whose aggressive questioning of Gestapo officers got him arrested on suspicion of espionage. Kept in solitary confinement for four months at Alexanderplatz and Moabit, he was threatened with execution while the Germans rebuffed diplomatic efforts for his release. Hottelet kept himself sane by reading the handful of books he was given by his guards, finding an unexpected emotional release in an English romance novel in the stack. In late June, Hottelet and Jay Allen of the North American Newspaper Alliance, who had been held by the Vichy French, were swapped for two Germans held by the United States.[6]

Aboard the big liner, as his regained freedom sank in, Hottelet sat silent for two days. The third night out, with Europe a thousand miles behind, Robertson and his dinner companions watched Hottelet "unfold like a flower," as out tumbled his recollections of imprisonment, of fearing not only for his life, but also for his sanity. While Hottelet came out of his shell, Allen talked nonstop, saying that after five months' imprisonment he felt like fizz water that had just been unstoppered. The tales told on the trip, Robertson wrote, led one to conclude "the country these Americans were talking about must surely be about the vilest mushroom ever to burst forth from the cellar of the earth." As the *West Point* arrived in New York, they were "home again and glad of it, and nearer than ever to war."[7]

Back in New York, Robertson prepared a series of articles for *PM* on Britain after two years of war. A run for office was also on his mind. His visions of a Congressional seat, however, were quickly dashed by the waiting mail. "I would so much like to see you run for Congress I am afraid I might be too optimistic about your chances," wrote Roger Peace, about to begin a temporary appointment to the United States Senate in the seat vacated by James F. Byrnes, now an associate justice of the Supreme Court. Although Peace felt Robertson was "the best fitted fellow I know of for the job," he warned that Hare was still popular and could be difficult to unseat, and counseled Robertson to wait a few years until Hare decided to retire.[8]

Less encouraging was the polite letter Byrnes sent. Now a member of the Court, Byrnes felt he needed to sever his ties to politics, so he refused to offer direct advice. "No man whose judgment was of value would advise me to be a candidate unless he was willing and ready to actively support my candidacy," he wrote, suggesting that Robertson delay his decision. "I know you would not want to give serious consideration to a political contest until you knew more about the situation than you now know or could possibly know at this time, even if you were at home."[9]

His ambitions punctured by political reality, Robertson decided not to run. His colleagues in London, who hoped he would soon return, were elated. Ed Murrow confessed to "the sneaking hope that your opponent will beat hell out of you . . . in order that you will the sooner come back to London!" Helen Kirkpatrick was likewise jubilant. "The place has gone mad with joy," she wrote him. "I'm sorry if your plans didn't go through, but we are all honestly so delighted at the prospect of seeing you again, that we're not as sorry as we should be."[10]

Instead, Robertson's friends at the *Greenville News* enlisted him to cover the final week of the campaign for Byrnes's Senate seat, which was to be filled in a special election. In late August, as he stood beneath oak trees in a Greenville park and watched candidates Burnet Maybank, Olin Johnston, and Joseph Bryson address the crowd, Robertson contrasted it to the vision Hitler had for Europe. The meeting, he wrote, "was the kind of meeting it has taken 30 generations of Englishmen and Americans a thousand years to develop . . . If the Germans have their way, it will be wiped out of existence—Hitler himself has told us it will be wiped out." He added that the meeting struck him as impressive considering his having just come from England, "where people are being bombed because they insist on such things as free political speech. It made me think we ought all to do our duty on this voting day—we ought all to go to the polls."[11]

In mid-August, Robertson's new series on the conditions in Britain began in *PM*. Predicting that the German bombing raids would permanently alter the British social system—bombs, after all, did not discriminate between rich and poor—Robertson also wrote about the future of the war, and of the esteem London had in the eyes of the world. "One conclusion we can draw from the first year of the Battle of Britain is that the Germans can't destroy London from the air," he wrote. "They have gone all out against the British capital with all the strength they have been able to put into the air, and they have failed. They have done their damnedest."[12]

Expanding on themes from six months before, Robertson explored how air raids had altered the British mindset, breaking down the caste system in society and turning the people into "a single community" whose members respected one another. He confessed to feeling in 1935 that the British were meek and too accepting of circumstances. Now he understood that feeling of acceptance, and beneath it was a strength and determination that made him understand what a Dover woman said to him: "No matter what happens, when the invasion comes, I am going to follow the instructions of the government. I am going to stay where I am, right here in Dover." In another piece, Robertson wrote an appreciation of Churchill's leadership of a nation at war, citing it as part of the country's strength. And, again, Robertson advocated for American help for Britain. "England has a quality that we don't understand in the U.S.A.," he wrote. "England knows how to wait. But even England knows that the British will never be able to invade the continent of Europe without enormous American aid."[13]

In addition, Robertson made promotional appearances and wrote articles to promote *I Saw England* and build support for American entry into the world war. He also tried to work, from afar, with Blanche Knopf on getting British officials to approve the English version of *I Saw England.* Mrs. Knopf, who wanted to go to London to see the war situation for herself and "gather material," asked Robertson to use his contacts to quietly secure her a flight. When he had no luck, Knopf delayed the matter until spring 1942. "The ground swells" of war were beginning, she wrote to Robertson, "and I will possibly be delayed on account of delayed sailings, and I just can't risk doing that."[14]

Robertson had begun considering another career move. Though his work at *PM* had brought his work to a new audience and resulted in a successful book, and though his reporting had allowed him to advocate for American intervention in the war, Robertson was working for a troubled newspaper. The ambitious *PM* had struggled with its finances from the start. Its expensive quest to present top-quality reporting and crisp printing with spot color on good paper was at odds with its policy of not selling advertisements, relying instead on newsstand sales and subscriptions. By the end of August 1940, *PM* was losing $40,000 a week, and only a buyout from Marshall Field had kept it in business. Although *PM* gained acclaim and circulation with its quality reporting from around the world, that hadn't been enough to pull the newspaper out of crisis. As war approached, the costs of printing went up. Furthermore, *PM*'s agreement with the Newspaper Guild made it difficult to cut staff members in order to reduce costs.[15]

Despite his personal friendship with Ralph Ingersoll and other *PM* staffers, Robertson began to have differences with *PM*'s editorial direction. He was also finding himself with less of a mission, and wondered if other opportunities were out there. Robertson wrote to Whitelaw Reid, hoping to get rehired by the *Herald Tribune.* While Reid replied that no openings were immediately available, he held open future possibilities. "I know the staff is keen to get your talent one of these days," Reid wrote.[16]

Other projects beckoned Robertson during the last months of 1941. The National Broadcasting Company persuaded Robertson to give a recorded talk on the battle for England. Associate editor Dorothy Hinitt of *Reader's Digest* asked Robertson to consider writing an article on the Commando regiments in England. But Robertson was busy on another work, of great personal importance.[17]

Right after he returned to America in August, Robertson wrote to Blanche Knopf and editor Bernard Smith. His plans for the fall were to either return to London, go to Egypt, or take the rest of the year off and write an autobiography. To Knopf and Smith he pitched a broad description. His new book would touch on the role of the South, race relations, his family connections with Thomas Wolfe and Daniel Boone, the relationship between those who leave home and those who stay home, his experiences in newspaper reporting around the world and in Washington, and his recent experiences in the war. "I've known a lot of people and I'd like to tell about them," he wrote. "I think at last I have learned how to write and I can do a good book."[18]

Knopf quickly requested that Robertson meet with her and Smith. Robertson, who was helping Burnet Maybank's campaign for the Senate, arranged a meeting for early September. At his New York townhouse, Robertson jotted down an outline for the book, sent it to Knopf and Smith, then headed to Wyoming for two weeks of vacation near Bob Neville's Montana ranch. Knopf and Smith accepted Robertson's outline, but asked him to keep the book focused on the South instead of following his original wide-ranging proposal. They agreed on a six-month deadline for the manuscript.[19]

In Wyoming, Robertson started roughing out the new book, then drove back to Clemson. There, he burrowed himself in a back room at his father's home, surrounded by maps, old family papers, books, pictures—all the material he had used to write *Travelers' Rest,* now brought back out for a new purpose. Along with them were the notes and outlines he'd made in Wyoming. Working away on his old typewriter, words tumbling out in his usual all-lower-case style, Robertson flew through page after typed page. As the pages piled up, they were sent off to Jeanne Gadsden, who made minor edits as she typed the final draft. Only she,

Knopf, Smith, and Robertson knew what the book was about. Friends and family assumed it would be about the war.

On December 5, Wright Bryan and his daughter drove to Clemson from Atlanta. En route to deliver a lecture at Converse College, Bryan had stopped in town to visit his father. While in the vicinity, he dropped by the Robertson home. In the back room they found Ben at his typewriter, working away. Bryan was curious about the new book's subject, but Robertson refused to tell him, claiming an old writer's custom not to divulge the topic. Instead he told Bryan, "I must work fast. We'll be in this war soon and my paper will want me to go abroad again."[20] The war, and America's lack of direct action, had been on Robertson's mind. In late November, at an American Legion convention in Columbia, Robertson had scorched the isolationist views of those such as Charles Lindbergh and Herbert Hoover—who "has been consistently wrong ever since that 'two chickens in every pot' affair"—and said the United States needed to declare war against the Axis.[21]

Two days after Bryan's visit, the Japanese attacked Pearl Harbor. The debate was over, and the United States was at war. "I feel you have done it this time," teased Nancy Astor by cable from England.[22] With his country suddenly in the fight, Robertson felt confused and frustrated. He was not sure if his book project, now at 35,000 words, would still matter. On the afternoon of December 7, he wrote a letter to Blanche Knopf. "Do you still want me to go on with this book now that we are at war?" As he stewed, Robertson banged out an editorial for the *Tiger.* He urged Clemson cadets to remain calm, work hard, and remember "this is a total war and that we will have to fight it, all men and all women, in factories, on farms and in classrooms, as well as in the air on every continent and on every ocean." He reminded cadets eager to get in the war that "the Army called upon Clemson in the other war and it will call upon Clemson again when the moment is ready." In words that could just as easily been directed to himself, Robertson wrote, "Until it does call, all of us here must do what Lincoln advised: 'We must learn wait.'"[23]

The next day, as his letter sped to Knopf and as President Roosevelt asked a joint session of Congress to declare war on Japan, Robertson hurried to Washington on a train, trying to figure out what to do next. A few days later, in a private screening arranged by intelligence contacts, he was shown the first films back from Pearl Harbor.[24]

Moved by the suddenness of events, Robertson agonized over what he should do next. The book about the South didn't seem to matter much, not with the country at war. In anguish, Robertson wrote two letters to Jeanne Gadsden, pouring out his frustrations and uncertainties, wondering if the book project was a waste of time, concerned Knopf wouldn't want it now that a war was on, worried about coastal bombings along the Atlantic, and wondering if Gadsden, who lived near Charleston, should build a shelter. Gadsden took time away from typing the new book's manuscript and composed a long, reassuring response. "Of course I know how you must feel," she wrote, knowing that he wanted to be on the scene. But she reminded Ben that his current project still mattered, and pleaded with him to complete it:

> But it will not be over soon. A few weeks can't make so very much difference. That is, if you can write this book now. You'll never write it again in quite the same way. Don't you think you should finish it—whether Mrs. Knopf thinks so or not?
>
> Get this down now. For yourself and for us—for your people and for South Carolina. Preserve this. She'll look at it from a publisher's view point—whether it will make a book that will sell. What do you care. No one knows what the next years will bring for any of us—how much it will change our viewpoints, etc. I don't think you will ever regret finishing it as you have started. . . .
>
> On the other hand I know how difficult it will be for you to work. You can't shut your mind to what is happening each day. It is our story now, and it will be difficult to escape what happens each day and to project yourself back into this.
>
> I feel that what you write will last, because people will always be able to refer to it as a true picture of its time—of the group, the place or the idea which you have intended to portray.[25]

Blanche Knopf also responded with a vote of confidence. "I think you should go right ahead," she wrote on December 10. "I certainly wouldn't let anything deflect me now. I am delighted that you are nearly finished and do please keep right on your way." Encouraged, Robertson returned to Clemson, completed his manuscript in two weeks, and had Gadsden type the final draft.[26]

Two days before Christmas, a telegram arrived from Ralph Ingersoll:

> HAVE EXTRAORDINARILY IMPORTANT SPECIAL JOB WHICH ONLY YOU CAN DO FOR PM. MAKES DIRECT CONTRIBUTION TO WINNING THE WAR. HOW SOON CAN YOU COME TO NEW YORK PM'S EXPENSE TO TALK TO ME ABOUT IT. HOW ABOUT MONDAY THE TWENTY NINTH. WIRE ANSWER. MERRY CHRISTMAS AND REGARDS.[27]

CHAPTER 14

Humble Times for Eagles

Now that the United States was involved in the war on both the European and Pacific fronts, *PM* could move to other crusades in its fight for democracy. Foremost in the mind of publisher Ingersoll, an ardent antifascist, was the total defeat of the Nazi regime. In 1940 and 1941, he had his newspaper take a very strong line against the Nazis. And one area that he believed held promise for defeating Germany was the Soviet Union.

In August 1939, the Soviet Union and Germany signed a nonaggression pact. Stalin hoped to stay out of a European war, and also felt the agreement could open an opportunity to rebuild a Tsarist empire in Europe. A week after the pact was signed, Germany invaded Poland. Two days later, Britain and France, with whom Russia had earlier tried but failed to forge an alliance, declared war on Germany. As Germany captured Polish territories, it persuaded the Russians to invade Poland from the east. Later in the year, Germany and the Soviet Union divided the Polish territories.[1]

For a time it seemed the Soviets had averted war with Germany. But Hitler, caught in a war of his own and fearing Soviet westward expansion that could threaten German resources, ordered plans for a military operation against Russia. Soviet military and intelligence leaders tried to persuade Stalin to prepare for a German assault. Stalin, who took the nonaggression pact seriously, believed an attack by Hitler would be irrational. The Germans began bombing Soviet cities on June 22, 1941. It was the start of Operation Barbarossa, the invasion of the Soviet Union.[2]

One week after Operation Barbarossa began, Ingersoll began seeking permission to visit the Soviet Union, believing that the Russians were key allies in the fight against Nazi Germany. He arrived in Moscow at the end of summer 1941, with Luftwaffe planes over the city and German troops 150 miles away. During his visit, Ingersoll saw Russian troops up close and spent an hour with Stalin himself. He returned convinced of the might of the Soviet Union against Germany. "The Russians will stick," Ingersoll wrote in a huge report published in

PM after his return. "I found them wholly prepared to see the war through, no matter how long it takes, no matter how much it costs." But in championing the Russians and in his warmth toward Stalin, Ingersoll disregarded the mounting reports of the Soviet leader's cruelty toward his own people, including the show trials and executions of his political opponents and perceived enemies during the purges of the 1930s, numbers eventually revealed to be in excess of a half million people. As a media historian would someday note, Ingersoll's belief "that *any* ally in the fight against Hitler was welcome" was "a tragic conclusion."[3]

Military analyst Leonard Engel, who wrote for *PM* under the byline "The General," had convinced Ingersoll of something else: the Nazis could be defeated only if a second front were opened somewhere on the European continent. Whether through the Middle East, Norway, Italy, or France, a second front would divide German forces, thus taking the pressure off the Russians and making it easier to defeat the Axis.[4]

After the attack on Pearl Harbor—and official American entry into the European war four days later—Ingersoll's main crusade was gone. America was in the war, taking on fascism. One of Ingersoll's lieutenants remembered the publisher in "a kind of vacant trance," saying at a staff meeting that "he was no longer certain of the paper's excuse for existence. Its mission was accomplished. The nation was at war."[5]

Now that America was in it, Ingersoll decided the paper's new cause would be championing ways the Allied powers could win. On the domestic front, Ingersoll decided the paper would crusade against fascist sympathizers, war profiteers, and domestic complacency. And on the international level, Ingersoll wanted to champion the idea of a second front, which would squeeze Axis resources.[6]

In mid-January, just before leaving for his next assignment, Robertson had given a blunt assessment of the task ahead. "Nobody who knows conditions believes it will be a short war," he told an audience in Greenwood. "There are many months ahead before America will be fully prepared." Robertson also spoke disapprovingly of the conduct of Sweden and Ireland, warned that bombing Tokyo would not be as destructive as people imagined, and stressed that an all-out campaign to win the war was important.[7]

Within days, he was off again. His sister Mary remembered years later how quickly he left. Ben "was packed up and gone to New York, and then abroad, without even contacting the many old friends he always looked up before taking a long trip," she wrote. "He called us he was leaving and we went over there just in time to see him leave."[8]

On January 18, Robertson was off to New York, headed to Iceland to report on military operations there. Then his orders changed, and Robertson went back to Washington, going through the long process of getting approvals to head to Australia. Five hours before he was to leave for Australia, the *PM* office called. Ingersoll and Marshall Field now wanted Robertson to go to India and Egypt, Palestine and Iran, then on to Russia. From there, his dispatches on the fighting might help build support for the opening of a second front.

All the preparations Robertson had made now had to be undone and redone. Back to Washington he went for approvals, passports, and visas. Then he had to wait for permission to board the African aircraft. While he waited, he wrote to a friend at the *Anderson Independent* about how Washington felt. "Washington must be like what it was under Lincoln in the early days with the Army and the Navy wanting the same sort of fighting force that McClellan wanted—a perfect fighting force," he wrote, understanding why the city seemed so impatient. "We are eight years behind and can't win the war in a couple of weeks . . . we must expect to have a tough time until we can catch up."[9]

As Robertson waited for clearance to travel, Knopf editor Bernard Smith, who had edited *I Saw England,* issued his preliminary estimate on Robertson's new manuscript. "I was deeply moved and impressed by it," he wrote, "and I congratulate you on a wonderful job. You have done exactly the kind of thing we wanted and you have done it well." However, Robertson's rush to finish the book after Pearl Harbor bothered Smith, who complained "the last few pages are rather weak—they sort of trail off." The unique sentiment of the book, he complained, was destroyed by a sudden "couple of pages about today . . . I think it is fine to bring the narrative up to the present moment, but it has to be done in the same style and with the same intensity as the bulk of the book."[10]

Robertson worked on manuscript revisions in between other tasks. As he waited stateside, *PM* asked him to investigate reports of friction between American servicemen and Royal Air Force trainees. Spending two weeks at training fields in Tennessee, Georgia, and Alabama, Robertson found that there had been misunderstandings. Some of the British personnel had chafed at the American system of military training: the grooming standards; the honor and demerit system, including the demerit system of punishment; the exercise regimen; the extensive use of quizzes that consumed hours they could have spent flying; and the prohibition against personal radios. Meanwhile, the Americans felt the British did not take their instruction seriously. "The trouble with you British," a young West Pointer said to a class of cadets, "is you laugh too damned much." A trainee responded, "Lieutenant, we laugh because it is so serious—everything about flying is serious, and if we didn't laugh we should burst into tears." Robertson saw some cultural and philosophical clashes between the American instructors and their British students, but found rumors of deep division unfounded. Instead he found the British and the Americans working on ways to resolve their differences, and that "both they and we are thrashing our way to a common understanding."[11]

February rolled into March. Still waiting in Washington, Robertson read through the Washington *Times-Herald.* Reading through the society column, he felt disgusted reading about Washington's elites having parties at one another's homes, shuttling from vacations in Florida back to fine homes in Washington, treating defense bonds as an attraction for throwing a turkey shoot at a society belle's country home, partying away while the free world fought for survival. "Day after day, the society columns of the Washington papers are filled with this sort of twaddle," he scolded in *PM.* "Meantime, on Saturday nights you see the streets of Washington crowded with soldiers and sailors who have nowhere to go."[12]

During the wait Robertson met up with his old friend Edgar Snow. Back in the United States after his extended stay in Asia, during which he reported on the Japanese offensive, Snow had been asked by the *Saturday Evening Post* to cover the war from India, China, and Russia. As the old friends talked, Snow confessed misgivings about the assignment. Robertson dismissed Snow's doubts. "I never had any doubts about this job of ours, Ed. We're worth as much as a couple of generals." Snow would thereafter tease Robertson by calling him "General," but Robertson didn't care for the jest. "He believed exactly what he said," Snow later wrote. "I never knew anybody in the business, except Ray Clapper, who managed to keep his respect for the press so intact and so helped to restore my own. Ben's sense of mission and obligation were still as crusader-like as when I first met him on the campus at Missouri, where we listened to old Walter Dean Williams preaching his creed of journalism."[13]

Still there was no clearance for Robertson to cross the Atlantic. Finally, *PM* called on help from friends on high. With orders from President Roosevelt, Robertson's passage was expedited, and he took the now-familiar Clipper flight across the Atlantic. In April Robertson arrived in Cairo, where he would await clearance to enter Russia. While in Egypt, he was to observe Allied forces as they prepared for a possible move against Egypt by German forces. Rumors flew of a strike through South Russia, a move through Turkey, an attempt at Syria or another strike at Egypt. "Everybody you talk to seems to think that something is about to happen," Robertson wrote. "Everyone seems assured that the Germans must try something desperate somewhere soon. However, nobody is certain of what and where it will be."[14]

Robertson's time in Cairo was frustrating. He was not allowed to get close to the front, and instead he spent days exploring the city, "a kind of uncaptured Shanghai . . . the night club of a conflagration . . . like an island, a sanctuary in a storm". He listened in as people from around the world expressed their hopes and fears about America. "They are counting on their arms, of course, and on our men to help them win the war. But more than that they are depending on our historical generosity to win for them victory after victory—to win for them the next peace." Some exiled allies hoped to reestablish their prewar boundaries after the war was over. And Robertson listened to American soldiers ponder why they were in the war and how the peace should be maintained once it was won. A soldier from Texas said, "I don't want to stay away from home enforcing any peace." One of his compatriots replied, "We will have to take turns about staying away from home."[15]

As Robertson listened to these soldiers, Rommel's forces were attacking British forces in a move toward the Libyan coast. But Robertson wouldn't be there to cover it, for his clearance had been issued and he was soon on the way to Russia via Teheran, where American crews ferried aircraft and cargo that was turned over to the Russians. A cable from Foreign Editor Alexander Uhl requested that Robertson file "three [or] four Palestine stories soonest then go to Russia quickest."[16]

Robertson found Jerusalem in early June free of pilgrims and tourists, with only local people and transiting service personnel stopping by the shrines. To Robertson, the lack of tourist bustle gave a visitor time to truly stop and think. With a group of American pilots, he went to Bethlehem and visited the Church of the Nativity, then the group returned to Jerusalem and visited the Mount of Olives. But within a holy land that spoke of peace, Robertson noted the air raid shelters on Mount Zion, its air raid organization, and its nightly blackouts. "The City of God is taking no chances with the frenzy of the Germans," he wrote.[17]

From Jerusalem Robertson went to Damascus, where he caught a bus ride to Baghdad, spending bumpy and dusty hours rolling across the desert, riding all night; the air conditioner broken, Robertson felt his body turning parched. After a night to recover at Baghdad's Hotel Sinbad, Robertson found Baghdad confident about the war, with locals believing if the Russians could hold the Caucasus until October 1, the Middle East would be saved. At the hotel, Robertson had breakfast on a terrace. An officer at a nearby table complained to a waiter that his egg was not fresh. The waiter cheerfully flung the bad egg into the nearby Tigris

River. The same waiter picked up cantaloupe rinds from Robertson's table and threw them into the river. "For the fish," he explained.

Robertson then boarded a truck and went to Habbaniyah Airport, where he climbed aboard a plane for Teheran. Bouncing over the mountains of Persia, Robertson "wished I had never heard of an airplane." In Iran, Robertson spent part of his visit on a cot at the Fedowski Hotel recovering from food poisoning, and part of his time reconnecting with several American friends and reading columns in American papers. "Home is a long distance from this ballroom but in other ways it is very near," he wrote.[18]

Days later Robertson boarded a Russian plane loaded with passengers and cargo. The heavily laden transport lumbered off the runway, stair-stepping across the Persian mountains. Robertson heard a woman retch as the plane bounced around in the turbulent air around the snowy peaks. But beyond the mountains were the long expanses of Russia, the miles of deserts and dunes giving way to green forests. "It is Russia," Robertson wrote. "Here is the battlefield on which so much depends. It is this faraway, isolated Russia that is fighting for our life." From above Robertson looked out across factories and houses, wheat fields, cattle grazing in vast yards, and felt an understanding, for these scenes reminded him of scenes back home. "An American who loves the great western U.S. spaces can understand at one glance why Russia is everything to 200,000,000 people."[19]

The plane landed at Kuibyshev, where Robertson spent the night at the American Embassy and met Ambassador William H. Standley. Then Robertson set out to know Russia during wartime. In Kuibyshev Robertson found scenes reminiscent of London, seeing a purpose and determination in how its people hurried to work in the city's new factories, and then hurried home. Robertson reflected that the Russian revolution's institution of five-year plans, sacrificing personal comfort to build industry, was making it possible to produce the tools to fight the Germans. "You think that perhaps in America we have thought too much of late about a standard of living," he wrote. "We have too often forgot that America originally was intended to be the home for the oppressed of the whole world, to be a land of the equal and free. In Russia you now remember that a standard of living is secondary to a standard of thought." And in conversations with the locals, Robertson found strong support for a second front. "Here it is nearly July and still the Russians alone are standing. Four and a half million of their people have been sacrificed. So who are we to talk?" He concluded, "You realize that, despite everything we can do for a long time, our standards today depend much on a Red Army of the Russians. These are humble times for eagles."[20]

The next day, Robertson watched an artillery unit in training, two weeks away from heading for the front. Vice General Victor Tikhonov showed Robertson and the other reporters around the training grounds and put the men of the unit through their paces. Tikhonov told the reporters that Stalin had ordered the Red Army to clear the Germans out of Russian territory in 1942, and that the Red Army would carry out that order. He told them that the Red Army wanted to see a second front in Europe, and that the sooner it was opened, the better. The Germans, Tikhonov said, had not achieved a strategic success in their spring operations, adding that the Red Army was stronger than the Germans. Robertson told Tikhonov about the exploits of American pilots ferrying bombers for Russia from America. "We don't doubt that you want to help us, and we already are beginning to feel that help," Tikhonov replied.[21]

Robertson watched mechanized artillery, then reviewed cavalry regiments of Cossacks practice in a recaptured area. Watching the horsemen swing sabres and yell their battle cries, Robertson heard their general tell of how this old form of fighting had bewildered German troops and had even routed a Panzer division, capturing tanks and supply train vehicles. Almost instantly Robertson was reminded of Civil War cavalry units, and the Russian general said the Red Army still studied cavalry campaigns of the American Civil War.[22]

As Americans celebrated Independence Day, Robertson thought about Russian sacrifice. Reports were coming in that Sevastopol had been captured after a long, grim siege. Robertson wrote of the sacrifices the people of Sevastopol had made, of the long odds against an increasing German campaign. In a July 4 dispatch, Robertson wrote of spending a "sober" Independence Day realizing that Russia "is as strong spiritually now as America was 200 years ago. This is a pioneer country and it has the same sort of spiritual strength that we had when Cotton Mather preached in Massachusetts." Thinking about how Russians had a cause for which they were willing to die, Robertson wrote, "I think of my grandfather when I talk to the Russians." And reflecting on how the Russians' drive was economic while the Puritans thought of religion, he wrote, "Any old-time American can understand the strength of such a drive. A star can mean as much to people as a cross."[23]

The fall of Sevastopol prompted Robertson to step up his calls for a second front. "We can now expect Hitler to make a supreme attempt to defeat the armies of the Soviet Union," he wrote on July 6. "Almost everything depends on the result of this great approaching battle in Russia, and on the battle now being fought against the Germans by the British in Egypt." To Robertson, the lack of a second front was as dire a situation as aid to Britain the year before. "Our help to Russia is now needed as urgently by the Soviet people as it was previously needed by the British. Of course, we understand this perfectly, but we cannot repeat it too frequently, for our position, and that of our allies, is both urgent and grave."[24]

As Robertson pondered the meaning of Sevastopol, and as a feeling of dread gripped Moscow after a number of setbacks including the abandonment of the overrun Rostov-on-Don, the second front became a recurring theme, tinged with desperation. "The Nazis are flooding Russia like water and they will try to flow wherever there is the least resistance," he wrote on July 17 as battles raged along the Don River. A second front, he insisted, "would have a magical effect on the men of the Soviet forces. In this regard, we as well as the Russians are approaching a crisis. We cannot afford to be wrong, we cannot miscalculate, for the outcome of the war depends on our immediate decisions—the future of the world depends on our immediate decisions.[25]

But just as had happened in Cairo, Robertson was frustrated in Russia. The Russian military officials would not let correspondents visit the front. Most often, the only exposure they had to the military came in sanctioned, carefully-planned trips to training exercises. Most information came from official communiques that frequently left out information about heavy losses. The correspondents' work was often heavily censored by Russian officials. And the Russian government kept tight rein on the Western correspondents, particularly the British and American reporters, suspecting they might be intelligence agents.[26]

His reporting constrained by the censors, unable to go to the front himself, Robertson looked around him for interest and inspiration. Just as the Savoy had been in London, the Hotel Metropole served as home to a small colony of American correspondents. There, Robertson and a dozen colleagues—including Henry Shapiro of the United Press, Robert Magidoff of NBC, whose ability to speak Russian helped the entire group, and Larry LeSueur of CBS—spent the days working, and their evenings having conversations over dinner. They often ended up in the room of the AP's Eddy Gilmore, which gratified Robertson. Not only was Gilmore from Alabama, but his room had a piano. "Sometimes Henry Cassidy or I will bang old time tunes that we learned years ago by heart," Robertson wrote, "sometimes we play hearts, but most of the time we read or we talk about war and about home." Another Southerner in the group was Janet Weaver of the *Daily Worker,* who unbeknownst to the correspondents was gathering intelligence for the Comintern. "She can make biscuits and can make old fashioned Southern gravy like nobody's business," Robertson noted. "We get along well together in Moscow. Often we quarrel and sometimes there are violent scenes but always after a few hours we quieten down and those who are wrong say they are sorry. We all unite when any of us is threatened from without."[27]

Deprived of the opportunity to see the war for himself, Robertson worked from official communiques and battle reports and newspapers—"which are more like textbooks than American newspapers," he noted—and he tried to piece together the best summary of the war that he could. Invariably, it was a dark vision of Red forces on the cusp of being outnumbered, and only prompt help from the United States could save them. "These days are as gloomy as any we have had since 1940. Again our cause is directly threatened," he wrote in late July. "Over here it seems to us we have but one issue before us in this struggle—does our mature country accept the responsibility or reject it? Do we help to develop the world or do we decay? Over here we know who our most vicious opponent is, for whoever has made peace with him soon has given up all power."[28]

For a month Robertson continued along this theme, his tone growing more urgent as the Russians tried to fight against a southern offensive by the Germans, as a decisive battle loomed for Stalingrad, and as the second front seemed less and less likely. Robertson described the response of eager young American pilots as it dawned on them just how big the battle was that they faced. "They begin to understand that Germany is waging war for time and that Germany is winning," he wrote. "You should see an American who realizes for the first time in his life that it is possible for the U.S.A. to lose a war."[29]

In mid-August, British Prime Minister Churchill and American ambassador Averell Harriman visited Moscow. Harriman, who said he came as a personal representative of President Roosevelt, said "The Americans will stand hand to hand and shoulder to shoulder with the Russians on the front." Robertson took cheer from this. "We think of our country far away and of the enormous difficulty of getting under way," he wrote. "Often we have hours of gloom. Then we remember some American something such as the statement by Averell Harriman." Noting the courage of the American spirit, Robertson wrote, "Our allies can trust us. We believe in open diplomacy openly arrived at and we believe that we have given our word to Russia for aid this year in Europe and we intend to keep our word. We do not expect anyone anywhere to fight our battles."[30]

But Robertson could not know what was happening at the highest levels. Britain, busy with a war in the North Atlantic and trying to hold Egypt, could not offer much help. The United States, with operations in both the Atlantic and Pacific, still building its military up to strength for both theaters, was likewise hard-pressed to assist in a second front. The Allies could offer only limited help to the Soviet Union, not the kind of commitment Stalin wanted or that *PM* had advocated.[31]

As Robertson saw no action on a second front, his spirits sank. "It is both inspiring and almost heartbreaking to be an American behind this Eastern battle line as the war goes into a new year," he wrote in early September. "It is inspiring to observe a nation resisting invasion as heroically as Russia. It is almost heartbreaking in the midst of death to see how much understanding there is of the situation in the U.S.A. The Russians are fighting for themselves, but you constantly realize that they consider themselves also to be fighting and dying to give America time . . . They believe we have promised the Second Front this year. They still believe us."[32]

Discouraged, tired of official censorship, and frustrated that the second front was unlikely to become reality, Robertson wired *PM* that he wanted to come back to the United States. Turner Catledge replied, "If mind is made up come home we naturally must agree any chance of returning via India."[33]

Glad to get out of Russia, where he had starved under strict rationing and had feared for his survival, Robertson leapt at the chance. From New Delhi, he summarized how he felt: "It is a saddening experience at this particular phase of the war for an American to be leaving Russia. You have a feeling of running away. You also have a sense of personal failure. All Americans in Russia have this feeling at this particular time. All of them feel that they have failed and that America has failed."[34] Although Robertson felt defeated as he left Russia, a more personal triumph was now his. On August 17, his book about the South had been published.

CHAPTER 15

A Southern Record

Red Hills and Cotton: An Upcountry Memory was several things. Part of it is a warm, autobiographical tribute to the South Robertson knew as a boy, a hymn to a simpler time, a love letter to his native region and a tribute to the people he came from. It was the story he had wanted to tell since those days he had lain ill in Surabaya, the words of Walt Whitman's *Leaves of Grass* making him yearn for home and inspiring him to write about the journey of a people through time and history. It was the story he struggled to tell in *Travelers' Rest:* the story of an old family in an old state. In fact, *Red Hills and Cotton* was so closely tied to *Travelers' Rest* that some passages and stories, this time attributed to real-life characters, came over intact. But by shedding the novel's melodrama, instead telling of his ancestors and his experiences in a more natural form, the compact *Red Hills and Cotton* succeeded where the meandering, overwritten novel had fallen short. An older Robertson had a perspective and clarity he hadn't possessed in 1937.

In this new book Robertson told stories of his ancestors, of the exploits of his family through the previous two centuries, the stories of his relatives who fought on the side of the Confederacy. He wrote of a childhood spent in the rural South, of the rhythms of farm life, of being poor in money but rich in everything else, of walks in the country and train trips and church services and stories told at kitchen tables. He wrote of lessons for an honorable life, taught by elders during long evenings on a front porch. And he meditated on where the South had been, on the places where it could improve, and on a vision for a South that was prepared for a changing age.

Robertson's pack-rat tendencies, his note-taking and diary-keeping over the years, made his task considerably easier than merely starting from scratch. His speeches and writings had served to sharpen his point of view, which he was able to express with eloquence in *Red Hills and Cotton.* The process of writing *Travelers' Rest* had let him organize his thoughts about his family's history, and had helped him further develop as a writer. And two years of covering the war from Britain, of witnessing danger and bravery firsthand, of experiencing a war of his own, had not only improved his ability to tell a story, but focused his perspective.

Robertson began the book with a stirring statement of his belief in his home state. "By the grace of God, my kinfolks and I are Carolinians," he wrote:

> My grandmother believed the finest country in the world was America and the most precious part of America was Carolina. The sun rose and set in our valley; it hovered between Glassy Mountain in the east and Six Mile in the west, then it dropped off into the darkness, into the dark night of despair; it sank off to shine for a few odd hours on the heathen down in China.
>
> I think my grandmother believed God had chosen us for our country, that He had said to us as He had to Joshua: "Arise and go over this Jordan, thou and all this people, unto the land that has been promised." A hundred and ninety years ago God had brought us into Canaan from eastern Pennsylvania.[1]

From this beginning Robertson expressed the values instilled from his childhood: belief in the independence and good of the common man, the goodness of the self-sufficient farmer, the admiration of his ancestors who had settled this wild country and then went on to fight for the South in the Civil War. Among those Robertson's family distrusted were bankers and merchants ("We hated them because they had robbed us—they should have been shot and we should have shot them, but always they have been so legal in their dirty business that we never felt quite justified in going after them with a gun," and the elites of Charleston.[2]

In among the warm memories, Robertson wrote of the choices the South had made. He told of the differences between the patrician Lowcountry planter mindset and the independent Scots-Irish upcountry farmers, of his belief that the planters dragged the South into the Civil War to defend their economic system; though the upcountrymen would never benefit from defending that system, their allegiance to South Carolina summoned them to fight.

Channeling the stories he had been taught since childhood, Robertson also wrote of Reconstruction excesses, of a belief that the federally imposed Reconstruction program was more interested in promoting blacks than actually caring for them, and of the excesses of carpetbaggers and scalawags. Robertson wrote of how the Ku Klux Klan and the Red Shirts organized to fight the Reconstruction government and of the changes made once Reconstruction ended. He wrote of all this in a matter-of-fact style, acknowledging the sins of the past but sparing harsh words of condemnation. He was, after all, writing about the activities his beloved grandparents and other ancestors had taken part in, and their stories undoubtedly were in the back of his mind as he wrote. He was too close to the subject to be truly objective.[3]

Robertson also offered a critique of the Southern economy. Though he wrote lyrically of the cotton grower's life and fondly recalled how its short growing season provided several months off to enjoy the freedom of rural life, he acknowledged that cotton had many shortcomings as a way of life. What had been a means to restart the Southern economy after the Civil War had become a habit; the habit became dependence, and eventually a trap. Cotton's selling price often fluctuated, and growing it was harsh on the soil, but to farm cotton was to feel comforted, to feel that cotton in the barn was as good as cash in the bank. Calls for farmers to diversify, grow different crops and keep more cattle in order to expand their opportunities to make money, were met with resistance because although cotton farmers were poor, they were comfortable growing a crop they knew so well.

Alongside this critique, Robertson explored the plight of the tenant farmer. As the price of cotton fell, tenant farmers could no longer survive, and many of them found jobs in the new textile mills that were opening in the upcountry. But to Robertson, this meant trading the freedom of farm life for long hours of work in a factory for a guaranteed wage. He wrote of seeing mill workers in the store after their pay periods, noting how pale they were from working indoors and how dispirited they seemed.

Culturally, Robertson brought to a national audience some of his beliefs about how clinging to the "Lost Cause" was holding the South back. In comments that were straight from his 1939 address in Charleston, Robertson urged the South to look to the challenges of tomorrow. And he wrote of the need to treat blacks as equal human beings—remembering the black servants who worked for his family, he wrote that "Jim and Mary raised me" and noted how much he had learned about life from their influence. But he issued his call for progress on the race issue by noting the errors of Reconstruction, of having racial equality suddenly forced upon the South. "Suddenness was not the way," Robertson counseled, noting that poverty and ignorance got in the way of understanding, and urging instead that the problem be worked out gradually, as each generation discovered it had nothing to fear from other races.

The influence of the coming war formed the book's final passages. Robertson observed that defeat in the Civil War left the South with the resolve never to lose another war again—and with that resolve, the South prepared for the war that came on a Sunday in December. Recalling the scene at his father's home as the news came in that cold day, as his family grieved privately before going to visit their kinfolks, Robertson wrote:

> Suddenly all the past seemed to sweep forward into the present, and we seemed again to take our place in the vast eternity of time. We were in trouble and our country was in trouble, and as always whenever there was trouble, we found that automatically we had come together. No longer were we merely ourselves. We were who we were because all of those who had lived before us had been what they had been. My cousin Billy said he was ready to go. So did my cousin George. So did J. B., Mary's nephew. We went alone to the cotton fields. There before us stood the hills. Our people had turned to them when the men had left for Kings Mountain; they had turned to them when our delegate had gone to vote against the Constitution; they had turned again when the news had come from Appomattox. The hills were eternal. Always they gave us strength.[4]

Robertson's book was an interesting contrast with other recent works on the South. Although he looked back with warmth on his rural Carolina boyhood, Robertson rejected the romanticism and anti-modernism of the Southern Agrarians' *I'll Take My Stand.* While the Agrarians argued against modernity in favor of an agrarian renaissance, Robertson suggested the solution would lie in merging "a Yankee mind and a Southern heart," adapting to more modern means of business while retaining the values that made the South special. And while Robertson was candid about what he felt were the South's many shortcomings, he also believed "our Southern problems were not beyond our ability to solve."[5]

While Robertson disagreed with the conservative case made by the Agrarians, he did not go as far as W. J. Cash had in *The Mind of the South,* published the year before. A South Carolinian like Robertson, Cash's observations about Southern culture and politics were not far removed at all from what Robertson had confided to journals and written to friends. But where Robertson had been inspired by Wolfe and Whitman, Cash had been inspired by H. L. Mencken. Where Robertson was lyrical, Cash was analytical. Where Robertson gently probed, Cash dissected. And while Robertson moderated his words in criticizing the South's racial and social attitudes and its lack of intellectual curiosity, Cash pulled no punches.[6]

Robertson was no less keen an observer of the Southern condition than Cash, and he reached similar conclusions. But it wasn't Robertson's style to write what Cash had, and their books served different purposes. Robertson's gentle nature would not have let him turn *Red Hills and Cotton* into the kind of book Cash wrote. Robertson's gentle book did not seek to confront the reader or inventory the region's shortcomings. It was instead part memoir, part love letter, part meditation, along the way gently nudging the South to look ahead and prepare for a changing world. He had promised Blanche Knopf a personal book about what it meant to be a Carolinian, not an analysis of the sort Cash had written (and that Knopf had also published). Robertson, as a native Southerner who took pride in his upcountry, Baptist, Democrat, Confederate pedigree, was able to make criticisms that, from a non-Southerner or even a non-Upstate native, would have been dismissed. Robertson's native voice gave his criticisms weight.

Robertson's moderate tone may have been influenced by another ambition. On at least two prior occasions, he had seriously explored running for public office. He often discussed this ambition with friends, and in a January 1941 interview Robertson admitted that when the war was over, he wanted to come back to South Carolina and run for Congress. "He had an urge to do public service as well as to report it," Wright Bryan wrote. "He felt, and rightly so, that he understood the people he would represent as well as anyone could."[7]

Privately, Robertson could discuss his strong and progressive beliefs about racial and economic matters with like-minded friends such as Bryan, David Bruce, John Lane and Bo Williams. But Robertson knew he would be selling a progressive message to a conservative constituency, and that a successful campaign would call for a lighter touch. Years earlier, in a note to himself after a speech on civil rights, he cautioned that calmness would make his message more persuasive. *Red Hills and Cotton* represents an older Robertson moderating his progressive message for a wider audience. Robertson also knew, having covered many a political campaign, how words could come back to haunt a candidate. He could do and say more later on. For now, Robertson tempered his language.

At the same time, *Red Hills and Cotton* made a slice of Southern culture accessible to a broader national audience. His *PM* readers, and the influential circle of friends that Robertson had cultivated through his years in New York, Washington, Honolulu, and elsewhere, had available to them a volume that outlined the influences of the man they knew. To those who knew him only through his newspaper stories, Robertson's book served as an ambassador, introducing new audiences to a warm and gentle view of the Southern way of life.

Robertson's friends knew he was working on a new book, but had no idea what it would be about. The mystery made *Red Hills and Cotton* an unexpected delight. "We were all quite surprised when the book finally came out," said Wright Bryan. "Everyone had expected another war book and instead Ben wrote a very gentle book, a book that is almost impossible to categorize."[8]

As the reviews came in, they were almost universally complimentary, whether in North or South. The *New York Times,* stating that the memoir "vivifies an energetic, rugged and self-confident South," noted that it "joins charm and humor and tenderness with wisdom and strength." The *Chicago Sun* called it "a book to come back to—a book to make one realize how fine (and rare) a thing it is when sense and beauty come in one cover," while the *San Francisco Chronicle* stated the book "was better than a tribute. It opens whole vistas to an understanding of a great part of America." *Time* called it "an eloquent hymn to one Southern way of life—that of the Hill Gentry. It is also an indigenous statement of the idea for which so many Southerners believe the South fought the Civil War—that only those governments are strong which are based on the land and its people, not on factories and the people who own or work in them." Stark Young of the *New Republic* wrote, "The whole material is so truly and deeply viewed, so proudly and deeply felt, and so steadily, intensely and simply put down, that I recognize without any reservations its validity as a Southern record. Liquor, pauperism, ignorance, fornication, miscegenation and all the stage thunder for Southern literary works are in this book; but they are in scale, incidental to the basic culture and way of living that the book is really about."[9]

Robertson's former and present employers joined in the acclaim. Rosemary Benet of the *Herald Tribune* wrote, "This is a delightful book. As far as I am concerned, it will go on that special, small shelf reserved for books that are to be re-read and cherished."[10] *PM,* which ran extracts in its "Good Writing" column, wrote, "Ben Robertson, *PM*'s Moscow correspondent, is a long way from South Carolina now. No doubt he finds it pleasant between air-raid alarms and battles to look back on the time he was a boy in the red hills at the foot of the Blue Ridge. That is the sort of book he has written, a reminiscence and appreciation of youth in the old time. He calls it *Red Hills and Cotton,* but the subtitle, *An Up-Country Memory,* is more descriptive."[11]

Southern reviewers found much to praise in the book, too. Another former employer of Robertson, the Charleston *News and Courier,* stated the book was "beautifully, simply, exquisitely written" and was "a contribution to South Carolina's literature; he has drawn a true picture, and it is and will be preservative." South Carolina's largest newspaper, the *State* of Columbia, said Robertson's book contained "a wealth of superb prose that brings to mind Thomas Wolfe, Walt Whitman and the Old Testament." Wright Bryan, in the *Atlanta Journal,* wrote that his friend's new book was "friendly and entertaining, as well as informative."[12]

Robertson's book was buoyed by positive assessments from the Book of the Month Club, which made it a selection for September 1942. "Out of its rambling back piazza talk there grows up, little by little, an admittedly sane, understandable interpretation of the Southern attitude. It is also one of the most persuasive and likable ever put into a book." Knopf produced newspaper advertisements that featured praise from Stephen Vincent Benet, who called *Red*

Hills and Cotton "one of the most beautiful and one of the truest books about the South that has ever been written."[13]

While most reactions to Robertson's new book showered it with praise, some readers found themselves at odds with its broader messages. Like Robertson, his friend Harry Ashmore had roots in the upcountry and was a Clemson graduate. He also shared Robertson's belief that the South needed to change its racial and economic philosophies. Ashmore would later become a vocal advocate for civil rights, earning a Pulitzer Prize for his editorials in support of school integration in Little Rock.[14]

When *Red Hills and Cotton* was released, Ashmore was going through Army training at Camp Swift, Texas. Excited to see his friend's new book, Ashmore devoured it in his spare time. Although he found much to admire about the book, he found himself in profound disagreement with some of Robertson's observations. In a lengthy letter to John Lane, Ashmore offered praise seasoned with critique. "It's a book that should have been written and Ben was the man for the job," Ashmore wrote, noting that Robertson's writing seemed to channel the gifts of Nathaniel Hawthorne, Walt Whitman, and Thomas Wolfe when describing how upcountry culture fit into the American story. Ashmore, who noted that his forebears had followed the same path as Robertson's in settling the hill country, praised Robertson's analysis of the upcountry character, and agreed that those who stuck to Jeffersonian principles were a bulwark against the Charleston mindset of "building white columns on all our houses, planting magnolias in all our yards, and placing a touch of lace at all our sleeves."

Ashmore, however, found himself at odds with Robertson's beliefs that there was no place for the upcountryman in an industrial world, and that if Southerners just lived a simple life the world would come back around to the Southern way. "We made a virtue out of poverty," Ashmore wrote, charging that this belief had become a fundamental truth handed down through the generations, discouraging intellectual curiosity, and leaving Southern children unprepared for the world that had replaced the frontiers their forebears tamed. For each one who survived, Ashmore wrote, "a thousand sank into the hopeless anonymity of the factories."

Ashmore scored Robertson's hope of "a Yankee mind and a Southern heart" as "a fatuous phrase." He elaborated: "The only future we have any right to hope for is the one we'll make for ourselves when we come out of our valleys, accept the fact that the only certainty is change, and go on to use the strength we brag about to make a place for ourselves in whatever world we have to face." To Ashmore, an upcountry that clung to the hopes of the past was no better than the Charleston mindset that Robertson criticized. "They have both served as a refuge for a people who ran and hid because their grandfathers once took a terrible licking for a people who said, 'They won't run the world the way I want it run, so the hell with it.'" Ashmore concluded, "Ben's subtitle for 'Red Hills and Cotton,' 'An Upcountry Memory,' is apt. He remembers Keowee the way any man remembers his childhood; the good things stand out, the bad things fade. But I would have subtitled it differently. I would have called it: 'Epitaph for the Upcountry—In Loving Memory Of a World That Existed Only In The Minds Of a Few Of Us.'"[15]

Red Hills and Cotton became popular, making the best-seller lists and steadily becoming a favorite of Southern literature. It was not a perfect book. It never meant to be anything other than one man's reflections on a region that made him who he was, set down for all time. Whatever else Ben Robertson might accomplish in his career, his hymn to the upcountry, the book whose heartfelt passages had taken a lifetime to build and years to express, lives on, between hard covers, as an enduring tribute to the region that made him, the people he loved, and the pioneer spirit of his beloved family.

CHAPTER 16

Cynical Men

In Moscow, Robertson boarded an airplane to retrace the route from months before back to Teheran. The plane took a pass over the city and Robertson looked down over the Kremlin—the Moscow river winding beneath—and he felt sadness and humiliation, a fear that by not following through on the second front, Americans had let down their Russian allies. The plane landed at Kubiyshev for the night, and Robertson spent eight hours in a tiny waiting room full of baggage, watching children play with puppies, while Soviet fighter pilots shared a watermelon with waiting passengers and women served tea.

The next morning, en route to Baku, Robertson cringed as the pilots flew their big plane low over haystacks and frightened herds of cattle, laughing while their nervous passengers sat in fear. Though the pilots claimed these risky maneuvers were done for reasons of security, Robertson opined "we think they like to hop hedges for the sheer hell of it. Russian pilots are magnificent, but they fly transport planes much in the same way Americans drive Ford cars." After a midday refueling stop in Baku, the plane climbed high over the mountains; with Teheran in sight, they dove in like a bomber and landed. Robertson was out of Russia, but his thoughts were still there. "We thought of Russia fighting on and on, regardless of odds. You leave part of your heart in Russia."[1]

After a brief stay in Teheran and a visit with American pilots who ferried planes from the United States, Robertson was off to New Delhi. Although the war against the Axis occupied some of his time there, and though he continued his personal form of journalism describing the people fighting the war, another story began to occupy more of his attention.

When war broke out in 1939, India had been brought into the conflict as part of the British Empire. That the British did this without consulting the Indian people angered Indian nationalists and intensified their desire for an independent India. Promises to address Indian self-governance after the war did not satisfy nationalist leaders. Meanwhile, the British felt Indian troops seemed discouraged, offering only halfhearted cooperation in the war effort. In 1942, Sir Stafford

Cripps made an effort to negotiate India's full cooperation in the war effort in exchange for a postwar resolution, but it failed. Late that summer, Gandhi and the other principals of the independence movement were imprisoned after he called for the British to leave India. The "Quit India" movement prompted acts of rebellion across the country, and British troops fought back.[2]

While all this was going on, Muslim leaders in India, who had supported British entry into the war and feared oppression from the Hindu majority, wanted part of India to be partitioned into a Muslim homeland. Mohammed Ali Jinnah, president of India's Moslem League, warned that the only hope for India was its division into separate Muslim and Hindu states. "It is impossible to run this subcontinent of 400,000,000 people as a united democratic country," Jinnah told Robertson. "If [the Hindus] are unwilling to let us have a quarter of India for ourselves, then God help the Hindus."[3]

The British, intent on demonstrating that all was well in India, took correspondents to watch cadets training to become officers. At a training camp near the base of the Himalayas, Robertson saw Hindu and Muslim troops train together, members of different castes working alongside one another with no difficulties. On the surface, all appeared well. But the unresolved tensions between Britain and India remained in the air.[4]

The British had installed General Archibald Wavell as commander-in-chief and Victor Hope, Lord Linlithgow, as the Viceroy, whose decrees could be overruled only by London. Heading the permanent civil government were Sir Reginald Maxwell and Sir Richard Tottenham, both of whom had been in India for three decades. The more Robertson talked to these men, the more appalled he became. "Maxwell and Tottenham believe in 'law and order' and they are perfectly willing to shoot to keep it," Robertson wrote after returning from India, when he no longer had to worry about his copy passing muster with British officials. "They are honest about their imperialism . . . Once I asked Tottenham what he thought of what Indians were saying about him and he replied, 'I have been here so long it doesn't matter.'" To Robertson, these "cynical men" were following a policy that was "resulting in failure for the allies for the reason that imperialism does not produce cooperation among citizens nor does it turn out the maximum number of guns and tanks."[5]

The disappointment with empire that had surfaced after his trip to Guam—when he saw the hardship that resulted from Washington's indifference and labored in vain to bring official action for the distant island territory—became disgust and anger in India as he watched the ruling "cynical men" use their power to enforce an imperial vision of order. Robertson later wrote of people being beaten and shot; poor citizens raising funds to pay a fine for civil disobedience;

Visiting the Taj Mahal in 1942. Special Collections & Archives, Clemson University Libraries, Clemson, South Carolina.

imprisoned girls, arrested after a demonstration; starvation and suppression; thousands of supporters of Gandhi and Nehru arrested; the incidents of sabotage against the British; the imprisonment of Gandhi; the hundreds of local constables, paid six dollars a month, hired to maintain order; and the differences between Hindu and Muslim, which the British used as one excuse to put off an agreement for Indian independence.[6]

Some leaders, including Chakravsti Rajagopalachari, the former premier of Madras, urged the Indian people to wait until the war was over; extreme moves, he worried, would be "an invitation" to Japan. "If we lose our country and fall into the hands of the Japanese, we may have to wait probably for another hundred years for our freedom," he warned.[7]

In November Robertson interviewed the Maharajah of Dholpur, who had ruled for thirty-one years and was well-connected with the ruling British. The Maharajah complained that British rule had lost its personal touch. "Dholpur holds that what India wants is kindness, friendliness and understanding, and that what it gets from Britain is coldness and abstract legal decisions," Robertson wrote. The Maharajah warned that the situation in India was deteriorating. "The British have shut one door. They must open another. If they cannot do something big, then they must do something. They must do something personal and monarchical. They cannot continue as they are at present in this country."[8]

When Robertson tried to question British officials, he met resistance. Sometimes they tried to say that India was a great burden, that Indians were too divided to govern themselves effectively. Other times, Robertson met hostility. "The British told me I was a fool to come out to India and spend three months and have nerve enough to talk to those who had been there for 200 years," he wrote. He replied that although there was much he would never know about India, "it did not take me 200 years to see starvation and suppression, and I could feel hatred when I felt it." They responded that Robertson was "negative and destructive—a technique they have developed to allay criticism," and asked him what they could do to help the situation. Robertson suggested several ideas, including talking to Manuel Quezon of the Philippines. But to every suggestion, Robertson wrote, the British "have an answer ready for anything that you say. The answer is 'No.'" On one occasion, General Wavell, who had been on good terms with the correspondents, issued a blistering reprimand to them in his official capacity as commander-in-chief in India.[9]

Increasingly, Robertson felt that India was not a political situation so much as it was "now a camp."[10] The correspondents were now at risk, as Wavell's angry reproof indicated. As Robertson composed a story back to New York, he wrote:

> Bill McGaffin of the Associated Press, who went through the blitz in England, is being threatened with disaccreditation by British authorities in India. McGaffin sent this message to his office in New York through the United States Army. Other American correspondents in India are considering resigning their accreditation to the British in this theater. Our relations with the authorities are getting worse.
>
> My personal opinion about British censorship in India is that it is exactly like that in Singapore and Burma, it is following the British colonial policy of not taking local people into confidence and of assuming always that everything everywhere is fine. I think the policy here means that the authorities are continuing the stand that has resulted in a defeat that has brought about the alienation of the oriental people that has demoralized Allied fighting units and that has hidden Allied faults. Those who would desire to change those faults if they knew about them are kept in ignorance. It seems to me that the aim of censorship out here is to conceal. I don't like it, and furthermore I think it is dangerous.[11]

The paragraph was struck through, and the rest of the story was transmitted back to America. Robertson put the typed page away in his notes. After the war was over, when he no longer had to worry about keeping war correspondent credentials, he wanted to be able to tell the whole story.[12]

In late November Robertson conducted visits to American air fields in India. He found the Americans worked to reach out to the people of the region and respected their customs. Robertson noted the contrast with the British and wrote that the American soldiers' efforts, as well as those of diplomats and military leaders, were building friends and raising hopes in India.[13]

During these visits Robertson also had encounters with Lt. Gen. Joseph Stilwell, commander of the China-Burma-India theater. The general, nicknamed "Vinegar Joe," came in "every other week or so. He would fly in and things would hum." Robertson found much to admire in Stilwell: he admired his unpretentious nature, and he found him "sometimes explosive but always patient about the things that mattered." With the correspondents, Robertson said, Stilwell was "both tough and gentle . . . his rule with the press is to tell the truth." After dealing with the difficulties of British rulers in India, Robertson found Stilwell's plain style refreshing. "He is an inspiring man, an impressive man," Robertson wrote. "I am willing to go with Gen. Stilwell wherever he decides to go."[14]

At the airfields Robertson did enjoy the opportunities he had to talk with servicemembers and pilots. The taste of home was refreshing half a world away. On a flight across India, a young captain told Robertson he wanted to become a writer. Pulling out a small notebook, the captain asked if he would look at a diary he had kept since Pearl Harbor. Looking through the little journal, Robertson was astonished by all the lengthy, sometimes hazardous journeys the young pilot had made in less than a year. "Some day I suppose there will live a generation that will look upon our air flights as we look now upon the sea voyages of Columbus," Robertson reflected. "Here in this little book I realized for the first time what it means to possess mobility over the earth. I realized how vast are the operations of our airmen."[15]

Soon it was time for Robertson to take his own lengthy voyage by air, to trade the disappointments of Russia and the frustrations of India for the familiarity of his home country. On Thanksgiving Day 1942, Robertson observed the holiday in New Delhi. Instead of turkey, he and his fellow celebrants shared a main course of peacock. Three days later, Robertson boarded an airplane heavily loaded with metal needed in the United States. "If you can clear the ground by four inches at the end of the field, you'll be all right," an officer told the airplane's commander. Robertson fretted about the heavy load and wondered if the runway was long enough. But the plane readily climbed into the sky. A sergeant sitting on a box of freight said to Robertson, "Boy, oh boy, these babies can take a beating."

On they flew to a staging area, and after a quick night of rest they spent the next day flying to the western coast of Africa. In Accra, Robertson waited a day and a half for a plane out. To his surprise, the base's chief pilot was Dallas Sherman, a fellow Clemson man, and the two passed the time catching up on stories.

The next night, in the midst of a thunderstorm, Robertson took off for South America aboard a four-engine Boeing transport full of ferry pilots headed back to the United States. They landed in Brazil, spending the night in a tent. When day broke, Robertson boarded another airplane for the next leg. As it bounced around the sky, a fellow passenger comforted the nervous Robertson: "Well, if we crack up, we won't know it." Two days of flying and one thunderstorm later, Robertson finally arrived in Miami.[16]

After one week and 12,000 miles of travel, Robertson was struck by what he encountered. Miami "seemed so warm and calm and quiet, the clouds were so soft and the city was dark and serious. You felt the country was at war, there was a new sort of silence." In the airfield's terminal, he and the pilots bought things they had gone so long without. Newspapers, candy, and chewing gum seemed like luxuries. They boarded a bus for their quarters. Too tired to eat, Robertson wrote, they "fell into the beds."[17]

Robertson was up at dawn. He and two of the officers he'd flown home with walked the quiet streets of Miami, stopping off at a drug store. At the lunch counter Robertson devoured a crisp salad and enjoyed a glass of fresh milk, the commonplace things of life seeming like riches after months of shortages in war zones. Soon Robertson was aboard a train for Atlanta, where he visited his old friend Wright Bryan. His sister Mary and her husband had come over from their home in Dalton, Georgia. The Bryans quickly laid out a platter of crackers and milk, which to Robertson they joked was "cheese and wine." And there, Robertson saw the published *Red Hills and Cotton* for the first time. Robertson picked up a pen and inscribed Bryan's copy, "Nine days out of India and on Peachtree Street."[18]

The next day, Edwin Camp, who broadcast over radio station WSB as "The Old Timer," was in his office. Camp had just read *Red Hills and Cotton* and was singing its praises to everyone he could. The phone rang. It was Wright Bryan, asking if the broadcaster wanted to meet the author of the book he so enjoyed. Camp, who knew of Robertson's many stations around the world, expected "a worldly, sophisticated globe-trotter, a dashing beau-sabreur of a war correspondent." Instead, Camp was surprised to meet

> a slender, grave yet smiling young man, whose voice was so low and so gentle and whose demeanor was so self-effacing, one got the idea that he was the shiest and most timid of mortals. Yet if you looked closely, you could see eyes that photographed all within their range; you could see a mental alertness that missed not an element in the scene, not a syllable of what was said, not an implication from a word or deed.
>
> His modulated voice, his slow speech, his deferential yet alert attitude and his utter lack of pose were parts of what we call manners. And in this young South Carolinian they were manners that made it possible for him to talk on terms of equality with the rudest longshoreman of the harbor of Sydney or the haughtiest functionary of No. 10 Downing Street.
>
> I didn't wonder that he was a great reporter. He could go anywhere and see anybody, and find the truth wherever he sought it, because he was keen and energetic, mentally and physically, and in his person he was still the well-bred South Carolinian of the Keowee Valley.[19]

From Atlanta, Robertson went to Washington for a series of meetings. One of the most important was a dinner with David Bruce. Joining them at the dinner was Robertson's former colleague John Whitaker, who had joined the Office of Strategic Services as a civilian intelligence officer and accepted an Army commission to run the OSS Psychological Warfare Branch.[20]

The timing of the meeting couldn't have been more apt, for Robertson was at a professional crossroads. While *PM* had provided him plenty of opportunities and had given him the chance to be an advocate, its editorial evolution and recurring financial crises had made him uncertain. Through 1942, Robertson had increasingly split his reporting duties between *PM* and the Chicago *Sun,* both owned by Marshall Field. And Robertson's sense of duty to his nation in wartime was also at work. He had considered joining the Army after Pearl Harbor. Now, here was a chance to serve his country, to carry on the family tradition. The appeals from his friends Bruce and Whitaker were strong. "I have to decide what to do," he wrote in his journal. "The army? The papers? Which—feel ought join the army but trained at propaganda."[21]

In New York, Blanche Knopf and Bernard Smith met with Robertson, offering to let him write another book. While in the city, Robertson called on Helen Rogers Reid, owner of the *Herald Tribune,* who quickly and gladly arranged to see him. She offered him not only a return to the *Herald Tribune* but a promotion to chief of its London bureau. That persuaded him. "Decided not to write book, not to leave papers—to go back to London," he wrote in his journal. Robertson then paid a courtesy call to Marshall Field.[22]

Between speaking engagements, Robertson describes the route of his flight home from India. Special Collections & Archives, Clemson University Libraries, Clemson, South Carolina.

After a quick visit to Texas to see the pilots he'd befriended on the trip back to the United States, Robertson finally returned to Clemson. There was so much to do, and so little time before he had to return to London. In a speech at Clemson on January 11, he told the crowd gathered in Memorial Chapel of the things he'd seen and what was needed to win the war, and while there the former yearbook editor visited the current staff of *Taps* and reviewed progress on the 1943 edition.[23]

The previous day, while Robertson was speaking in Anderson, his father had taken a fall. Growing frail in his advancing age, Ben Sr. had fractured his hip. At the theater, his son was told of the accident.[24] With Ben Jr. due to leave soon, no family members would be in Pickens County to see after Ben Sr. The only option was for Mary and her husband to care for him at their home in Georgia. Suddenly, the family was together one more time to help close out the house. For a moment, Ben Jr. looked out across the hills. They were "never clearer, the sky more clear." In that moment, Ben felt a sadness, and a premonition: "the feeling I so often have about the chance of return." But the relentless schedule continued: speeches around the upcountry, an upcoming trip to Vancouver, the letters and packages he had promised to send families of servicemen he had encountered, all up against an impending return to action.[25] There had been just enough time for a family reunion. Robertson spoke of his experiences in Russia, of the hard conditions, of losing twenty pounds to a meager diet of rationed black bread and cabbage. "I believe our next war will be with Russia," he told his relatives. "I do not believe it will be more than ten years away."[26]

Robertson also wrote one more series for *PM,* articles that prompted one of the most difficult decisions of his career. Robertson wanted to write candidly about what he had encountered in India. But he had not only the war correspondent's concern about printing material that might be helpful to an adversary, but the fear that writing too frankly could cost him his war correspondent's credentials. Robertson told his editor, John P. Lewis, that he was holding his notes against the end of the war, when he felt he could write the full story. As Lewis later wrote, "He thought for a time that political restrictions of war might prevent publication of the first of his India stories—his plea for freedom for the Indians—even though it gave no wisp of information or aid to the enemy. We talked it over, and Ben made his decision; that if publication were ordered withheld by officials, he was willing to have it printed anyway. The decision had to be his, for if the story had been printed in defiance of orders, he would have lost his credentials as a war correspondent. More than anything else, Ben wanted and needed those credentials, for he felt that he had a job to do. 'But I have to write what I feel about India,' he said. The thing that he feared didn't happen; the story was not ordered suspended."[27] Robertson did, however, distill his observations on India into a letter to President Franklin Roosevelt in mid-December.[28]

Soon it was time for Robertson to leave Clemson again, for duties awaited in Washington and New York before his return to London. His sister Mary was unhappy to see Ben leave. She not only worried for his safety, but also felt upset he would not be there to help with their father's care.

Just before they were to leave for the train station, Ben asked Mary to come outside. Together, they walked through the woods behind their father's house, the land they had known forever. It only made the looming farewell that much more painful. Mary protested Ben's departure for London, felt she was being left alone with a heavy burden. But her entreaties did not move her brother.

"I must go. You must understand that," Ben said. "A man's duty to his country comes before every personal consideration. Do you understand that?" Silent and mournful, she nodded her head.

They were soon off to the train station, Mary at the wheel. At the station, she gave her brother one last embrace before he boarded the train and headed back to war. She stayed behind until the train pulled away, then drove back to her father's house. As she got out of the car, a gleam of silver caught her eye. She looked down. In the floorboard was a bracelet. One side read, "Ben Robertson, Clemson College, S.C., U.S.A." The reverse read, "War Correspondent. Member of the Armed Forces of the United States of America." As she read the bracelet's inscription, Mary felt an ominous chill.[29]

CHAPTER 17

Trip 9035

Ben Robertson watched the last weeks of January disappear into a blur. He was back to New York, then back to Washington, then off to Vancouver to give another speech, and then back to Washington to deal with the bureaucratic necessities of travel, visas and inoculations. The women who took Robertson's fingerprints told him of a man whose fingerprints they had taken. When they learned he was killed in a crash in Guiana, "they sat down and cried."[1]

As Robertson's time vanished in endless meetings with officials, ambassadors, colleagues, and old friends, he felt a sense of disappointment. Life was disappearing before his eyes. Walking through the snowy streets of Washington, watching the flags fly in a cold westerly breeze, Robertson mused that over the last year, he had seen much, "but not satisfied with it—have not made as much of it as should—been solemn—am older." After a visit with Burnet Maybank, Robertson's sadness overflowed. He wrote of a feeling "of limited time, of not being able to see many old friends because of time limit—feel have friends in time & place and have let them exist alone in that time and space—sadness of feeling—feeling of all those left behind—on deserts, over the oceans, the men far away."[2]

In early February, Robertson was back in New York to await a flight to Europe. The *Herald Tribune* had arranged with the War Department for passage on a Pan Am Clipper for Robertson. Clipper flights required special dispensation from the government and were restricted to passengers on high-priority business. As Robertson waited, he made notes about how to cover the war, what to see, and what to avoid. He read the manuscript of *Retreat with Stilwell* by Jack Belden, a correspondent Robertson knew from New Delhi. Robertson, who admired and had interviewed General Stilwell, liked the manuscript and urged *Herald Tribune* literary critic Lewis Gannett to recommend its publication.

Robertson also wrote letters back home. "If I don't come back I will be sorry," he wrote Mary, "but I won't really regret it as one's personal life is not important while the United States is fighting. What is important is that all of us do what we can to win." He wrote a similar letter to John Lane, which years later Lane's widow described as "a short, touching letter" that "almost outlined a premonition of death."[3]

Not knowing when his flight out would be, he passed the days by visiting friends and associates. It helped him keep his mind off a dread that, despite his efforts, crept into his mind and into his notes. One afternoon Robertson went to Carnegie Hall to see the New York Philharmonic. As the orchestra performed a piece by Beethoven, Robertson reflected on the recent, stormy flight to Vancouver, writing that the music reminded him of "how feels after coming down from storms—the darkness & snow falling & ice on wings—the pureness of snowscape —blueness and white—green mountains—the oil pressure, turning back, going on—the lurching, anxiety—then ground—one of great feelings."[4]

The unease of flying mingled with the uncertainty over when he would depart. On February 11, Robertson wrote that he was still waiting. "War Dept. says 1st on priority list," he wrote. But the actual date of departure was classified, and Robertson wouldn't know until about a day or two beforehand.[5] The word finally came February 18, and Robertson called home to tell his family that he was departing three days later. He also wrote to Jeanne Gadsden, his beloved friend in Summerville, expressing his hopes that the war would be won. "Perhaps a lot of our people aren't doing what they should," he wrote. "Those of us who do care, then, must win it, and don't worry there are enough who do care enough—on the battlefields and at home, too."[6]

On the unseasonably warm morning of February 21, Ben Robertson arrived at the Marine Air Terminal at New York Municipal Airport. He walked inside the sleek and modern terminal building and waited for the boarding call. Other passengers joined him in the building's passenger rotunda, waiting on one of several benches beneath a brightly colored mural. There were thirty-three passengers on Trip 9035, all with some sort of special priority allowing them one of the Clipper's scarce seats. Among them were several members of a United Service Organization troupe, headed to entertain servicemen in Europe; the group included singers, dancers, and a puppeteer. An American diplomat was returning to his delegation in Lisbon. An architect from Chicago was going to Europe on business. Frank Cuhel was a former track star who had competed at the 1928 Olympics, and who was now a correspondent for the Mutual Broadcasting System. Like Robertson, he was headed back to Europe to cover the war. And in the USO group, Robertson saw a familiar face: Jane Froman had become famous as a singer in nightclubs and on radio programs in the 1930s, and had appeared in several motion pictures. And before she was a star, Ben Robertson had known her as a classmate when she briefly attended the University of Missouri's journalism school.[7]

Inside the terminal, a bell rang three times. The passengers gathered their belongings and headed out the door, walking along a long, narrow pier. At its end, a large airplane floated, bobbing gently on Bowery Bay, lines keeping the craft fast to the dock. The huge aircraft was of a type Ben Robertson knew well. At least three times before he had flown on one of Pan American's Boeing 314 flying boats, called "Clippers" after the swift ships of sailing days. In peacetime Pan Am had ordered twelve of the big, four-engine Boeings, whose long range and increased capacity made routes across the Atlantic and Pacific oceans easier and faster for passengers. They offered luxurious accommodations and a galley crewed by skilled chefs. Specially-designed seats folded out so passengers could sleep during the lengthy flights. Just as the supersonic Concorde would signal elite air travel to a future generation, the Boeing 314 symbolized airborne luxury to the travelers of 1938. "Fifty years from now," wrote Claire Booth Luce after a trip aboard a 314, "people will look back upon a Clipper flight of today as the most romantic voyage of history."[8]

But the luxury did not last long. Within three years of the 314s' entry into service, the United States was involved in World War II. Pan Am volunteered its assets for the war effort, and its Clippers were put to work shuttling high-priority personnel and cargo across the oceans. The bright silver aircraft were painted in muted camouflage to provide protection against enemy attack. Although they were officially under control of the American military, the aircraft were still operated by Pan Am pilots and crew.

The aircraft these passengers walked toward this morning had been the third Boeing 314 to enter service for Pan Am. Eleanor Roosevelt had christened the ship *Yankee Clipper* in March 1939. Since then, the *Yankee Clipper* had flown more than a million miles and crossed the Atlantic 231 times. In command of this trip was Captain R. O. D. Sullivan, one of the airline's most experienced pilots. A former Navy test pilot and a fourteen-year Pan Am veteran with more than fourteen thousand hours of flying time, Sullivan had logged more than 3,200 hours in the Boeing 314 and had flown the Atlantic a hundred times. Assisting him was a crew of twelve, including a copilot, navigator, and flight engineer.[9]

Aboard the *Yankee Clipper,* stewards guided the passengers to their seats in one of seven passenger compartments. Robertson stowed his bags, settled into his seat alongside his compartment mates, and waited for the plane to take off.

One by one, the plane's four engines coughed to life, and the fuselage thrummed with power. Lines were cast off. Captain Sullivan taxied the *Yankee Clipper* out of Bowery Bay, past Rikers Island, and into the East River. The plane's four engines roared to takeoff power. As the Clipper gained speed and its giant wings built lift, the boatlike bottom of its fuselage skimmed the water's surface, sending great clouds of spray from beneath. The misty clouds reminded Robertson of the huge clouds of dust that had billowed from the buses along the dusty roads to Baghdad the year before. As the *Yankee Clipper* roared into the skies over Long Island Sound, below sat Hart Island, from which Thomas Lafayette Robertson had begun his years-long walk back to South Carolina following the end of the Civil War.

The large Boeing 314 was more capable than the flying boats it had replaced. But even with its longer range, it could not make the Atlantic crossing in one jump. Fuel capacity and engine endurance required stops along the route. The first was in Bermuda later on the first day. After refueling and maintenance, the *Yankee Clipper* flew through the night to the Azores, touching down off Horta mid-morning. An hour later, the Clipper left Horta, climbing out for the seven-hour leg to Lisbon.

As the *Yankee Clipper* droned along at seven thousand feet above the Atlantic, as Captain Sullivan and his crew guided the big plane toward Lisbon, lively scenes unfolded in the passenger compartments. With a group of singers, dancers, and musicians aboard—and with creative and quick-witted people brought together in close quarters—entertainment was never far away. Several of them gathered in the midships lounge as Tamara Swann strummed her guitar; she sang along with Ellen Jane Ross and Yvette Silver. Soon others joined in the singing, including Ben Robertson, whose love of music continued to earn him friends. In between songs, the group in the lounge shared stories and told jokes, laughing the long hours away.

At about the same time the *Yankee Clipper* took off from Horta, *PM*'s distinctive delivery trucks were dropping off bundles of the day's edition at newsstands around Manhattan. That morning, atop *PM*'s front page were the words "Ben Robertson Tells Why We Are Failing in India." In the first installment of his final series for *PM,* Robertson began the story of his greatest reporting frustration, the story that he feared could cost him his war correspondent's credentials. "For four months I was in India," the story read, "and I want to say here and now that neither I nor many of the other Americans out there like what is going on. It is a sad and bitter experience to be in India when we are fighting to save the Four

Freedoms. India today makes you almost physically ill. You feel from the day you get there that you are enclosed in a solid circular wall and, day by day, this wall presses closer and closer. Getting out of India was like breaking out of jail."[10]

That afternoon, the *Yankee Clipper* cruised on toward Lisbon. It had been a long flight, but the ride had been smooth. The aircraft had performed without a problem. In fact, the flight was running about fifteen minutes ahead of schedule. At twenty minutes after 6 P.M., Captain Sullivan notified the crew that landing was about fifteen minutes away. Flight stewards went through the cabin and asked the passengers to return to their seats. The singing party in the lounge came to a reluctant end.

Eleven miles from Lisbon, Sullivan looked out the windscreen and saw the mouth of the Tagus River. He backed off the engines' power, gently descending the Boeing to six hundred feet for the last few miles in. The sun had just set in Lisbon, but the sky had not darkened. Still, the local Pan Am ground crew had set out a series of floating lights to mark the landing area off the seaplane base. Over the radio, the current weather conditions were reported to the flight crew. A thunderstorm had just passed south of the city, and intermittent light showers peppered the landing area. Although clouds lined the sky, visibility was very good and the winds were calm. The ground crew in Lisbon heard the roar of engines getting steadily nearer. Soon crewmen in nearby launches saw the familiar shape of the Clipper as it emerged in the gloaming. One more radio transmission brought last word on conditions before landing.

Captain Sullivan had made hundreds of landings in flying boats. He had helped turn the idea of Pan American's flying boat service into reality, commanding survey flights through the Pacific and captaining countless Clipper flights throughout the Pan Am empire. The last moment should have been routine. Sullivan eased the *Yankee Clipper* into a descending left turn as the landing lights came into view a mile ahead. But instead of lining up with the landing lights to land to the north, the aircraft continued to turn and lose altitude.

Inside the cabin, two passengers looked out their port side window just in time to see the left wingtip skim the surface of the river. On the flight deck, the assistant engineering officer heard a snap just after Captain Sullivan closed the throttles. The assistant traffic manager at Lisbon looked out his window just as the plane's lights disappeared from view and an explosion pierced the evening air. Horrified crewmembers in waiting boats watched the big airplane slam the surface of the Tagus at 130 miles an hour.

A Pan Am launch that had been standing by at the end of the water runway headed out to the site two miles away. Out in the river, the battered hulk of the

Yankee Clipper slowly slipped below the surface. Another Pan Am launch, as well as another owned by British Overseas Airways Corporation, hurried to the scene.

Some of the passengers and crew of the *Yankee Clipper* had not only survived, but swam to shore. Astonished onlookers watched a shocked but resolute Yvette Silver pull herself to safety and wade ashore. Out in the harbor, those in peril were picked up by the station boats. Fourth Officer John Burn kept vigil over a badly injured Jane Froman. Her seatmate Tamara Swann was nowhere to be found. Nor were twenty-three others, including Frank Cuhel and Ben Robertson.[11]

In Dalton, Georgia, Ben Robertson Sr. dozed in one of the Longleys' bedrooms. At their home, he could receive the ongoing care he now needed. Not only had he fractured his hip, but now he had contracted pneumonia. Mary had spent a long day looking after his needs, and now that he was resting, she stole a few moments to talk with relatives in the family room. In the background, a radio played.

Soon after six that evening, a newscast mentioned that a flying boat had crashed at Lisbon and that only some of those aboard were safe. Even though wartime restrictions prevented the naming of those aboard the aircraft, a chill went through Mary's body. She picked up the phone and called John Lane at Clemson. Meanwhile, the Longleys moved the radio out of earshot of Ben Sr. and spent the night and the following day awaiting further information.

The next several hours were uneasy. Was Ben actually on that flight? Was he still in New York? Had he been delayed in the Azores? Or, by any chance, was he one of the survivors? On the Clemson campus the next day, members of the college community stayed near radios waiting for additional word. John Lane's phone rang constantly as friends begged for the latest information. Around Greenville and Anderson, the question was the same: "Have you heard anything definite about Ben yet?"[12] Members of the community held out hope, but their hopes fell when Mrs. Ogden Reid of the *Herald Tribune* sent the family a telegram of condolence. "It meant so much to have him come back to the paper," she wired, "and he seemed happy among his old friends. We loved him too for himself and all his fine qualities." Reid eulogized Robertson as "one of the really great war correspondents of all time."[13]

The morning after the accident, salvage crews began retrieving the *Yankee Clipper*'s remains from the Tagus, and investigators puzzled over the flight's final moments. Inside the wreckage, a few more bodies were found. Ben Robertson was not among them. As the days passed, the likelihood of Ben's death began to sink in, and condolences from around the world streamed to the Longleys and to those Ben had worked for. Brendan Bracken, the British Minister of Information, who had befriended Ben during the Blitz, told the *Herald Tribune* that "Ben was one of the most captivating companions I have ever known. I was so sorry when this charming man went back to America. And you can imagine our delight when we heard he was to return to London . . . Now all our hopes of enjoying his friendship have been cruelly shattered."[14]

Harry Ashmore, briefly home from the Army, composed a tribute to his friend and mentor. "Nobody should have been particularly surprised when the newspapers reported that Ben Robertson was aboard the Atlantic clipper that disappeared in flames in Lisbon harbor," Ashmore wrote. "His friends were accustomed to having him turn up unexpectedly in far places, and the thoughtful ones knew that Ben lived on the thin edge of danger with death always standing by. The sentimental ones will say that Ben Robertson died with his boots on, his typewriter shoved under the seat of the plane, his wallet stuffed with a newspaper's expense money, a hot assignment in his pocket. And Ben will like that, for all his life he was, first of all, a sentimental South Carolinian who carried his dreams on the tip of his tongue."[15]

Perhaps the most heartfelt tribute came from CBS correspondent Edward R. Murrow, his fellow Carolinian, with whom he had watched the battles above Dover in the summer of 1940, who stood alongside him in stunned disbelief as they watched London burn one horrible evening. In a February 28 broadcast from London, Murrow eulogized the newspaperman he later remembered as "my best friend":

> Ben Robertson of the New York *Herald Tribune* died in a plane crash near Lisbon. He once wrote of an earlier flight from London to Lisbon, "The speed of that transition made me think of Christ saying to the thief on the cross of Calvary, 'Today thou shalt be with me in Paradise.'" He is out of the war and into peace.
>
> There never was a night so black Ben couldn't see the stars. This was his war from the moment he reached London. He understood it, for he understood the people who were fighting it. That soft, determined South Carolina voice was known to firemen and rescue workers in the slum districts, and to Cabinet Ministers. He was the least hardboiled newspaperman I've ever known. He didn't need to be, for his roots were deep in the red soil of Carolina. And he had a faith that is denied to many of us.
>
> Ben did a lot of traveling, and that means priorities. He told how familiar phrases kept going through his head. He told it like this. He said, "'Here is my

permission, here is my authority'—then I would be told, 'But your category is only B; you must have category A.' 'What must I do then, whom must I go see and where do I see them?' 'Have you priority?' 'I have priority.' 'But for this you must have double priority!'"

If any man I know ever had double priority for the long trip into the unknown, it was Ben Robertson.[16]

In early March, more bodies washed up along the shores of the Tagus. The bodies of Tamara Swann and another victim were recovered on March 6. About a week later, the body of a man was found about thirty miles from the scene of the crash, carried downstream by the swift currents of the Tagus. On one wrist was a heavy silver bracelet with his name engraved on it; the police cut off the bracelet to aid in identification. At a morgue in Lisbon, the body was identified as that of Ben Robertson, "the bearer of passport No. 678064 . . . a journalist, single . . . 69 Horatio St., N.Y. City." Medical authorities established the cause of death as drowning.[17]

On March 13 the Consular Section of the Department of State wired Mary that her brother's body had been identified. Keeping her promise to her brother, Mary took charge of his funeral arrangements. Pan American World Airways arranged to have the bodies of Robertson and nine other victims returned aboard the Portuguese liner *San Miguel,* which arrived in Philadelphia on April 11. The ancestors Ben Robertson venerated had arrived through Pennsylvania two hundred years before. Now, Ben Robertson's journey home brought him through there as well.[18]

From Philadelphia Robertson's body was sent to New York for positive identification, then taken for repose to the Fairchild Chapel in Brooklyn, near where his half-sister Hattie Wegener now lived with her husband. As Robertson's body lay in state in the Brooklyn church, Elmer Davis—the journalist turned head of the Office of War Information—paid tribute to Robertson and thirteen other fallen correspondents on April 14. Davis compared war correspondents to soldiers—the only difference, he noted, was that war correspondents "can't fight back, when as happens so often, their own lives are jeopardized."[19]

On April 16, Ben Robertson came home for the last time. His sister Mary and her husband accompanied him back to Clemson, his body in the same mahogany casket from Portugal, an American flag draped over its top. For one last night Ben was in his father's old home, the house where he had written his books, the home that had always called him back no matter how far he had traveled.

The next afternoon, under gray skies, Robertson's casket was taken to Clemson's Memorial Chapel for services. In the chapel, adjacent to the huge main building on the college campus, young Ben Robertson had played in the balcony as a child, attended services as a cadet, received his diploma as a graduate in 1923, and had addressed students and faculty as a distinguished journalist only weeks before. Flowers were arranged around the American and Clemson flags near the casket, On the back wall, in tribute to Robertson's wartime correspondent work and his affection for the valiant nation it represented, a Union Jack was displayed on the back wall. Hundreds of people from the community, some current Clemson cadets, and several members of Robertson's professional family joined Robertson's relatives at the service.

Dr. D. W. Daniel, Dean Emeritus of the Clemson School of General Science, who had been present at the wedding of Ben's parents, delivered a eulogy. "No other Clemson man was so widely known, so greatly admired; no other so keenly missed," Daniel said, before reading tributes from others and sharing Ben's most famous passage from *I Saw England,* about "losing a life in order to find it." Members of the Clemson glee club, and women of the Clemson community, performed special music, including a rendition of Wagner's "Song to the Evening Star" on piano, cello, and violin.[20]

As rain gently fell from an overcast sky, the funeral procession made its way the few miles from Clemson to the Robertson family plot at a cemetery in Liberty. There, in gently rolling countryside near a country road, Ben Robertson was laid to rest near his mother, his stepmother, his beloved grandfather and grandmother, and so many others who shaped his brief life. As Wright Bryan wrote, Robertson "was committed Sunday to the soil he loved best, the red clay hillsides of South Carolina."[21]

In time, a tall granite headstone was placed over his burial site. Carved into it was a passage from *Travelers' Rest,* four lines originally composed by Robertson years before for a homesick kinsman who had moved to Texas and had since yearned for the South:

> I rest in thy bosom, Carolina.
> Thy skies over me,
> thine earth and air above and around me.
> In my own country, among my own, I sleep.

Like the grandfather he had venerated, Ben Robertson had done his time in war. Now he would rest alongside him in the red hills he loved.

CHAPTER 18

An Upcountry Legacy

Tributes poured in, and those who knew Robertson continued to struggle with his loss. Edward R. Murrow grieved especially hard. His leading biographer noted that of all his friends who were killed in the war, Robertson's loss was the one Murrow could least reconcile himself to. Strom Thurmond, a Clemson classmate who was now serving as an Army officer in Europe, wrote to Robertson's family, "We were devoted friends . . . He was held in high esteem by so many people. Ben was able and profound, yet kind and affable."[1]

From Washington, James F. Byrnes, now a special assistant to President Roosevelt, eulogized Robertson as a war casualty. "He, like so many others in the newspaper and radio service, braved the hazards of war to give us here on the home front the news and deeds of our soldiers on the fighting front. . . . Ben gave his life in service to one of the freedoms, the preservation of which this war is being fought." Even the families of other victims of the *Yankee Clipper* accident wrote expressions of sympathy to the Robertson family.[2]

Robertson's father, already seriously ill, died not long after his son's funeral. But the Robertson heritage would live on. Hattie Wegener, Ben's half-sister, had given birth to a son on March 29. She and her husband named the child in honor of Ben Robertson. "We hope that our son will possess the same qualities as his namesake," she said. "If he does, he'll be tops."[3]

One particularly fitting honor came from the Overseas Press Club. The United States Maritime Commission, which oversaw American merchant shipping, had mounted an effort to build cargo ships that could be produced rapidly and in great numbers, building a merchant ships in a way that could outpace enemy submarines' efforts to sink them. These freighters, called "Liberty Ships," were crucial for transporting war supplies to ports in Europe and the Pacific. These ships were typically named in honor of distinguished Americans. But with so many ships being built so quickly, the Maritime Commission often sought outside help in naming them. And the Overseas Press Club was invited to submit names for Liberty ships that were under construction. One name the Club

Ben's sister Mary Longley prepares to christen the SS *Ben Robertson.* Special Collections & Archives, Clemson University Libraries, Clemson, South Carolina.

selected was that of Ben Robertson—appropriate not only because of Robertson's love of the sea and ships, but also because the ship was built to help win the war. A Liberty Ship to be built at a shipyard in Savannah, Georgia was chosen to bear the name. This would allow Robertson's family and friends to easily attend the christening.

On January 4, 1944, Ben's sister Mary smashed a champagne bottle against the freighter's looming gray hull and christened the ship *Ben Robertson.* His loved ones cheered as the ship slid down the building ways. Within weeks the SS *Ben Robertson* was ready for service. The ship was outfitted with a library, a portrait of its namesake, and a special plaque presented by the New York *Herald Tribune.* The *Ben Robertson* served nobly in the war, carrying supplies to support the Normandy invasion in June 1944, then taking emergency supplies to the Solomon Islands later that year. In a way, Ben Robertson was fighting in the war he had urged America to join. And Ben Robertson, who had loved ships and the sea, who had signed on with the crew of a freighter so he could chronicle the lives of the sailors he considered professional wanderers, was now honored as a part of the merchant marine he loved.[4]

Robertson's friends and relatives at the christening of the SS *Ben Robertson,* January 4, 1944. Leslie Phillips, the English boy Robertson sent to live in South Carolina during the war, stands at center left between two shipyard workers. Behind him is Ben's sister, Mary Longley. Jeanne Gadsden, one of Robertson's closest friends and typist for all his books, is at center right holding a purse. Special Collections & Archives, Clemson University Libraries, Clemson, South Carolina.

At the christening ceremony for the SS *Ben Robertson,* family and friends assembled for a group portrait. Standing at the front of the party was Leslie Phillips, the English boy whose passage to the safety of America had been arranged by Robertson in the early days of the war. Under the devoted care of Ben's beloved friend Jeanne Gadsden, Leslie came to enjoy life in the United States and decided to make his home in his adopted country. In time, he enlisted in the United States Air Force and built a career in service to America.[5]

Old friends still on the war front could not forget Robertson. Ernie Pyle, who would also be killed before the war ended, wrote of a voice he heard during a night maneuver with the 34th Division in Italy, a voice whose easygoing qualities stirred memories of a friend he missed. "The voice was that of PFC Eddie Young of Pontiac, Michigan, the company's runner and message carrier," Pyle wrote. "A person gets to know voices very quickly. Newcomer that I was, there were a dozen men I could name in the blackness. Eddie Young's voice especially haunted me. It was soft, and there was a tolerant and gentle humor in it. It was a perfect duplicate of the voice of my friend Ben Robertson . . . Whenever Eddie spoke, I could not help feeling that Ben was marching behind me."[6]

After the war ended the SS *Ben Robertson,* which had honored its namesake with its participation in both theaters of the war, sailed back to the United States to be taken out of service. As the ship was prepared for layup, its captain, Ernest N. Kettenhofen, praised the ship and the contributions its namesake's friends and family had made. "Although I am a young man," he wrote, "I have been captain of three different vessels, and I will truthfully say that none of them had the personality and prestige equal to the S.S. *Ben Robertson.* I also know for a fact of many a long dark night at sea for the captain and the men was made less long and less dark and less lonely because of the books and literature put on board through the thoughtfulness and love of the friends and family of Mr. Ben Robertson. For this generosity, every man of the crew of the S.S. *Ben Robertson* send their sincere gratitude." With Kettenhofen's help, the book collection and other items related to its namesake were removed from the ship and brought to Clemson, where they formed the basis of a Ben Robertson Memorial Reading Room in the college library.[7]

In October 1948, Secretary of Defense James Forrestal dedicated a memorial at the Pentagon in honor of all the American war correspondents who had died in the line of duty. Ben Robertson was one of the many correspondents honored in the display, which included his friend Ernie Pyle and fellow *Yankee Clipper* passenger Frank Cuhel.[8]

But those who knew Ben Robertson as a friend or as a relative kept his memory alive. Three years after the end of the war, Lady Astor came to Atlanta for a speaking engagement. Her one special request was to travel to Dalton, to meet Ben's sister Mary Longley. On a stop in Atlanta, Lady Astor and Margaret Mitchell met with Wright Bryan at his home. The three talked about the Battle of Britain and about *Gone with the Wind.* But, inevitably, their conversations came back around to their old friend Ben Robertson.[9]

In 1960, as the nation approached the hundredth anniversary of the Civil War, the University of South Carolina Press was about to issue a new edition of *Red Hills and Cotton.* With substantial assistance from Mary Longley, who had become a loving caretaker of her brother's memory, Wright Bryan contributed a warm biographical sketch for the introduction. Bryan, who was by then editor of the Cleveland *Plain Dealer,* focused on the memories of the youth he and Ben spent together in the upcountry, and reflected on Ben's circle of friends, "a fraternity, world-wide yet intimate, non-selective yet always congenial. . . . the fraternity is *The Friends of Ben Robertson.*"[10]

The republication of *Red Hills and Cotton* inspired Mary to finish a task her brother had left undone. Having kept his papers, she located his notes and outline from his 1937 sea voyage and spent four years adapting his notes and unpublished manuscript into a novel titled *The Pilgrim: Voyage 37.* The central character of the book, a young man named John Clayton Clemson, was based substantially on her brother; the voyage of the *Pilgrim* likewise traced the voyage of the *City of Rayville* in 1937. And, as with her brother and the ship he sailed aboard in 1937, both John Clayton Clemson and the *Pilgrim* become victims of the world war that erupts not long after the voyage. Even the book's title was a tribute to Ben Robertson—not only was *The Pilgrim* his working title for the book about life at sea, but with that title his sister paid tribute to Ben's wandering nature and the spirit of adventure he explored in his writing. *The Pilgrim* was published in 1966 and, while it never achieved the reach of *Red Hills and Cotton,* the book was received warmly by those who knew Robertson.[11]

As the years went by, those who knew Ben Robertson and those who worked with him passed away, and the man himself faded into obscurity. Brief flashes of interest occurred at times—an occasional graduate student would write a paper or a thesis on Robertson, and those still alive who knew him would contribute recollections. In 1982, a large trove of Robertson's personal papers were donated to Clemson University, opening new materials to Southern historians. Occasional journal articles analyzed *Red Hills and Cotton,* and in 1990 the University of South Carolina Press issued a new trade-paper version of Robertson's classic with an extensive biographical introduction. A 2000 miniseries on the Public Broadcasting Service about the Battle of Britain, titled *Finest Hour,* featured segments about Robertson's reporting from wartime Britain; passages from *I Saw England* were read by a voice actor who provided a subtle Southern accent. And even Robertson's self-published novel *Travelers' Rest,* which had dwindled into hard-to-find obscurity, was rescued in 2015 when the Clemson University Press reissued it with a modern reappraisal.

Clemson University continues to take great pride in claiming Robertson as one of its own. A group of students and faculty members formed the Ben Robertson Society, a campus group "dedicated to promoting the ideals of Clemson alumnus, Ben Robertson, through service and scholarship." The Society seeks to carry on Robertson's legacy by contributing "to common good without South Carolina and beyond as he fought for human rights locally and throughout the world."[12]

Ben Robertson would find the South of today a puzzling place. The man who championed Jeffersonian values, who felt an attachment to the land and believed in the good of agriculture, who was suspicious of big business and championed the cause of labor, would have mixed feelings about the modern, industrialized South. He would be heartened by the advances brought about by the civil rights movement, advances that have brought equal rights and equal votes for minorities, efforts that have desegregated schools. But in many other areas, Robertson would feel gloom.

Large industries—in many cases, large international companies—have placed factories and facilities in the South, attracted by right-to-work laws, low labor costs, political opposition to organized labor, and massive tax incentives. While such "economic development" incentives have become a pastime for politicians who are interested in luring business, they have meant lawmakers are not keeping the watchful eye on capitalism that Robertson urged. Now even the working-class people of the South, who once distrusted big business, look with distrust toward both organized labor and the government—the government that was, as one historian notes, "the entity Robertson saw as protector against the scourges of the business cycle."[13]

Robertson's vision of "a Northern mind and a Southern heart," of a progressive mindset rooted in Southern values, did not prevail. Instead, it was the vision of his Clemson classmate Strom Thurmond that signaled where the South was heading. While Robertson was reporting from around the United States and around the world, sometimes toying with a run for Congress, Thurmond built a political base in South Carolina, worked his way up the political ladder through the state Senate to the governorship and the United States Senate, and became a strong voice for states' rights and as an opponent of federally ordered desegregation. In so doing, Thurmond twice broke away from the Democratic Party. The first time was in 1948, when he ran for President on the Dixiecrat ticket, as part of a Southern revolt against the addition of a civil rights to the Democratic platform.

But as a United States Senator, Thurmond played a major role in a transformation that would forever change the region's politics. For in 1964, Thurmond became one of the first prominent Southern politicians to switch to the Republican Party, a party that had become more socially conservative as the Democratic Party grew more liberal. In the wake of court-ordered desegregation, in the midst of the civil rights movement, Thurmond channeled backlash and resentment against those advances into enduring political power. In changing parties, Thurmond became a major figure in helping turn the South toward the party of Lincoln—a change that, decades before, would have been unthinkable. Other Southern political figures soon followed suit. Within three decades, the South was solidly Republican, with South Carolina one of the strongest bastions of Republican power in the country.

In the end, it was the conservatism of Strom Thurmond, not the progressive view Robertson championed, that won out. Even Democratic politicians feel that to win in the South, they must espouse conservative views. Robertson's politics—politics that championed independent farms, that envisioned a pragmatic South that retained its traditions yet had gotten over the "lost cause," that accepted progress in civil rights, now seem relics of a different time.

Instead, the end of *Travelers' Rest,* with Stephen John putting the house and farm land up for sale, presaged what would eventually take place. The South turned industrial while farms disappeared. While some family farms remain here and there in the 21st century, they are exceptions to the rule. More often, family farms have been sold off, their once-cherished land developed for industrial or business use, or purchased by real-estate developers and turned into subdivisions that house workers for the South's corporate and industrial economy. The mills, the factories, the big-box stores, and the other figures of industry won out. Now, in practical terms, there is now little to distinguish South Carolina's economy from that of any other state. Even the textile mills whose morning whistles prompted dread in young Robertson's heart have been replaced as major figures in the state's economy. Now the major players in South Carolina's economy are huge corporations with international reach—BMW, Michelin, Fuji, Boeing, and Samsung among them.

Meanwhile, a sizable number of white Southerners still cling to the concept of the "lost cause." The symbols of the Confederacy, the cause for which Robertson's ancestors fought, have gone from historical artifacts to weapons in a cultural war. The Confederate battle flag was co-opted as a symbol of resistance to civil rights in the 1950s and 1960s, and in some Southern states it was prominently flown from state houses. While the Confederate flag is now gone from the South Carolina State House, removed from the dome after a protracted political battle and removed entirely from the grounds after a horrific racially-motivated hate crime in 2015, the banner remains popular with a significant number of white Southerners, many of whom insist it represents "heritage, not hate." But to many minority and progressive communities, the Confederate flag is seen as a painful symbol of white supremacy. In the second decade of the 21st century, the battle has extended beyond the flag, to the status of Confederate monuments on public grounds, all taking place in a splintered and superheated political environment.

In 1939, as he delivered his "Forget Gettysburg" speech in Charleston, Robertson outlined his hope that the South would bind its wounds, put the past behind it, and come together as Americans to face the challenges of the future. Robertson would have wanted a way to both acknowledge the Confederacy and to honor the sacrifice his and other Southern families made, while looking ahead to a South and an America free of racial and cultural division, in which everyone worked together, equal in the eyes of the law, to build a better future. Instead, the South enters a new era with deep cultural rifts, with significant backlash against advances in civil rights, with organized labor virtually wiped out, with one political party dominating the governments of most Southern states, and with the economic system Robertson hoped for nowhere to be seen.

Aside from his book about the South, Ben Robertson is little-remembered. The major newspapers he wrote for in his career—the *Herald Tribune* and *PM*—have long disappeared. Most of Robertson's newspaper work was specific to a moment in time, particularly his war dispatches and *I Saw England.* His one effort at fiction, *Travelers' Rest,* was not a critical or literary success. For many, the legacy of Ben Robertson is a charming little book, his love letter to the South, that even six decades later remains a Southern classic, that remains required reading in literature, social science, and history courses in high schools and universities.

Yet there was more to the story of Ben Robertson than just one beloved book. The story of Ben Robertson was the story of the South, and of a nation, across four decades, a story that took him around the world and made him an advocate for freedom, a journey that took him from the hills of South Carolina to Hawaii, from the tropics of Java to the Depression of New York, from the Washington of the New Deal to the fires of London and the struggles in India. It is the story of one Southerner's political evolution, and the story of a political ambition that might have offered an alternative vision for the South.

Ben Robertson should not be remembered merely for one beloved book. He was more than just an author; he was one of the most influential journalists South Carolina has ever produced, and a thoughtful and persuasive voice at a crucial time in history. Nothing less than the full measure of Ben Robertson should be remembered, and his legacy should never fade into the red hills from which he came.

Notes

Prologue

1. Ann M. Sperber, *Murrow: His Life and Times* (New York: Bantam, 1986), 381.

Chapter 1—American Pilgrims

1. Ben Robertson, *Red Hills and Cotton: An Upcountry Memory* (New York: Knopf, 1942), 3–4.

2. Robertson, *Red Hills and Cotton,* 191.

3. Robertson, *Red Hills and Cotton,* 192.

4. Robertson, *Red Hills and Cotton,* 190–200. A thinly fictionalized version of this story appeared in the first chapter of Robertson's novel *Travelers' Rest* (Clemson, S.C.: Cottonfield Publishers, 1938).

5. Robertson, *Red Hills and Cotton,* 22.

6. Dot Jackson, in "Benjamin Franklin Robertson," Clemson University Alumni website, https://cualumni.clemson.edu/page.aspx?pid=1558 (accessed November 1, 2017); Charles H. Busha, "Ben Robertson of Pickens County: A Brief Biographical Sketch" (paper presented at Pickens County Historical Society, Pickens, S.C., November 19, 1982), 4; Lacy K. Ford Jr., introduction to *Red Hills and Cotton: An Upcountry Memory* by Ben Robertson (Columbia: University of South Carolina Press, 1990), xiii.

7. Busha, "Ben Robertson of Pickens County" (1982), 4; Robertson, *Red Hills and Cotton,* 28; Charles H. Busha, "Ben Robertson of Pickens County," *Old Pendleton District Messenger* 27 no. 13 (December 2013), 6. For more information on Hart Island, see Lonnie Speer, *Portals to Hell: Military Prisons of the Civil War* (Mechanicsburg, Pa.: Stackpole, 1997), 253–54.

8. Ben Robertson, genealogical summary dated September 1, 1938, Narcissa Clayton Papers, South Caroliniana Library, University of South Carolina; Robertson, *Red Hills and Cotton,* 51; 10. Busha, "Ben Robertson of Pickens County" (2013), 6.

9. Busha, "Ben Robertson of Pickens County" (1982) 4; Busha, "Ben Robertson of Pickens County" (2013), 6–7; Ford, introduction, xiv; William S. Walker Jr., "Ben Robertson, War Correspondent," (M.A. thesis, University of South Carolina, 1971), 2; Beatrice Naff Bailey, "Losing a Life to Find It: Ben Robertson Jr.'s Freedom Quest," (M.A. thesis, Clemson University, 2011), 32–33. Bailey's thesis, which made considerable use of the Robertson Papers at Clemson as well as interviews with members of the Robertson family, interprets Ben Robertson's life as the journey of a man who became a leader in a struggle for freedom. It

is an insightful examination of Robertson's life and the author recommends it to this book's readers. Bailey's thesis is available through Clemson's TigerPrints scholarship portal at https://tigerprints.clemson.edu/all_theses/1544/ (accessed July 17, 2018).

10. "William Thomas Bowen," Find A Grave, https://www.findagrave.com/cgi-bin/fg.cgi?page=gr&GRid=10854187 (accessed November 1, 2017); Busha, "Ben Robertson of Pickens County" (2013), 7–8.

11. William J. Cooper Jr. and Thomas E. Terrill, *The American South: A History* (New York: McGraw Hill, 1998) 389–400; Walter Bryan Cisco, *Wade Hampton: Confederate Warrior, Conservative Statesman* (Washington, D.C.: Potomac Books, 2004), 226; Robertson, *Red Hills and Cotton*, 263.

12. "Another Old Soldier Gone," *Pickens Sentinel,* March 23, 1922, 1; Robertson, *Red Hills and Cotton,* 75.

13. "Chronology," Winthrop University, https://www.winthrop.edu/aboutus/secondary.aspx?id=31352 (accessed November 1, 2017); Cooper and Terrill, *The American South,* 502; Busha, "Ben Robertson of Pickens County" (1982), 4; Busha, "Ben Robertson of Pickens County" (2013), 7; Ford, introduction, xiv–xv.

14. "Robertson – Bowen," undated clipping in Narcissa Clayton Papers, South Caroliniana Library, University of South Carolina; Busha, "Ben Robertson of Pickens County" (1982), 3.

Chapter 2—A Childhood in the Red Hills

1. This overview of the history of Clemson University is indebted to Jerome V. Reel, *The High Seminary, Vol. 1: A History of the Clemson Agricultural College of South Carolina, 1889–1964* (Clemson, S.C.: Clemson University Digital Press, 2011, 2013), 3–96. Information about Benjamin Robertson Sr.'s time at Clemson comes from Busha, "Ben Robertson of Pickens County" (1982), 3; and Walker, "Ben Robertson," 2.

2. Wright Bryan, "About Ben Robertson," in *Red Hills and Cotton: An Upcountry Memory* by Ben Robertson (Columbia: University of South Carolina Press, 1960), ii.

3. Bailey, "Losing a Life to Find It," 35.

4. "Happenings of Local and Personal Nature," *Pickens Sentinel-Journal,* July 11, 1906, 3; Busha, "Ben Robertson of Pickens County" (2013), 8; "Local and Personal," *Keowee Courier,* December 28, 1910, 10. Busha's account places Mary's typhoid struggle in 1908, but the *Sentinel-Journal* item, which clearly identifies Mary and her parents, is from 1906.

5. Busha, "Ben Robertson of Pickens County" (2013), 8; "A Marriage and Other Liberty News," *Pickens Sentinel,* July 3, 1913, 1; Bailey, "Losing a Life to Find It," 47.

6. Robertson, *Red Hills and Cotton,* 95. The train, which ran to Easley, got its nickname because in its earliest years it had no place to turn around at the end of the line. It ran in reverse to Easley and forward to Pickens. Locals said when the train backed out, it "looked like a doodle-bug." Passenger service ended in 1928, and the last train ran in 2013. The rails were removed and the old route was converted into the "Doodle Trail," a multi-purpose recreational trail. See "A Condensed Timeline of Pickens County History" on the Pickens County website, http://www.co.pickens.sc.us/History/default.aspx (accessed July 7, 2018).

7. Robertson, *Red Hills and Cotton,* 76.

8. Robertson, *Red Hills and Cotton,* 3.

9. Tony Stanley Cook, "Remembering the South Carolina Upcountry: Ben Robertson's *Red Hills and Cotton,*" *Southern Studies* (Fall 1987): 222.

10. Robertson, *Red Hills and Cotton,* 220, 14.

11. Robertson, *Red Hills and Cotton,* 88.

12. Robertson, *Red Hills and Cotton,* 26; Cooper and Terrill, *The American South,* 432–35.

13. Robertson, *Red Hills and Cotton,* 26–28.

14. Robertson, *Red Hills and Cotton,* 79.

15. Robertson, *Red Hills and Cotton,* 180; Bailey, "Losing a Life to Find It," 41–47.

16. Robertson, *Red Hills and Cotton,* 247, 257.

17. Robertson, *Red Hills and Cotton,* 31–33.

18. Robertson, *Red Hills and Cotton,* 84, 129–30; Cook, "Remembering the South Carolina Upcountry," 220.

19. Robertson, *Red Hills and Cotton,* 3, 220.

20. Robertson, *Red Hills and Cotton,* 7, 9–10.

21. Robertson, *Red Hills and Cotton,* 10–11, 218–19, 6–7.

22. Robertson, *Red Hills and Cotton,* 218.

23. Robertson, *Red Hills and Cotton,* 221–23.

24. Robertson, *Red Hills and Cotton,* 210, 223–27.

25. Robertson, *Red Hills and Cotton,* 219, 59.

26. Busha, "Ben Robertson of Pickens County" (1982), 4; M. D. Klaas, "Lest We Forget: Ben Robertson, Foreign Correspondent" (seminar paper, San Francisco State College, 1966), 9; Bryan, "About Ben Robertson," iii–iv.

27. Robertson, *Red Hills and Cotton,* 232–34.

28. Bryan, "About Ben Robertson," iii; Ben Robertson, "Remember When," *Clemson (S.C.) Commentator* (June 1938); "William Wright Bryan," Find A Grave, https://www.findagrave.com/cgi-bin/fg.cgi?page=gr&GRid=14236139 (accessed November 1, 2017); "William Bryan; First Newsman to Broadcast D-Day Invasion Report," *Los Angeles Times,* February 15, 1991, http://articles.latimes.com/1991–02–15/news/mn-996 1 william-bryan (accessed November 1, 2017).

29. Ben Robertson, "Remember When," *Clemson Commentator* (June 1938); Reel, *The High Seminary, Vol. I,* 185.

30. Robertson, *Red Hills and Cotton,* 5–6.

31. Robertson, *Red Hills and Cotton,* 157. A very thorough treatment of the boll weevil's effect on Southern agriculture, and the ways in which planters responded, is James Conrad Giesen's doctoral dissertation, "The South's Greatest Enemy? The Cotton Boll Weevil and Its Lost Revolution, 1892–1930" (Ph.D. diss., University of Georgia, 2004).

32. Robertson, *Red Hills and Cotton,* 161.

33. Robertson, *Red Hills and Cotton,* 160, 224, 155. Information on the arrival of textile mills in Pickens County comes from G. Anne Sheriff, "Pickens County: A Brief History," reprinted on the website of Pickens County, South Carolina, http://www.co.pickens.sc.us/History/default.aspx (accessed July 7, 2018).

34. Ben Robertson, genealogical summary dated September 1, 1938, Narcissa Clayton Papers, South Caroliniana Library, University of South Carolina; Robertson, *Red Hills and Cotton,* 11, 154, 169, 268–75; Bailey, "Losing a Life to Find It," 38–40.

35. Reel, *The High Seminary, Vol. I,* 210–11; Stanford University Human Virology, "The Influenza Pandemic of 1918," https://virus.stanford.edu/uda/ (accessed November 7, 2017).

36. Busha, "Ben Robertson of Pickens County" (2013): 8; Reel, *The High Seminary, Vol. I,* 210–11; "Death of Mrs. B.F. Robertson," *Pickens Sentinel,* October 24, 1918, 1.

Chapter 3—An Education

1. Busha, "Ben Robertson of Pickens County" (1982), 5.

2. Walker, "Ben Robertson, War Correspondent," 2.

3. *Clemson College Catalogue, 1918–19* (Clemson College, 1918), 24.

4. Reel, *The High Seminary, Vol. I,* 100–103. Though this account is based on what Clemson's early cadets faced, the routine had not changed appreciably by the time Robertson enrolled.

5. *Clemson College Catalogue, 1918–19,* 26–27, 38–40.

6. "Many Cadets on Honor Roll," *Tiger,* January 22, 1920, 1; "Many Students on Honor Roll for Second Term," *Tiger,* April 12, 1922, 3; Bryan, "About Ben Robertson," xi.

7. Reel, *The High Seminary, Vol. I,* 127, 155; "For Particulars, See Below," *Clemson College Chronicle* (October 1919): 23–24.

8. Ben Robertson, "The Part South Carolina Played in the Confederacy," *Clemson College Chronicle* (May 1921): 20–21. Whether intentionally or not, Robertson's view in this passage echoed Atlanta newspaper editor Henry Grady's insistence in his famous 1886 "New South" speech that "the South has nothing for which to apologize." See Cooper and Terrill, *The American South,* 430.

9. Ben Robertson, "Clemson in 1776," *Clemson College Chronicle* (October 1921): 1–2.

10. Ben Robertson, "The Old Stone Church," *Clemson College Chronicle* (February 1922): 9–10.

11. Ben Robertson, "The Calhoun Mansion," *Clemson College Chronicle* (November 1922): 5–6.

12. Ben Robertson, "General Andrew Pickens," *Clemson College Chronicle* (November 1921): 5; Ben Robertson, "Christmas Legends," *Clemson College Chronicle* (December 1921): 6; "The Palmetto," *Tiger,* September 28, 1921, 3; "Chronicle '22 Staff Elected," *Tiger,* May 18, 1921, 1.

13. "Clemson News Boy's [*sic*] Attend Press Asso. In Greenville," *Tiger,* December 7, 1921, 1; "Reporters' Club," *Tiger,* October 4, 1922, 2; "Juniors Elect Taps '23 Staff," *Tiger,* February 8, 1922, 1.

14. "Glee Club Gives Entertainment," *Tiger,* March 30, 1921, 1; "Campus News," *Tiger,* November 16, 1921, 2; Klaas, "Lest We Forget," 10–11; Busha, "Ben Robertson of Pickens County" (1982), 3–4.

15. "Dancing Clubs Have Organized," *Tiger,* September 27, 1922, 1; Bryan, "About Ben Robertson," v; Clemson College, *Taps* (Clemson College: 1923), 74.

16. Mary B. Longley, letter to M. D. Klaas, April 14, 1966. Folder 22, Box 2, Ben Robertson Papers, Special Collections and Archives, Clemson University Libraries, Clemson, South Carolina.

17. Robertson, *Red Hills and Cotton,* 16.

18. Robertson, *Red Hills and Cotton,* 143.

19. Robertson, *Red Hills and Cotton,* 16.

20. Klaas, "Lest We Forget," 10; Bryan, "About Ben Robertson," vi.

21. Ronald T. Farrar, *A Creed for My Profession: Walter Williams, Journalist to the World* (Columbia: University of Missouri, 1998), 132–138, 182.

22. Farrar, *A Creed for My Profession,* 52–53.

23. Farrar, *A Creed for My Profession,* 147–54.

24. Walker, "Ben Robertson, War Correspondent," 3; "William Bryan; First Newsman to Broadcast D-Day Invasion Report," *Los Angeles Times,* February 15, 1991, http://articles.latimes.com/1991–02–15/news/mn-996_1_william-bryan (accessed November 1, 2017).

25. Farrar, *A Creed for My Profession,* 141, 159, 202–203.

26. Farrar, *A Creed for My Profession,* 159. Robertson's Missouri notebooks are in Folders 23 and 24, Box 2, Ben Robertson Papers, Special Collections and Archives, Clemson University Libraries, Clemson, South Carolina.

27. Capt. Thomas E. May, letter to Ben Robertson, September 13, 1923. Folder 13, Box 1, Ben Robertson Papers, Special Collections and Archives, Clemson University Libraries, Clemson, South Carolina; Klaas, "Lest We Forget," 12.

28. Report card, Folder 13, Box 1, Ben Robertson Papers, Special Collections and Archives, Clemson University Libraries, Clemson, South Carolina; "Mountain View," Salem (Oregon) *Daily Capital Journal,* February 16, 1924, 12.

29. Walker, "Ben Robertson, War Correspondent," 3; Ford, introduction, xvii; Ben Robertson, "Southern is Easy for Bantam Crew," *Charleston News and Courier,* undated clipping, Folder 5, Box 1, Ben Robertson Papers, Special Collections and Archives, Clemson University Libraries, Clemson, South Carolina.

30. "Colleton Lads Unable to Withstand Experience and Drive of Local Players," *Charleston News and Courier,* undated clipping; "Telephone Girls Have Busy Times," *Charleston News and Courier,* undated clipping; "Lady Misunderstands, Thinks Scout Who Came To Her Assistance Was Fresh," *Charleston News and Courier,* undated clipping; "Strange Entries on Hotel Books," *Charleston News and Courier,* undated clipping, Folder 5, Box 1, Ben Robertson Papers, Special Collections and Archives, Clemson University Libraries, Clemson, South Carolina.

31. Ledger in Folder 5, Box 1, Ben Robertson Papers, Special Collections and Archives, Clemson University Libraries, Clemson, South Carolina. Some stories do not have bylines but their style is unmistakably Robertson's.

32. Farrar, *A Creed for My Profession,* 167.

Chapter 4—In Exile

1. Farrar, *A Creed for My Profession,* 166.

2. Walker, "Ben Robertson, War Correspondent," 3.

3. "All Southerners Become Gentlemen," *Atlanta Journal,* June 11, 1939. Folder 65, Box 6, Ben Robertson Papers, Special Collections and Archives, Clemson University Libraries, Clemson, South Carolina.

4. Klaas, "Lest We Forget," 13; Ben Robertson, "Cowboys, Outlaws in Gleeful Tale," *Honolulu Star-Bulletin,* May 21, 1927, 54; Ben Robertson, "Kilauea Apparently Entering Stage of Upward Activity, Wilson Asserts," *Honolulu Star-Bulletin,* July 11, 1927, 13–14.

5. Ben Robertson, "The Hawaiian Melting Pot." *Current History* (June 1932): 312–15.

6. Bailey, "Losing a Life to Find It," 57; "Greet Noted Journalist," *Honolulu Star-Bulletin,* July 30, 1927, 30; J. E. Davidson, letter to Walter Williams, October 19, 1927. Folder 26, Box 2, Ben Robertson Papers, Special Collections and Archives, Clemson University Libraries, Clemson, South Carolina; Klaas, "Lest We Forget," 14; "Aloha Dinner Given Two Going to Antipodes," *Honolulu Star-Bulletin,* January 21, 1928, 32; "Little Interviews," *Honolulu Star-Bulletin,* January 19, 1928, 2.

7. Ben Robertson, postcard to Ben Robertson Sr., February 1928, Folder 27, Box 3, Ben Robertson Papers, Special Collections and Archives, Clemson University Libraries, Clemson, South Carolina.

8. Ben Robertson, "Australia's Sons of Perdition," *Travel* (July 1929): 35; Ben Robertson with McCoy Hill, "At the Heart of Desolation," *Travel* (February 1929): 38.

9. Ben Robertson, "No Sunday-School Town," *Asia* (August 1929): 612–17.

10. Klaas, "Lest We Forget," 14; Ben Robertson, "That Yellow House in Surabaya," *Asia* (May 1933): 314–16.

11. Robertson, "That Yellow House in Surabaya," 314–16.

12. Robertson, *Travelers' Rest,* vii; Ben Robertson, "Heavy Traffic in Surabaya," *Travel* (July 1929): 35–37, 58. The Red Bridge later became famous as the site near which British brigade commander Brigadier A. W. S. Mallaby was killed in October 1945 during the Battle of Surabaya, part of the Indonesian National Revolution.

13. Robertson, *Travelers' Rest,* vii.

14. Robertson, "That Yellow House in Surabaya," 316; Ben Robertson, letter to Wright Bryan, January 29, 1929, Folder 14, Box 1, Ben Robertson Papers, Special Collections and Archives, Clemson University Libraries, Clemson, South Carolina; Ben Robertson, "The Mattress-Stuffing Tree," *Asia* (August 1931): 492.

15. Robertson, "That Yellow House in Surabaya," 314; Ben Robertson, letter to R. N. Brackett, January 1929, Folder 28, Box 3, Ben Robertson Papers, Special Collections and Archives, Clemson University Libraries, Clemson, South Carolina; Ben Robertson, letter to Wright Bryan, January 29, 1929, Folder 28, Box 3, Ben Robertson Papers, Special Collections and Archives, Clemson University Libraries, Clemson, South Carolina; E. A. Smyth, letter to Ben Robertson, April 4, 1929, Folder 28, Box 3, Ben Robertson Papers, Special Collections and Archives, Clemson University Libraries, Clemson, South Carolina.

16. Robertson, *Travelers' Rest,* vii.

17. Robertson, *Travelers' Rest,* viii.

18. Klaas, "Lest We Forget," 15; Walker, "Ben Robertson," 12.

Chapter 5—The Hope of the *Herald Tribune*

1. Richard Kluger, *The Paper: The Life and Death of the New York Herald Tribune* (New York: Knopf, 1986), 242–43.

2. Kluger, *The Paper,* 242–43.

3. Ben Robertson, letter to Ben Robertson Sr., January 24, 1930, Folder 14, Box 1, Ben Robertson Papers, Special Collections and Archives, Clemson University Libraries, Clemson, South Carolina.

4. Walker, "Ben Robertson, War Correspondent," 5; Ben Robertson, "Cats Create Trouble for Stage Folks," *Oakland Tribune,* June 8, 1930, 79; Ben Robertson, personal journal, 1930,

Folder 30, Box 3, Ben Robertson Papers, Special Collections and Archives, Clemson University Libraries, Clemson, South Carolina. Syndication agreements often meant Robertson's *Herald Tribune* articles appeared in papers far and wide.

5. Quoted in Walker, "Ben Robertson, War Correspondent," 63–64.

6. "Pearl Harbor is Dr. Jekyl and Mr. Hyde To New York Writer," *Honolulu Star-Bulletin,* October 31, 1931, 39; Klaas, "Lest We Forget," 16.

7. Ben Robertson, "Pele's Return to Halemaumau," *New York Herald Tribune,* January 3, 1932; Ben Robertson, "Edi-San, a Cook," *Honolulu Advertiser,* January 14, 1930, 14; Ben Robertson, "Hawaii to Be a State?" *Decatur Evening Herald,* June 4, 1931, 6; "Uncle Sam's Boys in East Indies," *Fairmount News,* December 10, 1931, 7.

8. Edgar Snow, letter to Ben Robertson, April 15, 1930; Mrs. W. B. Meloney, letter to Ben Robertson, January 23, 1930, Folder 14, Box 1, Ben Robertson Papers, Special Collections and Archives, Clemson University Libraries, Clemson, South Carolina; Ben Robertson, "Australia's Labor Prime Minister," *New York Herald Tribune Sunday Magazine,* October 12, 1930, 15; Ben Robertson, "A Hero of the Frozen South," *New York Herald Tribune Sunday Magazine,* February 9, 1930, 3; Ben Robertson, "He Never Went to College," *New York Herald Tribune Sunday Magazine,* November 23, 1930, 10.

9. Ben Robertson, personal journal, entry of August 3, 1930, Folder 30, Box 3, Ben Robertson Papers, Special Collections and Archives, Clemson University Libraries, Clemson, South Carolina.

10. "Robert Neville, Writer, is Dead; A Former Time Correspondent," *New York Times,* Feb. 18, 1970, 42; "Says New York Should Ape Us in Dry Puzzle," *Greenville News* January 4, 1931, 13. Tom Waring went on to a lengthy career at the *News and Courier* and as its editor he was an outspoken defender of segregation in the South.

11. Ford, introduction, xviii; Kluger, *The Paper,* 264–67; "A Quick One at Bleeck's," Grade "A" Fancy, http://www.grade-a-fancy-magazine.com/2014/09/a-quick-one-at-bleecks.html (accessed November 1, 2017).

12. Edgar Snow, letter to Ben Robertson, April 15, 1930; T. E. May, letter to Ben Robertson, June 26, 1930, Folder 14, Box 1, Ben Robertson Papers, Special Collections and Archives, Clemson University Libraries, Clemson, South Carolina; Ben Robertson, letter to Alan Villiers, January 14, 1937, Folder 15, Box 2, Ben Robertson Papers, Special Collections and Archives, Clemson University Libraries, Clemson, South Carolina.

13. Mary B. R. Longley, *The Pilgrim: Voyage 37* (New York: Vantage, 1965), 18–19.

14. Ben Robertson, personal journal entry, March 23, 1935, Folder 15, Box 2, Ben Robertson Papers, Special Collections and Archives, Clemson University Libraries, Clemson, South Carolina; Thomas A. Sheridan, letter to Ben Robertson, June 3, 1933, Robertson Papers, CU; "College Crew to Try Atlantic in Sailing Ship," undated New York *Herald Tribune* clipping, Folder 6, Box 1, Ben Robertson Papers, Special Collections and Archives, Clemson University Libraries, Clemson, South Carolina.

15. William Manchester, *The Glory and the Dream: A Narrative History of America, 1932–1972* (New York: Bantam, 1973), 3–17.

16. Ben Robertson, entry in personal journal, August 3, 1930, Folder 30, Box 3, Ben Robertson Papers, Special Collections and Archives, Clemson University Libraries, Clemson, South Carolina.

17. Ben Robertson, entry in personal journal, undated (August 1930), Folder 30, Box 3, Ben Robertson Papers, Special Collections and Archives, Clemson University Libraries, Clemson, South Carolina.

18. Ben Robertson, "Our Sailors Sleep in the Palace of the Czar," *Scribner's Magazine* (May 1932): 298–99.

19. This account is summarized from a thorough analysis of the "Aunt Molly" story, and the Dreiser group's involvement, in Bailey, "Losing a Life to Find It," 77–82.

20. Vladimir P. DeLevitt, letter to Ben Robertson, October 8, 1933, Folder 14, Box 1, Ben Robertson Papers, Special Collections and Archives, Clemson University Libraries, Clemson, South Carolina.

21. Robertson, *Red Hills and Cotton,* 28–29.

22. Marietta Huff, letter to Ben Robertson, November 16, 1932, Folder 14, Box 1, Ben Robertson Papers, Special Collections and Archives, Clemson University Libraries, Clemson, South Carolina; Ben Robertson, "King of the Bush Country," *New York Herald Tribune Sunday Magazine,* July 3, 1932, 6; George Shively, letter to Ben Robertson, November 10, 1932, Folder 14, Box 1, Ben Robertson Papers, Special Collections and Archives, Clemson University Libraries, Clemson, South Carolina.

23. George Shively, letter to Ben Robertson, February 13, 1933, Folder 14, Box 1, Ben Robertson Papers, Special Collections and Archives, Clemson University Libraries, Clemson, South Carolina; Sydney A. Sanders, letter to Ben Robertson, November 6, 1933, Folder 14, Box 1, Ben Robertson Papers, Special Collections and Archives, Clemson University Libraries, Clemson, South Carolina; Sydney A. Sanders, letter to Ben Robertson, November 24, 1933, Folder 14, Box 1, Ben Robertson Papers, Special Collections and Archives, Clemson University Libraries, Clemson, South Carolina; Sydney A. Sanders, letter to Ben Robertson, January 3, 1934, Folder 14, Box 1, Ben Robertson Papers, Special Collections and Archives, Clemson University Libraries, Clemson, South Carolina.

24. For more information on the struggles facing the *Herald Tribune* in these years, see Kluger, *The Paper,* 269–305.

25. "Lester Walton Quits N.Y. Herald-Tribune," *Pittsburgh Courier,* April 25, 1931, 2. It is worth noting that Ben Robertson developed a friendship with Dr. George Washington Carver of the Tuskegee Institute. Its origins are not fully clear, although it may have developed through collaborations Carver had made with Clemson, and professional affiliations he shared with Robertson's father. This may have played a role in why Robertson took on the Tuskegee Institute story for the *Herald Tribune.* In any event, the friendship between Ben Jr. and Carver is evidenced by an especially warm letter of January 1, 1934 in which Carver passes along greetings for the new year and states, "I thank God for you, many, many times each day." The letter is in the Ben Robertson Papers at Clemson University.

26. Kluger, *The Paper,* 306–14; Tom Waring, letter to Jeanne Gadsden, March 1, 1943, Folder 21, Box 2, Ben Robertson Papers, Special Collections and Archives, Clemson University Libraries, Clemson, South Carolina.

27. Ben Robertson, "Free Philippines Feared by T. R. Jr.," *Morning News* (Wilmington, Del.), April 26, 1934, 8.

28. Edgar Snow, letter to Ben Robertson, June 6, 1932, Folder 14, Box 1, Ben Robertson

Papers, Special Collections and Archives, Clemson University Libraries, Clemson, South Carolina.

29. Ben Robertson, "Grand Fleet of U.S. Is Reviewed by Roosevelt," *Richmond Item*, June 1, 1934, 1; Ben Robertson, "Survivors Give Lurid Versions of Fire Horror on Ocean Liner," *Miami Daily News-Record* (Miami, Okla.), September 9, 1934, 1; Ben Robertson, "Airliner is Found Wrecked; Seven Aboard Are Dead," *Gazette and Daily* (York, Pennsylvania), June 12, 1937, 1.

Chapter 6—Hitting at Windmills

1. Ben Robertson, personal journal, February 1, 1935, Folder 33, Box 3, Ben Robertson Papers, Special Collections and Archives, Clemson University Libraries, Clemson, South Carolina.
2. Ben Robertson, personal journal, February 6, 1935, Folder 33, Box 3, Ben Robertson Papers, Special Collections and Archives, Clemson University Libraries, Clemson, South Carolina.
3. Ben Robertson, personal journal, February 8, 1935, Folder 33, Box 3, Ben Robertson Papers, Special Collections and Archives, Clemson University Libraries, Clemson, South Carolina.
4. Ben Robertson, personal journal, February 15, 1935, Folder 33, Box 3, Ben Robertson Papers, Special Collections and Archives, Clemson University Libraries, Clemson, South Carolina.
5. Ben Robertson, personal journal, February 11, 1935, Folder 33, Box 3, Ben Robertson Papers, Special Collections and Archives, Clemson University Libraries, Clemson, South Carolina.
6. Ben Robertson, personal journal, March 9, 1935, Folder 33, Box 3, Ben Robertson Papers, Special Collections and Archives, Clemson University Libraries, Clemson, South Carolina.
7. Ben Robertson, journal entries of March 20, 1935 and April 1, 1935, Folder 33, Box 3, Ben Robertson Papers, Special Collections and Archives, Clemson University Libraries, Clemson, South Carolina.
8. Ben Robertson, personal journal, April 13, 1935, Folder 33, Box 3, Ben Robertson Papers, Special Collections and Archives, Clemson University Libraries, Clemson, South Carolina.
9. Ben Robertson, personal journal, March 16 and 17, 1935, Folder 33, Box 3, Ben Robertson Papers, Special Collections and Archives, Clemson University Libraries, Clemson, South Carolina.
10. Ben Robertson, personal journal, April 3, 1935, Folder 33, Box 3, Ben Robertson Papers, Special Collections and Archives, Clemson University Libraries, Clemson, South Carolina.
11. Ben Robertson, personal journal, April 3, 1935, Folder 33, Box 3, Ben Robertson Papers, Special Collections and Archives, Clemson University Libraries, Clemson, South Carolina.
12. Ben Robertson, personal journal, March 17, 1935, Folder 33, Box 3, Ben Robertson Papers, Special Collections and Archives, Clemson University Libraries, Clemson, South Carolina.
13. Ben Robertson, personal journal, April 15, 1935, Folder 33, Box 3, Ben Robertson Papers, Special Collections and Archives, Clemson University Libraries, Clemson, South Carolina.

14. Busha, "Ben Robertson of Pickens County" (1982), 6; Klaas, "Lest We Forget," 16–17; Ben Robertson, personal journal, May 15–30, 1936, Folder 35, Box 4, Ben Robertson Papers, Clemson University Libraries, Clemson, South Carolina. Hattie went on to join the faculty of the Washington School for Secretaries, working in its New York branch. In May 1940 she married Frederick W. Wagener of Brooklyn. See "Miss Hattie Robertson Wed To F. W. Wagener," *Brooklyn Daily Eagle,* May 5, 1940, 17.

15. Ben Robertson, "Train Tears Bus in Half, 14 High School Students Killed," *Akron Beacon Journal,* April 12, 1935, 1; Ben Robertson, "Navajos See Capital, But Like Zoo Best," *Oakland Tribune,* July 2, 1935, 3.

16. David Kennedy, *Freedom from Fear: The American People in Depression and War, 1929–1945* (New York: Oxford, 1999), 398; Ben Robertson, letter to Edgar Snow, January 3, 1937, Folder 15, Box 2, Ben Robertson Papers, Special Collections and Archives, Clemson University Libraries, Clemson, South Carolina.

17. Ben Robertson, letter to Jean Muir, January 18, 1937, Folder 15, Box 2, Ben Robertson Papers, Special Collections and Archives, Clemson University Libraries, Clemson, South Carolina.

18. William Hillman, "Japan Wrecks Naval Parley," *Pittsburgh Post-Gazette,* January 16, 1936, 1; "King George's Illness Alarms His Physicians as Cold Weakens Heart," *Philadelphia Inquirer,* January 18, 1936, 1; "Britons Kneel in Prayer for King at Palace Gates," *Philadelphia Inquirer,* January 19, 1936, 1; "Ben Robertson Says Nazi Bombs Have Destroyed British Social Barriers, Building a New Belief in Community Life," *PM,* August 17, 1941, 5.

19. Ben Robertson, "Hamlet Lived at Elsinore," *Travel* (March 1937), 15–17.

20. Ben Robertson, letter to Edgar Snow, January 3, 1937, Folder 15, Box 2, Ben Robertson Papers, Special Collections and Archives, Clemson University Libraries, Clemson, South Carolina.

21. Ben Robertson, letter to John Whitaker, January 3, 1937, Folder 15, Box 2, Ben Robertson Papers, Special Collections and Archives, Clemson University Libraries, Clemson, South Carolina; Don Wharton, letter to Ben Robertson, September 29, 1936, Folder 15, Box 2, Ben Robertson Papers, Special Collections and Archives, Clemson University Libraries, Clemson, South Carolina.

22. Ben Robertson, letter to Edgar Snow, January 3, 1937, Folder 15, Box 2, Ben Robertson Papers, Special Collections and Archives, Clemson University Libraries, Clemson, South Carolina.

Chapter 7—A Vague, Confused Plan

1. Bett Anderson, "Book Marks," *Pittsburgh Press,* November 16, 1941, 21; Ben Robertson, personal journal, September 21, 1936, Folder 35, Box 4, Ben Robertson Papers, Special Collections and Archives, Clemson University Libraries, Clemson, South Carolina.

2. Ben Robertson, personal journal, September 24, 1936, Folder 35, Box 4, Ben Robertson Papers, Special Collections and Archives, Clemson University Libraries, Clemson, South Carolina.

3. Ben Robertson, letter to Edgar Snow, January 3, 1937; Ben Robertson, letter to Don Wharton, September 29, 1936, Folder 15, Box 2, Ben Robertson Papers, Special Collections and Archives, Clemson University Libraries, Clemson, South Carolina.

4. Ben Robertson, letter to Edgar Snow, January 3, 1937, Folder 15, Box 2, Ben Robertson Papers, Special Collections and Archives, Clemson University Libraries, Clemson, South Carolina.

5. Some of the family letters and papers Robertson used while writing *Travelers' Rest* were later donated to the South Caroliniana Library of the University of South Carolina, where they are catalogued as the Narcissa Clayton Papers. Robertson wrote a two-page summary of his family's history and acknowledged that the papers in the collection were used while writing *Travelers' Rest.*

6. Harry Ashmore, "Robertson Kept Mind Clear in Midst of Furies of War," *Greenville News,* February 25, 1943, 6.

7. Ben Robertson, letter to Jean Muir, January 18, 1937; Ben Robertson, letter to Bud Fisher, January 16, 1937, Folder 15, Box 2, Ben Robertson Papers, Special Collections and Archives, Clemson University Libraries, Clemson, South Carolina.

8. Ben Robertson, letter to Bud Fisher, January 16, 1937, Folder 15, Box 2, Ben Robertson Papers, Special Collections and Archives, Clemson University Libraries, Clemson, South Carolina.

9. Ben Robertson, letter to Dorothy Spalding, January 31, 1937, Folder 15, Box 2, Ben Robertson Papers, Special Collections and Archives, Clemson University Libraries, Clemson, South Carolina.

10. Ben Robertson, letter to Thomas Wolfe, January 24, 1937; Thomas Wolfe, letter to Ben Robertson, February 5, 1937, Folder 15, Box 2, Ben Robertson Papers, Special Collections and Archives, Clemson University Libraries, Clemson, South Carolina. When Wolfe died the following year, Robertson wrote to Wolfe's mother expressing his own grief at Wolfe's death. "I have never been so moved in my life as I have been by your son's great, superlative prose. I felt by instinct what he was trying to put down. I never questioned, never doubted." Ben Robertson, letter to Julia Wolfe, September 15, 1938, Manuscripts Division, South Caroliniana Library, University of South Carolina.

11. Ben Robertson, undated journal entry, February 1937, Folder 37, Box 4, Ben Robertson Papers, Special Collections and Archives, Clemson University Libraries, Clemson, South Carolina.

12. Ben Robertson, notes from February 1937, Folder 37, Box 4, Ben Robertson Papers, Special Collections and Archives, Clemson University Libraries, Clemson, South Carolina.

13. Ben Robertson, notes from February 1937, Folder 37, Box 4, Ben Robertson Papers, Special Collections and Archives, Clemson University Libraries, Clemson, South Carolina. Robertson's Red Cross card from this period is also preserved in the Robertson Papers.

14. Ben Robertson, journal entries of March 31 and April 5, 1937, Folder 37, Box 4, Ben Robertson Papers, Special Collections and Archives, Clemson University Libraries, Clemson, South Carolina.

15. Ford, introduction, xxi.

16. Giles Stedman of the United States Lines was the first master of the liner SS *America* in 1940, and he took the ship to war as the troopship *West Point.* Harry Manning was not only a master mariner with United States Lines but also an aviator; he was Amelia Earhart's original navigator on her ill-fated 1937 round-the-world flight, but he was replaced by Fred Noonan when Manning had to go back to sea. He was later the first master of the record-breaking liner

SS *United States* in 1952. Frederick Fender of United States Lines retired in May 1964 as the last master of the SS *America.*

17. Ben Robertson, letter to Edgar Snow, January 3, 1937, Folder 15, Box 2, Ben Robertson Papers, Special Collections and Archives, Clemson University Libraries, Clemson, South Carolina; Thomas A. Sheridan, letter to Ben Robertson, June 26, 1935, Folder 14, Box 1, Ben Robertson Papers, Special Collections and Archives, Clemson University Libraries, Clemson, South Carolina.

18. Thomas A. Sheridan, letter to Ben Robertson, January 12, 1937; Ben Robertson, letter to Edgar Snow, January 3, 1937, Folder 15, Box 2, Ben Robertson Papers, Special Collections and Archives, Clemson University Libraries, Clemson, South Carolina.

19. This account is constructed from Mary Longley's book *The Pilgrim: Voyage 37* and from the detailed account at "Sawokla, City of Rayville, City of Dalhart & Yomachichi," http://www.derbysulzers.com/shipsawokla.html (accessed November 1, 2017). Robertson's notebooks from the voyage have disappeared; they were likely among items unintentionally discarded by Mrs. Longley's family after her death. See the February 1986 note from Bessie Mell Lane in Folder 34, Box 1, John Dewey Lane Papers, Special Collections and Archives, Clemson University Libraries, Clemson, South Carolina.

Chapter 8—A Literary Gale

1. Robertson, *Travelers' Rest,* 56; Walker, "Ben Robertson, War Correspondent," 17.

2. Robertson, *Travelers' Rest;* Walker, "Ben Robertson, War Correspondent," 17.

3. Robertson, *Travelers' Rest,* 101.

4. Robertson, *Travelers' Rest,* 60.

5. Robertson, *Travelers' Rest,* 69–70. In her presentation "Ben Robertson's Red Hills," Dianne Luce noted that *Travelers' Rest* "lacks a dramatic center and the sustained momentum readers seek in a novel," making it "a curiously static work." Dianne Luce, "Ben Robertson's Red Hills" (conference paper, undated), 15–16.

6. Jeanne Gadsden, letter to Tom Waring, February 26, 1943, Folder 4, Box 23, William Wright Bryan Papers, Special Collections and Archives, Clemson University Libraries, Clemson, South Carolina.

7. Ben Robertson, undated personal memorandum, Folder 39, Box 4, Ben Robertson Papers, Special Collections and Archives, Clemson University Libraries, Clemson, South Carolina.

8. Ben Robertson to unknown recipient, January 12, 1938, Folder 15, Box 2, Ben Robertson Papers, Special Collections and Archives, Clemson University Libraries, Clemson, South Carolina.

9. Walker, "Ben Robertson, War Correspondent," 16; Ben Robertson, letter to the R. L. Bryan Company, November 10, 1937, Folder 15, Box 2, Ben Robertson Papers, Special Collections and Archives, Clemson University Libraries, Clemson, South Carolina. There is a South Carolina town named Travelers Rest about forty miles from Clemson, but the town does not figure in the novel, at least by name.

10. "Conquest of Keowee, Story of Carolina, Told by Carolinian," Charleston *News & Courier,* May 15, 1938, Folder 7, Box 1, Ben Robertson Papers, Special Collections and Archives, Clemson University Libraries, Clemson, South Carolina.

11. Ben Robertson, letter to John Whitaker, January 3, 1937, Folder 15, Box 2, Ben Robertson Papers, Special Collections and Archives, Clemson University Libraries, Clemson, South Carolina.

12. Ben Robertson, journal entry of November 30, 1937, Folder 38, Box 4, Ben Robertson Papers, Special Collections and Archives, Clemson University Libraries, Clemson, South Carolina; Walker, "Ben Robertson, War Correspondent," 16. According to Jeanne Gadsden, the manuscript for *The Pilgrim* was rejected by at least one publisher. Jeanne Gadsden, letter to Tom Waring, February 26, 1943, Folder 4, Box 23, William Wright Bryan Papers, Special Collections and Archives, Clemson University Libraries, Clemson, South Carolina.

13. Cooper and Terrill, *The American South,* 659–60.

14. Ben Robertson, letter to Dorothy Spalding, January 31, 1937, Folder 15, Box 2, Ben Robertson Papers, Special Collections and Archives, Clemson University Libraries, Clemson, South Carolina.

15. Ben Robertson, text of speech delivered before Anderson Kiwanis Club, November 1937, Folder 38, Box 4, Ben Robertson Papers, Special Collections and Archives, Clemson University Libraries, Clemson, South Carolina.

16. This theme is also explored in Lacy K. Ford Jr., "The Affable Journalist as Social Critic: Ben Robertson and the Early Twentieth-Century South," *Southern Cultures* 2.3 no. 4 (1996), 353–71.

17. Ben Robertson, letter to B. O. Williams, December 6, 1937, Folder 15, Box 2, Ben Robertson Papers, Special Collections and Archives, Clemson University Libraries, Clemson, South Carolina. Ben Robertson, letter to Turner Catledge, March 1, 1938, Folder 15, Box 2, Ben Robertson Papers, Special Collections and Archives, Clemson University Libraries, Clemson, South Carolina.

18. "Ben Robertson's Book," *Charleston News & Courier,* May 6, 1938. Folder 7, Box 1, Ben Robertson Papers, Special Collections and Archives, Clemson University Libraries, Clemson, South Carolina.

19. Harry Ashmore, "Robertson Kept Mind Clear in Midst of Furies of War," *Greenville News,* February 25, 1943, 6. Lacy Ford outlined a similar belief in his introduction to the 1990 reissue of *Red Hills and Cotton.*

20. "Clemson Man's Book Attacked," *Anderson Daily Independent,* June 14, 1936, Folder 7, Box 1, Ben Robertson Papers, Special Collections and Archives, Clemson University Libraries, Clemson, South Carolina.

21. "Robertson Defending Book; Mrs. Johnston Will Read It." Anderson *Daily Independent,* June 15, 1936, Folder 7, Box 1, Ben Robertson Papers, Special Collections and Archives, Clemson University Libraries, Clemson, South Carolina.

22. "We may be poor but we are very proud." —Mrs. Johnston. Ibid.

23. "Robertson Defending Book; Mrs. Johnston Will Read It." Anderson *Daily Independent,* June 15, 1936, Folder 7, Box 1, Ben Robertson Papers, Special Collections and Archives, Clemson University Libraries, Clemson, South Carolina.

24. Ben Robertson, "Statement from Ben Robertson to Be Used If Desired When Mrs. Johnston's Reply Has Been Received," Folder 15, Box 2, Ben Robertson Papers, Special Collections and Archives, Clemson University Libraries, Clemson, South Carolina. Robertson also had it printed as a column in a small Clemson paper, the Clemson *Commentator,* that summer.

25. "Robertson Defending Book; Mrs. Johnston Will Read It." Anderson *Daily Independent,* June 15, 1938; Alester G. Holmes, "Frontier Life Dramatized by South Carolina Author," *Charlotte Observer,* June 12, 1938, Folder 7, Box 1, Ben Robertson Papers, Special Collections and Archives, Clemson University Libraries, Clemson, South Carolina.

26. Ben Robertson, letter to George Chaplin, June 1938, Folder 15, Box 2, Ben Robertson Papers, Special Collections and Archives, Clemson University Libraries, Clemson, South Carolina.

27. George Chaplin, letter to *Time* magazine, June 17, 1938, Folder 15, Box 2, Ben Robertson Papers, Special Collections and Archives, Clemson University Libraries, Clemson, South Carolina. The ambitious Chaplin added, "Incidentally, if you have no *Time* correspondent in upper–South Carolina, I should like to apply for the job."

28. Ben Robertson, letter to George Chaplin, June 1938, Folder 15, Box 2, Ben Robertson Papers, Special Collections and Archives, Clemson University Libraries, Clemson, South Carolina; "Clan Supports Ben Robertson," undated clipping, Folder 7, Box 1, Ben Robertson Papers, Special Collections and Archives, Clemson University Libraries, Clemson, South Carolina; "Book Assailed, Clemson Author Fortifies Home," undated clipping from *Charleston News and Courier,* Folder 7, Box 1, Ben Robertson Papers, Special Collections and Archives, Clemson University Libraries, Clemson, South Carolina.

29. George Chaplin, letter to Ben Robertson, June 1938, Folder 15, Box 2, Ben Robertson Papers, Special Collections and Archives, Clemson University Libraries, Clemson, South Carolina.

30. See, among others, "Man About Manhattan," Jersey City *Jersey Journal,* June 16, 1938. Other clippings of the column in the Robertson Papers are from as far west as Oakland, California. Folder 7, Box 1, Ben Robertson Papers, Special Collections and Archives, Clemson University Libraries, Clemson, South Carolina.

31. Fred T. Marsh, "Fiction in Many Moods," New York *Herald Tribune,* June 19, 1938; G. O. Mudge, "Review of Travelers Rest," undated clipping, Folder 7, Box 1, Ben Robertson Papers, Special Collections and Archives, Clemson University Libraries, Clemson, South Carolina.

32. "Descendant's Novel," *Time,* July 4, 1938, Folder 7, Box 1, Ben Robertson Papers, Special Collections and Archives, Clemson University Libraries, Clemson, South Carolina.

33. Irving Deakin, letter to Ben Robertson, June 13, 1938; Macmillan Publishing Company, postcard to Ben Robertson, June 20, 1938, Folder 15, Box 2, Ben Robertson Papers, Special Collections and Archives, Clemson University Libraries, Clemson, South Carolina.

34. Ole H. Lexau, "Caldwell Family," *Atlanta Journal Sunday Magazine,* undated clipping, Folder 7, Box 1, Ben Robertson Papers, Special Collections and Archives, Clemson University Libraries, Clemson, South Carolina.

35. Undated typewritten copy, c. September 1938, Folder 15, Box 2, Ben Robertson Papers, Special Collections and Archives, Clemson University Libraries, Clemson, South Carolina. The story about McJunkin's protest appears to have been written in advance of the event. A draft is in the Robertson papers. "Uncle Charlie" McJunkin, a favorite subject of Greenville *News* columnist Carter "Scoop" Latimer, often attempted unusual feats, such as attempting to enter a Golden Gloves boxing match at age seventy-six. See, for instance, "One-Round McJunkin Scares 'Em," *Greenville News,* January 10, 1937, 15.

36. Ford, introduction, xxiv.

Chapter 9—A New South

1. Cooper and Terrill, *The American South,* 662.

2. Ben Robertson, "Maybank Under Fire as Candidates Move into Piedmont Region," *Anderson Independent,* August 3, 1938, 1.

3. Ben Robertson, "King George Strives to Please," *Saturday Evening Post,* February 4, 1939, 5–7, 69.

4. Ben Robertson, letter to Dorothy Spalding, September 1, 1939, Folder 16, Box 2, Ben Robertson Papers, Special Collections and Archives, Clemson University Libraries, Clemson, South Carolina.

5. Ben Robertson, letter to Thomas R. Waring Jr., January 18, 1939; Thomas R. Waring Jr., letter to Ben Robertson, January 19, 1939, Folder 16, Box 2, Ben Robertson Papers, Special Collections and Archives, Clemson University Libraries, Clemson, South Carolina.

6. Arthur Williams, *Tales of Clemson, 1936–1940* (Clemson University Press, 1992), 43.

7. Ben Robertson, diary entry for March 6, 1939, Folder 40, Box 4, Ben Robertson Papers, Special Collections and Archives, Clemson University Libraries, Clemson, South Carolina.

8. "Kingfish Called 'Public Enemy,'" *Greenville News,* April 10, 1935, 1; Ben Robertson, diary entry for March 6, 1939, Folder 40, Box 4, Ben Robertson Papers, Special Collections and Archives, Clemson University Libraries, Clemson, South Carolina; Cooper and Terrill, *The American South,* 598–99, 645; Kennedy, *Freedom from Fear,* 236–38.

9. Ben Robertson, "The Lucky Girls of Aruba," *Saturday Evening Post,* July 8, 1939, 8–9+.

10. Frank L. Martin, letter to Ben Robertson, May 25, 1939, Folder 16, Box 2, Ben Robertson Papers, Special Collections and Archives, Clemson University Libraries, Clemson, South Carolina; Ben Robertson, diary entry for May 11, 1939, Folder 40, Box 4, Ben Robertson Papers, Special Collections and Archives, Clemson University Libraries, Clemson, South Carolina.

11. Ben Robertson, letter to Ben Robertson Sr., July 28, 1940, Folder 16, Box 2, Ben Robertson Papers, Special Collections and Archives, Clemson University Libraries, Clemson, South Carolina.

12. "Urges Democratic Women to Advance A New South In '40," *Index-Journal* (Greenwood, S.C.), February 26, 1939, 11; "Not to Be Found," *Anniston Star,* June 2, 1939, 4.

13. Ben Robertson, diary entry for May 10, 1939, Folder 40, Box 4, Ben Robertson Papers, Special Collections and Archives, Clemson University Libraries, Clemson, South Carolina. Before he left Atlanta, Robertson joined some friends at the Piedmont Driving Club where they met up with golfing legend Bobby Jones. The antics of one of Robertson's older acquaintances on the course repulsed him. "Chip Robert there, zippy, dancing," he wrote in his journal. "God deliver me from the men who get rejuvenated at fifty . . . or worse yet from those like Senator McAdoo who get that way at seventy. The ends that people go to keep the illusion of youth. McAdoo and Robert just as repulsive as Fanny Ward."

14. John A. Lomax and Ruby T. Lomax, "Southern Recording Trip, March 31–June 14, 1939"; John A. Lomax, letter to Burnet R. Maybank (undated); Ben Robertson, letter to John A. Lomax, June 27, 1939, John A. Lomax Collection, Library of Congress.

15. John A. Lomax and Ruby T. Lomax, field notes for June 9–11, 1939, John A. Lomax Collection, Library of Congress.

16. Much of the speech was reprinted as Ben Robertson, "Forget Gettysburg," in the *Anderson Independent,* July 2, 1939, Folder 8, Box 1, Ben Robertson Papers, Special Collections and Archives, Clemson University Libraries, Clemson, South Carolina.

17. Ben Robertson, "Forget Gettysburg."

18. Ben Robertson, "Forget Gettysburg."

19. Quoted in Ford, introduction, ix.

20. "Ben Robertson Is Opportunity School Speaker This Week," *Index-Journal* (Greenwood, S.C.), August 11, 1939, 2.

21. J. P. Richards, letter to Ben Robertson, June 29, 1939; Burnet Maybank, letter to Ben Robertson, July 1, 1939, Folder 16, Box 2; undated letter from "George," Folder 19, Box 2, Ben Robertson Papers, Special Collections and Archives, Clemson University Libraries, Clemson, South Carolina. On the letter from "George," Robertson's sister Mary added a note reading, "Ben helped many college students with loans."

22. Ben Robertson, letter to Martin Sommers, July 18, 1939, Folder 16, Box 2, Ben Robertson Papers, Special Collections and Archives, Clemson University Libraries, Clemson, South Carolina.

23. Martin Sommers, letter to Ben Robertson, July 21, 1939, Folder 16, Box 2, Ben Robertson Papers, Special Collections and Archives, Clemson University Libraries, Clemson, South Carolina; J. S. Harrison, letter to Sherwood Anderson, July 15, 1939, Folder 16, Box 2, Ben Robertson Papers, Special Collections and Archives, Clemson University Libraries, Clemson, South Carolina.

24. Ben Robertson, letter to Margaret Mitchell, July 24, 1939, Folder 16, Box 2, Ben Robertson Papers, Special Collections and Archives, Clemson University Libraries, Clemson, South Carolina.

25. Margaret Mitchell, letter to Ben Robertson, July 28, 1939, Folder 16, Box 2, Ben Robertson Papers, Special Collections and Archives, Clemson University Libraries, Clemson, South Carolina. The manuscript of the article is in the Robertson Papers.

26. Ben Robertson, letter to Jack Alexander, July 30, 1939, Folder 16, Box 2, Ben Robertson Papers, Special Collections and Archives, Clemson University Libraries, Clemson, South Carolina.

27. Ben Robertson, letter to Robert Neville, July 30, 1939, Folder 16, Box 2, Ben Robertson Papers, Special Collections and Archives, Clemson University Libraries, Clemson, South Carolina.

28. Ben Robertson, letter to Dorothy Spalding, September 1, 1939, Folder 16, Box 2, Ben Robertson Papers, Special Collections and Archives, Clemson University Libraries, Clemson, South Carolina.

29. Ben Robertson, letter to Dorothy Spalding, September 1, 1939, Folder 16, Box 2, Ben Robertson Papers, Special Collections and Archives, Clemson University Libraries, Clemson, South Carolina.

30. Ben Robertson, journal entry, September 3, 1939, Folder 16, Box 2, Ben Robertson Papers, Special Collections and Archives, Clemson University Libraries, Clemson, South Carolina.

31. Klaas, "Lest We Forget," 19; "Robertson to Write Isle Article for Satevepost," *Honolulu Star-Bulletin,* January 8, 1940, 3; Ben Robertson, "Real Hawaii Seen at Ewa Celebration,"

Honolulu Star-Bulletin, February 3, 1940, 36; "Via Clipper," *Honolulu Star-Bulletin,* February 3, 1940, 5.

32. "Judge Thurmond and Ben Robertson Speak at Clemson," The *Index-Journal* (Greenwood, S.C.), April 10, 1940, 6; Ben Robertson, notes for "What Are We Doing in Guam?," Folder 91, Box 9, Ben Robertson Papers, Special Collections and Archives, Clemson University Libraries, Clemson, South Carolina; immigration manifest for MS *Torrens,* sailing from Manila to Los Angeles, March 21, 1940. On Midway, Robertson learned the only two cars on the island had been involved in a head-on collision. At Guam, he told a radio operator that such a story didn't seem possible. "The hell it doesn't," the radioman shot back. "I was driving one of those cars."

33. Mary B. R. Longley, letter to Wright Bryan, September 10, 1960, Folder 4, Box 23, William Wright Bryan Papers, Special Collections and Archives, Clemson University Libraries, Clemson, South Carolina. Some of Robertson's notes from his Pacific trip are in the Robertson papers, and although some of the items his sister noted do not appear to be in the collection, certain other items, including a very detailed description of certain military installations, lend some credence to the possibility this trip had more than journalism at its core.

Chapter 10—"My God, what a war!"

1. Paul Milkman, *PM: A New Deal in Journalism,* 1940–1948 (New Brunswick: Rutgers, 1997), 12.

2. Roy Hoopes, *Ralph Ingersoll: A Biography* (New York: Atheneum, 1985), 152–53.

3. Hoopes, *Ralph Ingersoll,* 157–58.

4. Hoopes, *Ralph Ingersoll,* 166–87. For more information on Luce's conservative views, see David Halberstam, *The Powers That Be* (New York: Dell, 1979) and Robert Herzstein, *Henry R. Luce: A Political Portrait of the Man Who Created the American Century* (New York: Scribners, 1994).

5. Milkman, *PM: A New Deal in Journalism,* 1–40.

6. Quoted in Milkman, *PM: A New Deal in Journalism,* 41.

7. "New journalism" means not only substance, in the way *Time*'s articles synthesized and interpreted an entire week's events into a brief story, but also the snappy syntax *Time* employed, with a jazzy tone and dramatic effect. Wolcott Gibbs's famous 1936 profile of Henry Luce for the *New Yorker,* written entirely in "Timestyle," was a delicious send-up that included such gems as "Backward ran sentences until reeled the mind" and "Certainly to be taken with seriousness is Luce at thirty-eight, his fellowman already informed up to his ears, the shadow of his enterprises long across the land, his future plans impossible to imagine, staggering to contemplate. Where it will all end, knows God!" See Milkman, *PM: A New Deal in Journalism,* 12, and Wolcott Gibbs, "Time . . . Fortune . . . Life . . . Luce," *New Yorker,* November 28, 1936, 20–25.

8. Earl Mazo, letter to Ben Robertson, May 11, 1940. Folder 16, Box 2, Ben Robertson Papers, Special Collections and Archives, Clemson University Libraries, Clemson, South Carolina; "Biographical Note, Butler Black Hare Papers, 1900–1966," South Carolina Political Collections, the University of South Carolina, http://library.sc.edu/scpc/Hare.pdf (accessed November 2, 2017).

9. Walker, "Ben Robertson, War Correspondent," 6; Klaas, "Lest We Forget," 20; Ford, introduction, xxix.

10. Here, and at many points throughout the narrative of Robertson's war tours, the author is grateful for the guidance of two major sources. The first is Juliet Gardiner, *Wartime Britain 1939–1945* (London: Headline Publishing, 2004), a comprehensive and incredibly readable account of England at war. More specific to Robertson is William Walker's 1971 M.A. thesis "Ben Robertson, War Correspondent," a chronological survey and analysis of Robertson's *PM* work.

11. Ben Robertson, *I Saw England* (New York: Knopf, 1941), 3–4.

12. Robertson, *I Saw England,* 5.

13. Robertson, *I Saw England,* 7–8.

14. Robertson, *I Saw England,* 8–9.

15. Robertson, *I Saw England,* 9–10.

16. Robertson, *I Saw England,* 10–12.

17. Robertson, *I Saw England,* 12–13.

18. Robertson, *I Saw England,* 14–16.

19. Robertson, *I Saw England,* 17.

20. Vincent Sheean, *Between the Thunder and the Sun* (New York: Macmillan, 1943), 214.

21. Ben Robertson, "Britons Firm, Await Nazi Attack . . . London Feverishly Prepares, *PM,* June 28, 1940, 5; Ben Robertson, "British Train for Defense by Drilling on Roofs, Streets, Yards," *PM,* July 1, 1940, 6; Robertson, *I Saw England,* 26; Ben Robertson, "This Is How Britons React To Threat of Invasion," *PM,* July 10, 1940, 5.

22. Robertson, *I Saw England,* 31–35; Ben Robertson, "British Trains Go Through on Schedule Despite Bombs," *PM,* August 9, 1940, 6.

23. Ben Robertson, "England's Plymouth Ready for Blitzkrieg," *PM,* July 22, 1940, 6; Robertson, *I Saw England,* 36.

24. Harry Ashmore, "Robertson Becomes Fabulous Character," *Greenville News,* January 28, 1941, 1.

25. Sheean, *Between the Thunder and the Sun,* 214; Helen Kirkpatrick Milbank, oral history, Washington Press Club Foundation, April 4, 1990; Ben Robertson, letter to Ben Robertson Sr., July 28, 1940. Folder 16, Box 2, Ben Robertson Papers, Special Collections and Archives, Clemson University Libraries, Clemson, South Carolina; Helen Kirkpatrick, letter to Ben Robertson, September 15, 1941, Folder 17, Box 2, Ben Robertson Papers, Special Collections and Archives, Clemson University Libraries, Clemson, South Carolina; Robertson, *I Saw England,* 25.

26. Robertson, *I Saw England,* 36–43; Ben Robertson, "British Trains Go Through on Schedule Despite Bombs," *PM,* August 9, 1940, 6.

27. Ben Robertson, letter to Ben Robertson Sr., July 28, 1940. Folder 16, Box 2, Ben Robertson Papers, Special Collections and Archives, Clemson University Libraries, Clemson, South Carolina.

28. Ben Robertson, letter to George Chaplin, August 2, 1940, Folder 16, Box 2, Ben Robertson Papers, Special Collections and Archives, Clemson University Libraries, Clemson, South Carolina.

29. Ben Robertson, letter to Lord and Lady Astor, July 28, 1940, Folder 16, Box 2, Ben Robertson Papers, Special Collections and Archives, Clemson University Libraries, Clemson, South Carolina.

30. Ben Robertson, letter to Earl Mazo, August 2, 1940, Folder 16, Box 2, Ben Robertson

Papers, Special Collections and Archives, Clemson University Libraries, Clemson, South Carolina.

31. Ben Robertson, letter to Lord and Lady Astor, July 28, 1940, Folder 16, Box 2, Ben Robertson Papers, Special Collections and Archives, Clemson University Libraries, Clemson, South Carolina.

32. Robertson, *I Saw England,* 45–46, 54.

33. Ben Robertson, letter to Millard Tydings, July 28, 1940; Ben Robertson, letter to Henry Cabot Lodge, July 28, 1940. Folder 16, Box 2, Ben Robertson Papers, Special Collections and Archives, Clemson University Libraries, Clemson, South Carolina.

34. Robertson, *I Saw England,* 63–64; Ben Robertson, "British See Official Immorality as Source of Quick French Defeat," *PM,* July 31, 1940, 7.

35. "Young Refugee Arrives from Hull, England," *Index-Journal* (Greenwood, S.C.), August 4, 1940, 1; Jeanne Gadsden, letter to Ben Robertson, November 6, 1940, Folder 16, Box 2, Ben Robertson Papers, Special Collections and Archives, Clemson University Libraries, Clemson, South Carolina.

Chapter 11—London Is Burning

1. Robertson, *I Saw England,* 46–47.

2. Robertson, *I Saw England,* 50–52.

3. Robertson, *I Saw England,* 70–71; Ben Robertson, "'Duignan's Yanks' Are Coming . . . Adolf Better Beware!" *PM,* August 5, 1940, 7.

4. Robertson, *I Saw England,* 72–84; Ben Robertson, "Reporters See RAF in Action," *PM,* August 8, 1940, 4.

5. Robertson, *I Saw England,* 86–87.

6. Robertson, *I Saw England,* 88.

7. Quoted in Nancy Caldwell Sorel, *The Women Who Wrote the War* (New York: Arcade, 1999), 97.

8. Robertson, *I Saw England,* 86–93, 102; Helen Kirkpatrick Milbank, oral history.

9. Helen Kirkpatrick Milbank, oral history; Nelson D. Lankford, *The Last American Aristocrat: The Biography of Ambassador David K. E. Bruce* (New York: Little, Brown, 1996), 116.

10. Stanley Cloud and Lynne Olson, *The Murrow Boys: Pioneers on the Front Lines of Broadcast Journalism* (New York: Houghton Mifflin, 1996), 63–64.

11. Robertson, *I Saw England,* 97; Klaas, "Lest We Forget," 22.

12. Ben Robertson, "I Saw Five Planes Crash! PM Man on Chalk Cliff Watches Air Battle." *PM* August 29, 1940, 5; Robertson, *I Saw England,* 93.

13. Quentin Reynolds, Only the Stars are Neutral (New York: Random House, 1942). Quoted in Bailey, "Losing a Life to Find It," 149. In the same passage, Reynolds told of an instance when Robertson wrote of two girls, one a niece of Lady Astor, who were serving refreshments to the men of the barrage balloon stations around London's East End. The troops, happy to see the young women, sometimes made playful remarks; the women laughed along, taking the flirtations as the jests they were meant to be. The censor ordered the lines removed because it made His Majesty's armed forces look unmannered. As Reynolds wrote, "Robertson was kept from tossing himself into the Thames only when we reminded him that Berlin censorship was probably even worse."

14. Robertson, *I Saw England,* 110.

15. Robertson, *I Saw England,* 111–13; Ben Robertson, "British Courage Withstands Raids," *PM,* September 3, 1940, 5.

16. Robertson, *I Saw England,* 113.

17. Ben Robertson, letter to Wilton Hall, August 5, 1940, Folder 16, Box 2, Ben Robertson Papers, Special Collections and Archives, Clemson University Libraries, Clemson, South Carolina.

18. Ben Robertson, "Hail of Nazi Bombs Turns London Into Hell on Earth," *PM,* September 9, 1940, 4.

19. Robertson, *I Saw England,* 121–23.

20. Robertson, *I Saw England,* 126–27.

21. Robertson, *I Saw England,* 128–29; Ben Robertson, "London 'Carries On' Amid Ruin and Tragedy Left by Nazi Raids," *PM,* September 10, 1940, 4.

22. Robertson, *I Saw England,* 130–33; Ben Robertson, "London 'Carries On' Amid Ruin and Tragedy Left by Nazi Raids," *PM,* September 10, 1940, 4; Ben Robertson, "London's Diners Calmly Share Dangers of Battlefield," *PM,* September 13, 1940, 4.

23. Robertson, *I Saw England,* 130–31, 151.

24. Robertson, *I Saw England,* 138–40.

25. Robertson, *I Saw England,* 142.

26. Robertson, *I Saw England,* 144–47.

27. Ralph Ingersoll, telegram to Ben Robertson, September 24, 1940; Robert Neville, letter to Ben Robertson Sr., September 26, 1940, Folder 16, Box 2, Ben Robertson Papers, Special Collections and Archives, Clemson University Libraries, Clemson, South Carolina.

28. Robertson, *I Saw England,* 152–56.

29. Helen Kirkpatrick Milbank, oral history; Robertson, *I Saw England,* 159–61; Ben Robertson, "British Industry Winning a Battle," *PM,* October 8, 1940, 6.

30. Robertson, *I Saw England,* 167–70.

31. Ben Robertson, "War Has Changed the Dour Scots," *PM,* October 16, 1940, 5.

32. Robertson, *I Saw England,* 180–81.

33. Helen Kirkpatrick Milbank, oral history; Ben Robertson, "London This Winter: 'Hardships in Windowless Homes in Chill and Fog," *PM,* October 20, 1940, 6.

34. Robertson, *I Saw England,* 181–82; Ralph Ingersoll, telegram to Ben Robertson Sr., November 13, 1940, Folder 16, Box 2, Ben Robertson Papers, Special Collections and Archives, Clemson University Libraries, Clemson, South Carolina.

35. "Ben Robertson Says U.S. Newsmen in Britain Believe 'England Will Come Through,'" *Index-Journal* (Greenwood, S.C.), December 5, 1940, 16.

36. Gardiner, *Wartime Britain 1939–1945,* 436–45.

37. Robertson, *I Saw England,* 183–84; Ben Robertson, "Dublin Street Lights Give Real Thrill After London Blackouts," *PM,* November 12, 1940, 4.

38. Robertson, "Dublin Street Lights Give Real Thrill"; Robertson, *I Saw England,* 182–83.

39. Robertson, *I Saw England,* 186–87.

40. Helen Kirkpatrick Milbank, oral history; James F. Byrnes, letter to Ben Robertson, December 9, 1940, Folder 16, Box 2, Ben Robertson Papers, Special Collections and Archives, Clemson University Libraries, Clemson, South Carolina.

41. Robertson, *I Saw England,* 189–96; Ben Robertson, "By Ben Robertson: The Truth About Coventry," *PM,* January 20, 1941, 6–7.

42. Gardiner, *Wartime Britain 1939–1945,* 350–54.

43. Robertson, *I Saw England,* 195.

44. Robertson, *I Saw England,* 199.

45. Robertson, *I Saw England,* 207; "Rayville Officers Tell of Ship Blast," *PM,* November 13, 1940, 4.

46. Ben Robertson, "British Women at War: Robertson Picks London's Six Bravest," *PM,* December 11, 1940, 5; Ben Robertson, "The 'Weaker Sex' Gives England Strength," *PM,* December 16, 1940, 5; Ernie Pyle, "Rambling Reporter," *Pittsburgh Press,* January 17, 1941, 25.

47. Ben Robertson, "How Churchill Relaxes," *PM,* January 21, 1941, 6. Beatrice Naff Bailey makes a convincing case that during the group singing described in the article, Robertson was playing the piano and leading the group in song, and that Robertson provided the albums of the Southernaires to Churchill. See Bailey, "Losing a Life to Find It," 107–12.

48. Ben Robertson, "Britain Resumes Lisbon Air Service . . . But Ambassadors Get First Choice," *PM,* December 20, 1940, 6; Harry Ashmore, "Robertson Becomes Fabulous Character," *Greenville News,* January 28, 1941, 1.

49. Robertson, *I Saw England,* 210–11. Merrill "Red" Mueller later became a correspondent for NBC News.

50. Robertson, *I Saw England,* 213.

Chapter 12—"What are we going to do about it?"

1. Ben Robertson, "Ben Robertson, Back from London's Blackouts, Finds N.Y. Leisurely, and Ice Cream Fun," *PM,* January 8, 1941, 4.

2. Ralph Ingersoll, "Explaining the Paradox of Joe Kennedy . . . Ralph Ingersoll Interviews Ben Robertson," *PM,* January 19, 1941, 10–11.

3. Ben Robertson, "By Ben Robertson: About Britain's War Aims . . . ," *PM,* January 30, 1941: 8.

4. Harry Ashmore, "Robertson Becomes Fabulous Character," *Greenville News,* January 28, 1941, 1.

5. Laura Claridge, *The Lady with the Borzoi: Blanche Knopf, Literary Tastemaker Extraordinaire* (New York: Farrar, Straus and Giroux, 2016), 211; Bernard Smith, letter to Ben Robertson, February 5, 1941, Folder 17, Box 2, Ben Robertson Papers, Special Collections and Archives, Clemson University Libraries, Clemson, South Carolina.

6. "Robertson Sees Good Chance for British Victory," *Greenville News,* February 1, 1941, 5.

7. Koji Ariyoshi, "Robertson Traces War to Manchuria," *Honolulu Star-Bulletin* February 17, 1941, 11; Burnet Maybank, telegram to Ben Robertson, February 10, 1941, Folder 17, Box 2, Ben Robertson Papers, Special Collections and Archives, Clemson University Libraries, Clemson, South Carolina; Bailey, "Losing a Life to Find It," 9; Klaas, "Lest We Forget," 26.

8. Ben Robertson, "*PM's* Ben Robertson Gets Back to London," *PM,* March 11, 1941, 7.

9. Ben Robertson, "Getting Used to Bombs Again," *PM,* March 20, 1941, 6.

10. Ben Robertson, "*PM's* Ben Robertson Gets Back to London," *PM,* March 11, 1941, 7.

11. Ben Robertson, "Getting Used to Bombs Again," *PM,* March 20, 1941, 6.

12. Ben Robertson, "FDR's Speech Gives Britain a New Optimism," *PM,* March 18, 1941, 5.

13. Ben Robertson, "How Plymouth Was Blitzed Two Nights in a Row," *PM,* March 24, 1941, 4.

14. Rosina Harrison, *Rose: My Life in Service* (Worthing, U.K.: Littlehampton Book Services, 1975), 181–83.

15. Ben Robertson, "How Plymouth Was Blitzed Two Nights in a Row," *PM,* March 24, 1941, 4.

16. Ben Robertson, "Ben Robertson Wonders If Americans Take Air Raids on Britain for Granted," *PM,* March 25, 1941, 6.

17. Ben Robertson, "Ben Robertson Wonders If Americans Take Air Raids on Britain for Granted," *PM,* March 25, 1941, 6.

18. Cherry Kearton, letter to Ben Robertson, April 21, 1941; Blanche Knopf, telegram to Ben Robertson, March 31, 1941, Folder 17, Box 2, Ben Robertson Papers, Special Collections and Archives, Clemson University Libraries, Clemson, South Carolina.

19. John Cournos, "An Eyewitness of England at War," *New York Times Review of Books,* April 6, 1941, 5; Frank Kelley, "Stars Above the Blackout," New York *Herald Tribune,* April 6, 1941, Folder 11, Box 1, Ben Robertson Papers, Special Collections and Archives, Clemson University Libraries, Clemson, South Carolina; clipping from *Foreign Affairs,* August 1942, Folder 11, Box 1, Ben Robertson Papers, Special Collections and Archives, Clemson University Libraries, Clemson, South Carolina.

20. Ben Robertson, "One of the World's Most Important Places Inside a Spitfire Factory," *PM,* April 4, 1941, 6; Ben Robertson, "Springtime in London: Flowers Try to Hide the Scars," *PM* April 6, 1941, 6.

21. Ben Robertson, "This War Has Now Become a Matter of Food and Ships," *PM,* April 9, 1941, 6.

22. Ben Robertson, "'British Morale, as a Whole, Is Unshattered': A Tour of Seaports," *PM,* April 21, 1941, 8.

23. Ben Robertson, letter to Ben Robertson Sr., April 13, 1941, Folder 17, Box 2, Ben Robertson Papers, Special Collections and Archives, Clemson University Libraries, Clemson, South Carolina.

24. Ben Robertson, "What Is More Important, Bombs or Chiffon Scarfs?," *PM,* April 25, 1941, 19. This article ran the same day Ingersoll inaugurated the "What Are We Going to Do About It?" crusade for American involvement in the war.

25. Ben Robertson, "A Cable from Ben Robertson," *PM,* April 20, 1941, 5.

26. "A Cable from Our London Correspondent," *PM,* April 25, 1941, 7.

27. Ben Robertson, "Is It All Big Talk . . . Or Do We Really Mean Business?," *PM,* April 27, 1941, 15.

28. Ben Robertson, "U.S.-Anglo Navies, World's Biggest, Might Lick Nazis," *PM,* April 28, 1941, 15; Ben Robertson, "The Hour for the U.S.A. to Act," *PM,* April 30, 1941, 8; Ben Robertson, "Food Still Is Plentiful in London . . . But for How Long?" *PM,* May 2, 1941, 22; Ben Robertson, "England Is Losing More Ships Than She Can Build," *PM,* May 9, 1941, 2; Ben Robertson, "Bombs on the White House? Robertson Says It Can Happen," *PM,* May 7, 1941, 20.

29. Cloud and Olson, *The Murrow Boys,* 142.

30. Helen Kirkpatrick Milbank, oral history.

31. For a description of how the role of the war correspondent took on additional meaning

in a new generation, see William Prochnau, *Once Upon a Distant War: Young Foreign Correspondents and Their Early Vietnam Battles* (New York: Vintage, 1997).

32. Cloud and Olson, *The Murrow Boys,* 142.

33. Ben Robertson, letter to Lord Beaverbrook, undated, Folder 17, Box 2, Ben Robertson Papers, Special Collections and Archives, Clemson University Libraries, Clemson, South Carolina.

34. Ben Robertson, letter to Winston S. Churchill, May 2, 1941, Folder 17, Box 2, Ben Robertson Papers, Special Collections and Archives, Clemson University Libraries, Clemson, South Carolina.

35. Ralph Ingersoll, letter to Ben Robertson, June 6, 1941, Folder 17, Box 2, Ben Robertson Papers, Special Collections and Archives, Clemson University Libraries, Clemson, South Carolina.

36. Ben Robertson, "Tears and Trouble: Another 'Blitz' Tries London's Courage," *PM,* May 12, 1941, 3.

37. Ben Robertson, "Commons Carries On Despite Nazi Bombs," *PM,* May 15, 1941, 11.

38. Ben Robertson, telegrams to Barry Bingham, Frank Martin, and Paul Smith, undated (probably May 1941), Folder 17, Box 2, Ben Robertson Papers, Special Collections and Archives, Clemson University Libraries, Clemson, South Carolina. Also see Kennedy, *Freedom from Fear,* 494, and Manchester, *The Glory and the Dream,* 232.

Chapter 13—The Advocate

1. Ben Robertson, "Bombs Still Rock Dover . . . But They Fall on France," *PM,* June 24, 1941, 4.

2. Ben Robertson, letter to James F. Byrnes, July 5, 1941, Robertson Papers, CU.

3. Harry Ashmore, "Robertson Becomes Fabulous Character," *Greenville News,* January 28, 1941, 1; Ben Robertson, letter to James F. Byrnes, July 5, 1941, Folder 17, Box 2, Ben Robertson Papers, Special Collections and Archives, Clemson University Libraries, Clemson, South Carolina.

4. Ben Robertson, letter to Lewis Gannett, August 8, 1941, Folder 17, Box 2, Ben Robertson Papers, Special Collections and Archives, Clemson University Libraries, Clemson, South Carolina. Robertson noted in his letter that when Lady Astor told the Shaws that they could come to Cliveden, the old writer replied, "Cliveden isn't a place you enjoy — if I had Cliveden I'd burn it to the ground and build one of the *Daily Mail*'s Ideal Homes on the site"; Douglas Williams, letter to Portuguese Consul-General, July 16, 1941, Folder 17, Box 2, Ben Robertson Papers, Special Collections and Archives, Clemson University Libraries, Clemson, South Carolina.

5. John Hennessey Walker, "Navy Liner Returns with Strange Cargo from Darkest Europe," *PM,* August 3, 1941, 7; Ben Robertson, "*PM* Writer Describes Strange Voyage Home," *PM,* August 3, 1941, 8–9.

6. Cloud and Olson, *The Murrow Boys,* 199–201.

7. Ben Robertson, "*PM* Writer Describes Strange Voyage Home," *PM,* August 3, 1941, 8–9.

8. Roger C. Peace, letter to Ben Robertson, July 23, 1941, Folder 17, Box 2, Ben Robertson Papers, Special Collections and Archives, Clemson University Libraries, Clemson, South Carolina.

9. James F. Byrnes, letter to Ben Robertson, July 23, 1941, Folder 17, Box 2, Ben Robertson Papers, Special Collections and Archives, Clemson University Libraries, Clemson, South Carolina.

10. Edward R. Murrow, letter to Ben Robertson, August 4, 1941, Folder 17, Box 2, Ben Robertson Papers, Special Collections and Archives, Clemson University Libraries, Clemson, South Carolina; Helen Kirkpatrick, letter to Ben Robertson, September 15, 1941, Folder 17, Box 2, Ben Robertson Papers, Special Collections and Archives, Clemson University Libraries, Clemson, South Carolina.

11. Ben Robertson, "Ben Robertson to Write on Senate Campaign in S.C.," *Greenville News,* August 24, 1941, 5.

12. Ben Robertson, "Ben Robertson Says the Germans Can't Destroy London from the Air; 98% of City Still Stands," *PM,* August 15, 1941, 8–9.

13. Ben Robertson, "Nazi Bombs Have Destroyed British Social Barriers, Building a New Belief in Community Life," *PM,* August 17, 1941, 5; Ben Robertson, "Churchill, the Gargantuan, Still Rules Unchallenged," *PM,* August 18, 1941, 6; Ben Robertson, "Britain's Reasons for Not Invading Continent Now," *PM,* August 19, 1941, 8. Author Phillip Knightley argued in his book *The First Casualty* that the "social leveller" stories of the Blitz were exaggerated, often to help stories gain approval under wartime censorship. However, Robertson's observations about cooperation among social classes in wartime London remained consistent, whether they were filed from London where they would be subject to censorship, filed in New York with no censorship, or written as part of a book. See Knightley, *The First Casualty: From the Crimea to Vietnam: The War Correspondent as Hero, Propagandist, and Myth Maker* (New York: Harcourt Brace Jovanovich, 1975), 238–39.

14. Blanche Knopf, letter to Ben Robertson, October 13, 1941, Folder 17, Box 2, Ben Robertson Papers, Special Collections and Archives, Clemson University Libraries, Clemson, South Carolina.

15. Milkman, *PM: A New Deal in Journalism,* 54–55; Hoopes, *Ralph Ingersoll,* 254–55; Mary B. R. Longley, letter to Wright Bryan, undated (1960), Folder 4, Box 23, William Wright Bryan Papers, Special Collections and Archives, Clemson University Libraries, Clemson, South Carolina.

16. Mary B. R. Longley, letter to Wright Bryan, undated, Folder 4, Box 23, William Wright Bryan Papers, Special Collections and Archives, Clemson University Libraries, Clemson, South Carolina; Whitelaw Reid, letter to Ben Robertson, October 15, 1941, Folder 17, Box 2, Ben Robertson Papers, Special Collections and Archives, Clemson University Libraries, Clemson, South Carolina. For more information on the financial health of *PM,* see Milkman, *PM: A New Deal in Journalism,* 54–55.

17. Dorothy Hinitt, letter to Ben Robertson, December 2, 1941; John F. Royal to Ben Robertson, November 22, 1941, Folder 17, Box 2, Ben Robertson Papers, Special Collections and Archives, Clemson University Libraries, Clemson, South Carolina.

18. Ben Robertson, letter to Blanche Knopf and Bernard Smith, August 11, 1941, Alfred A. Knopf Papers, Harry Ransom Center, The University of Texas at Austin.

19. Ben Robertson, letter to Blanche Knopf, August 25, 1941; Blanche Knopf, letter to Ben Robertson, August 28, 1941; Ben Robertson, letter to Blanche Knopf and Bernard Smith,

September 3, 1941; Blanche Knopf, letter to Ben Robertson, September 5, 1941, Alfred A. Knopf Papers, Harry Ransom Center, The University of Texas at Austin.

20. Bryan, "About Ben Robertson," xv; Ford, introduction, xxx; Busha, "Ben Robertson of Pickens County" (1982), 7; Klaas, "Lest We Forget," 27.

21. "Ben Robertson Makes Sharp Criticism of Isolationist Group," *Index-Journal* (Greenwood, S.C.), November 26, 1941, 7.

22. Nancy Astor, telegram to Ben Robertson, December 10, 1941, Folder 17, Box 2, Ben Robertson Papers, Special Collections and Archives, Clemson University Libraries, Clemson, South Carolina.

23. Ben Robertson, letter to Blanche Knopf, December 7, 1941, Alfred A. Knopf Papers, Harry Ransom Center, The University of Texas at Austin; "Ben Robertson Advises Clemson Students to Study Hard, Wait," *Greenville News,* December 12, 1941, 10.

24. Mary B. R. Longley, letter to Wright Bryan, September 10, 1960, Folder 6, Box 23, William Wright Bryan Papers, Special Collections and Archives, Clemson University Libraries, Clemson, South Carolina.

25. Jeanne Gadsden, letter to Ben Robertson, December 13, 1941, Folder 17, Box 2, Ben Robertson Papers, Special Collections and Archives, Clemson University Libraries, Clemson, South Carolina.

26. Blanche Knopf, letter to Ben Robertson, December 10, 1941, Folder 17, Box 2, Ben Robertson Papers, Special Collections and Archives, Clemson University Libraries, Clemson, South Carolina.

27. Ralph Ingersoll, telegram to Ben Robertson, December 22, 1941, Folder 17, Box 2, Ben Robertson Papers, Special Collections and Archives, Clemson University Libraries, Clemson, South Carolina.

Chapter 14—Humble Times for Eagles

1. Richard Overy, *Russia's War: A History of the Soviet War Effort, 1941–1945* (New York, Penguin, 1997), 44–51.

2. Overy, *Russia's War,* 58–73.

3. Milkman, *PM: A New Deal in Journalism,* 100; Hoopes, *Ralph Ingersoll,* 250–52; Christopher B. Daly, "When the 99% Had a Paper: The Brief, Wondrous Life of *PM,*" *Columbia Journalism Review* January/February 2012, http://archives.cjr.org/essay/when_the_99_had_a_paper.php (accessed November 2, 2017).

4. Milkman, *PM: A New Deal in Journalism,* 102.

5. Hoopes, *Ralph Ingersoll,* 254–55.

6. Hoopes, *Ralph Ingersoll,* 255.

7. "Robertson Answers Many Questions About the War," *Index-Journal* (Greenwood, S.C.), January 17, 1942, 1.

8. Mary B. R. Longley, letter to Wright Bryan, September 10, 1960, Folder 22, Box 2, Ben Robertson Papers, Special Collections and Archives, Clemson University Libraries, Clemson, South Carolina.

9. "Robertson to Australia," *Index-Journal* (Greenwood, S.C.), March 9, 1942, 5; "Brief City News," *Index-Journal* (Greenwood, S.C.), March 16, 1942, 5.

10. Bernard Smith, letter to Ben Robertson, January 29, 1942, Folder 18, Box 2, Ben Robertson Papers, Special Collections and Archives, Clemson University Libraries, Clemson, South Carolina.

11. Ben Robertson, "Friction with RAF Students in U.S.A.? Here Are the Facts," *PM,* February 11, 1942, 10; Ben Robertson, "American Cadets, RAF Agree! No Hazing for British Pilots," *PM,* February 15, 1942, 9; Ben Robertson, "British RAF Cadets in U.S.A. Grade Exams, Give Each Other 100," *PM,* February 16, 1942, 10.

12. Ben Robertson, "Nero Did It, Can't They?" *PM,* March 18, 1942, 12.

13. Edgar Snow, *People on Our Side* (New York: Random House, 1944), 6. Quoted in Bailey, "Losing a Life to Find It," 16.

14. Milkman, *PM: A New Deal in Journalism,* 90; Walker, "Ben Robertson, War Correspondent," 44–46; Ben Robertson, "Germans Keep Allies Guessing," *PM,* May 3, 1942, 15.

15. Ben Robertson, "Cairo's Beer from Jersey." *PM,* May 4, 1942, 19; Ben Robertson, "Allied Soldiers in Cairo Talk of Post-War World." *PM,* May 24, 1942: 17.

16. Alexander Uhl, telegram to Ben Robertson, May 26, 1942, Folder 18, Box 2, Ben Robertson Papers, Special Collections and Archives, Clemson University Libraries, Clemson, South Carolina.

17. Ben Robertson, "Holy Land is at Peace in the Midst of War," *PM,* June 5, 1942, 13.

18. Ben Robertson, "Robertson Rides the Dust – Damascus to Baghdad," *PM,* June 26, 1942, 4.

19. Ben Robertson, "Journey into Russia One Year After," *PM,* June 25, 1942, 15.

20. Ben Robertson, "It's Total War in Kubiyshev," *PM,* June 28, 1942: 14.

21. Ben Robertson, "Robertson Finds U.S. Jeeps Popular with Red Army Men," *PM,* June 29, 1942, 18.

22. Ben Robertson, "How Cossacks Fight Panzers," *PM,* July 2, 1942, 18.

23. Ben Robertson, "Sevastopol Isn't a City . . . It's Men Dying for a Cause," *PM,* July 3, 1942, 18; Ben Robertson, "Ben Robertson Finds the July 4 Spirit," *PM,* July 5, 1942, 18.

24. Ben Robertson, "Russia Needs Aid Now as Britain Did in 1940," *PM,* July 6, 1942, 14.

25. Ben Robertson, "Nazis Are Flooding Russia Like Water," *PM,* July 17, 1942, 15; Ben Robertson, "Second Front Would Boom Soviet Morale," *PM,* July 15, 1942, 18; Overy, *Russia's War,* 157–58.

26. Knightley, *The First Casualty,* 245–51.

27. Ben Robertson, draft of undated dispatch, Folder 95, Box 9, Ben Robertson Papers, Special Collections and Archives, Clemson University Libraries, Clemson, South Carolina. "Janet Weaver," whose name was Janet Ross, was a longtime Communist who used her access to the American embassy to gather information for the Comintern. See Harvey Klehr, John Earl Haynes and Fridrikh Igorevich Firsov, *The Secret World of American Communism* (New Haven: Yale University Press, 1996), 286–87.

28. Ben Robertson, "Russians Now Look to Urals," *PM,* July 22, 1942, 15.

29. Overy, *Russia's War,* 158–69; Ben Robertson, "We Play as Russia Burns," *PM,* August 17, 1942, 14.

30. Ben Robertson, "We'll Fight Beside Soviets," *PM,* August 20, 1942, 19.

31. Overy, *Russia's War,* 166–68.

32. Ben Robertson, "Russia Still Trusts U.S.A.," *PM,* September 2, 1942, 17.

33. Turner Catledge, telegram to Ben Robertson, undated, Folder 18, Box 2, Ben Robertson Papers, Special Collections and Archives, Clemson University Libraries, Clemson, South Carolina.

34. Ben Robertson, "A Humiliating Summer for Americans in Russia," *PM,* Sept 28, 1942, 19.

Chapter 15—A Southern Record

1. Robertson, *Red Hills and Cotton,* 3–4.

2. Robertson, *Red Hills and Cotton,* 82.

3. Here the author must credit the eminent historian John Hammond Moore, who shared a similar observation with the author during a journalism conference in March 2001.

4. Robertson, *Red Hills and Cotton,* 294–95.

5. Robertson, *Red Hills and Cotton,* 288.

6. W. J. Cash, *The Mind of the South* (New York: Knopf, 1941); Louis D. Rubin, "W. J. Cash after Fifty Years," *Virginia Quarterly Review,* Spring 1991, http://www.vqronline.org/essay/wj-cash-after-fifty-years (accessed November 2, 2017).

7. Harry Ashmore, "Robertson Becomes Fabulous Character," *Greenville News,* January 28, 1941, 1; Bryan, "About Ben Robertson," viii.

8. Quoted in Walker, "Ben Robertson, War Correspondent," 8.

9. Katherine Woods, "In South Carolina's Upcountry," *New York Times Review of Books,* August 23, 1942, 5; unsigned clipping, *Chicago Sun,* November 1, 1942; Georgiana G. Stevens, "The New South Explained," San Francisco *Chronicle,* August 9, 1942; "The Hill Gentry," *Time,* September 28, 1942, Folder 12, Box 1, Ben Robertson Papers, Special Collections and Archives, Clemson University Libraries, Clemson, South Carolina; Stark Young, "More Souths," *New Republic,* October 5, 1942, Folder 12, Box 1, Ben Robertson Papers, Special Collections and Archives, Clemson University Libraries, Clemson, South Carolina.

10. Rosemary Benet, "Kinfolks by the Blue Ridge in Carolina," *New York Herald Tribune,* August 16, 1942, Folder 12, Box 1, Ben Robertson Papers, Special Collections and Archives, Clemson University Libraries, Clemson, South Carolina.

11. "Ben Robertson Writes of Southern Memories," *PM,* August 16, 1942, Folder 12, Box 1, Ben Robertson Papers, Special Collections and Archives, Clemson University Libraries, Clemson, South Carolina.

12. "Red Hills and Cotton," Charleston *News and Courier,* August 16, 1942; Jacob H. Lowrey, "Carolinian's Book Is as Honest as It Is Puritan," Columbia (S.C.) *State,* August 16, 1942; Wright Bryan, "Red Hills and Cotton," Atlanta *Journal,* undated, Folder 12, Box 1, Ben Robertson Papers, Special Collections and Archives, Clemson University Libraries, Clemson, South Carolina.

13. Dorothy Canfield, "Red Hills and Cotton," *Book of the Month Club News,* September 1942; advertisement for *Red Hills and Cotton,* August 1942, Folder 12, Box 1, Ben Robertson Papers, Special Collections and Archives, Clemson University Libraries, Clemson, South Carolina.

14. Ford, introduction, xxxii. The best source of information on the varied career of Harry Ashmore is Nathania K. Sawyer, "Harry S. Ashmore: On the Way to Everywhere" (M.A. thesis, University of Arkansas at Little Rock, 2001). The author thanks Sawyer for her generous assistance with this biographical sketch.

15. Harry Ashmore, letter to John D. Lane, October 15, 1942, Folder 2, Box 1, John Dewey Lane Papers, Special Collections and Archives, Clemson University Libraries, Clemson, South Carolina. Ashmore later adapted the phrase into the title of his book *An Epitaph for Dixie* (New York: Norton, 1958).

Chapter 16—Cynical Men

1. Ben Robertson, "A Humiliating Summer for Americans in Russia," *PM,* Sept 28, 1942, 19.

2. For more on the "Quit India" movement, see Srinath Raghvan, *India's War: World War II and the Making of Modern South Asia* (New York: Basic Books, 2016), 256–75.

3. Ben Robertson, "Divide India Into Two States," *PM,* October 11, 1942, 14; Ben Robertson, "Yanks in India Avert Malaria," *PM,* October 23, 1942, 19.

4. Ben Robertson, "Indians Train in Himalayas," *PM,* October 28, 1942, 16; Walker, "Ben Robertson: War Correspondent," 57.

5. Ben Robertson, "British Colonial Imperialism and Four Freedoms Clash in India; United Nations Are the Losers," *PM,* February 22, 1943, 8; Ben Robertson, "How Britain's 'Practical' Men Rule Over India," *PM,* February 23, 1943, 4.

6. Ben Robertson, "Gandhi – Alive or Dead – Holds Key to India," *PM,* February 24, 1943, 7.

7. Ben Robertson, "Yanks in India Avert Malaria," *PM,* October 23, 1942, 19.

8. Ben Robertson, "The Mind of a Maharajah," *PM,* November 22, 1942, 15.

9. Ben Robertson, "British Colonial Imperialism and Four Freedoms Clash in India; United Nations Are the Losers," *PM,* February 22, 1943, 8; Ben Robertson, "How Britain's 'Practical' Men Rule over India," *PM,* February 23, 1943, 4.

10. Ben Robertson, "India Is Now a Camp . . . ," *PM,* November 4, 1942, 19.

11. Ben Robertson, dispatch for Chicago *Sun,* undated (November 1942), Folder 93, Box 9, Ben Robertson Papers, Special Collections and Archives, Clemson University Libraries, Clemson, South Carolina. It is very likely that Robertson was among those correspondents who considered resigning their credentials.

12. John P. Lewis, "An Editorial: On a Newspaperman," *PM,* February 24, 1943, 17.

13. Ben Robertson, "Our Soldiers Keep Their Points of View," *PM,* November 27, 1942, 16; Ben Robertson, "India Looks to U.S. for Help in the Future; American Troops Have Made Friends for Us," *PM,* February 25, 1943, 5–6.

14. Ben Robertson, "What an American Ferry Pilot Goes Through," *PM,* February 28, 1943, 6.

15. Ben Robertson, "What an American Ferry Pilot Goes Through," *PM,* February 28, 1943, 6.

16. Bryan, "About Ben Robertson," xvi; Ben Robertson, "Ben Robertson's Last Story – Home from India," *PM,* March 1, 1943, 8.

17. Ben Robertson, entry in personal journal, undated (1942), Folder 46, Box 5, Ben Robertson Papers, Special Collections and Archives, Clemson University Libraries, Clemson, South Carolina.

18. Ben Robertson, entry in personal journal, undated (1942), Folder 46, Box 5, Ben Robertson Papers, Special Collections and Archives, Clemson University Libraries, Clemson, South

Carolina; Mary B. R. Longley, letter to Wright Bryan, undated, Folder 4, Box 23, William Wright Bryan Papers, Special Collections and Archives, Clemson University Libraries, Clemson, South Carolina. According to one story, a copy of *Red Hills and Cotton* had been sent with Wendell Willkie when he went to Russia in the autumn; Willkie was to have given Robertson the book and some letters from home when he arrived in Moscow, but by the time Willkie arrived Robertson had already left for India. "He brought the pkg. back to us—a war casualty." See also Lem Jones, letter to Jeanne Gadsden, September 1, 1942, Folder 18, Box 2, Ben Robertson Papers, Special Collections and Archives, Clemson University Libraries, Clemson, South Carolina.

19. Edwin Camp, radio script of February 25, 1943, Folder 3, Box 23, William Wright Bryan Papers, Special Collections and Archives, Clemson University Libraries, Clemson, South Carolina.

20. Ben Robertson, entry in personal journal, undated (1942), Folder 46, Box 5, Ben Robertson Papers, Special Collections and Archives, Clemson University Libraries, Clemson, South Carolina.

21. Ben Robertson, entry in personal journal, undated (1942), Folder 46, Box 5, Ben Robertson Papers, Special Collections and Archives, Clemson University Libraries, Clemson, South Carolina.

22. Ben Robertson, entry in personal journal, undated, (1942), Folder 46, Box 5, Ben Robertson Papers, Special Collections and Archives, Clemson University Libraries, Clemson, South Carolina.

23. "Ben Robertson Addresses Students, Faculty Monday," *Tiger,* January 14, 1943, 1.

24. "Miss Inez McCoy Enlists In WAAC," *Greenville News,* January 17, 1943, 14.

25. Ben Robertson, entry in personal journal, undated (1942), Folder 46, Box 5, Ben Robertson Papers, Special Collections and Archives, Clemson University Libraries, Clemson, South Carolina; "Clemson Cadets to Hear Robertson," *Greenville News* January 11, 1943, 10; "Robertson Talks at Meeting Here," *Greenville News,* January 12, 1943, 2; Mary B. R. Longley, notes for revised preface to "Red Hills and Cotton," undated (1960), Folder 6, Box 23, William Wright Bryan Papers, Special Collections and Archives, Clemson University Libraries, Clemson, South Carolina.

26. Klaas, "Lest We Forget," 29.

27. John P. Lewis, "An Editorial: On a Newspaperman," *PM,* February 24, 1943, 17.

28. Stephen Early, letter to Ben Robertson, December 29, 1942, Folder 18, Box 2, Ben Robertson Papers, Special Collections and Archives, Clemson University Libraries, Clemson, South Carolina.

29. Klaas, "Lest We Forget," 33.

Chapter 17—Trip 9035

1. Ben Robertson, entry in personal journal, undated (1943), Folder 46, Box 5, Ben Robertson Papers, Special Collections and Archives, Clemson University Libraries, Clemson, South Carolina.

2. Ben Robertson, entry in personal journal, undated (1943), Folder 46, Box 5, Ben Robertson Papers, Special Collections and Archives, Clemson University Libraries, Clemson, South Carolina.

3. Mary B. R. Longley, letter to Wright Bryan, undated (1943), Folder 4, Box 23, William Wright Bryan Papers, Special Collections and Archives, Clemson University Libraries, Clemson, South Carolina; Bessie Mell Lane, memorandum, February 1986, Folder 34, Box 1, John Dewey Lane Papers, Special Collections and Archives, Clemson University Libraries, Clemson, South Carolina.

4. Ben Robertson, entry in personal journal, February 4, 1943, Folder 46, Box 5, Ben Robertson Papers, Special Collections and Archives, Clemson University Libraries, Clemson, South Carolina.

5. Ben Robertson, entry in personal journal, February 1943, Folder 46, Box 5, Ben Robertson Papers, Special Collections and Archives, Clemson University Libraries, Clemson, South Carolina; Klaas, "Lest We Forget," 34.

6. Jeanne Gadsden, letter to Tom Waring, February 26, 1943, Folder 21, Box 2, Ben Robertson Papers, Special Collections and Archives, Clemson University Libraries, Clemson, South Carolina.

7. "Toll of Yankee Clipper Crash: 4 Dead; 20 Missing; 15 Living," *Chicago Tribune,* February 24, 1943, 6; "Historic Missourians: Ellen Jane Froman," State Historical Society of Missouri website, http://shsmo.org/historicmissourians/name/f/froman/ (accessed November 2, 2017).

8. Klaas, "Lest We Forget," 33–35; "Model 314, Where Are You?" *Boeing Magazine,* June 1965, 3–6.

9. "Model 314, Where Are You?," 5; "Report of the Civil Aeronautics Board on the Investigation of an Accident Involving Aircraft of United States Registry NC18603, in the Tagus River, Lisbon, Portugal, on February 22, 1943 (Washington: Civil Aeronautics Board, 1943). The author is indebted to Ned Preston, retired historian for the Federal Aviation Administration, for providing a copy of the CAB report.

10. Ben Robertson, "British Colonial Imperialism and Four Freedoms Clash in India; United Nations Are the Losers," *PM,* February 22, 1943, 8.

11. This account draws on several sources, including Klaas, "Lest We Forget," and the Civil Aeronautics Board report. Captain Sullivan was found by the CAB investigation to be responsible for the crash. He lost his job with Pan Am but entered the Navy and served for the remainder of the war. A story persists that the *Yankee Clipper* crashed in a thunderstorm, but the thunderstorm was clear of the landing site when the aircraft was on approach.

12. Joe Sherman, "Ben Robertson, Noted Reporter, Lost on *Clipper,*" *Greenville News,* February 25, 1943, 1.

13. Ogden and Helen Reid, telegram to Ben Robertson Sr., February 24, 1943, Folder 21, Box 2, Ben Robertson Papers, Special Collections and Archives, Clemson University Libraries, Clemson, South Carolina.

14. Brendan Bracken, letter to New York *Herald Tribune,* February 1943, Folder 21, Box 2, Ben Robertson Papers, Special Collections and Archives, Clemson University Libraries, Clemson, South Carolina.

15. Harry Ashmore, "Robertson Kept Mind Clear in Midst of Furies of War," *Greenville News,* February 25, 1943, 6.

16. Edward R. Murrow, CBS radio broadcast, February 28, 1943. Several copies of the transcript may be found in Folder 105, Box 11, Ben Robertson Papers, Special Collections and Archives, Clemson University Libraries, Clemson, South Carolina.

17. "Report of The Death of an American Citizen, 353.113: Robertson, Ben," U.S. Department of State, April 16, 1943; "Ben Robertson's Body Recovered," *Greenville News,* March 17, 1943, 3.

18. "Ben Robertson's Body Reaches U.S.," *Greenville News,* April 12, 1943, 1.

19. Klaas, "Lest We Forget," 42.

20. Joe Sherman, "Ben Robertson Laid to Rest in Red Hills of Carolina," *Greenville News,* April 19, 1943, 2; Wright Bryan, "Ben Robertson Is Buried Near Scenes of Boyhood," *Atlanta Journal,* April 19, 1943, 24.

21. Wright Bryan, "Ben Robertson Is Buried Near Scenes of Boyhood," *Atlanta Journal,* April 19, 1943, 22.

Chapter 18—An Upcountry Legacy

1. Sperber, *Murrow: His Life and Times,* 261; J. Strom Thurmond, letter to Ben Robertson Sr., March 9, 1943, Folder 21, Box 2, Ben Robertson Papers, Special Collections and Archives, Clemson University Libraries, Clemson, South Carolina.

2. James F. Byrnes, letter to Ben Robertson Sr., April 14, 1943, Folder 21, Box 2, Ben Robertson Papers, Special Collections and Archives, Clemson University Libraries, Clemson, South Carolina. For condolence letters see, for instance, the letter from Mrs. Frank Cuhel to Mary Longley in the Robertson Papers. Mrs. Longley even wrote letters of condolence to Pan American World Airways, and even Captain Sullivan. "He is a crushed, despondent man," she noted. "Pilot error was declared responsible. Ben would have been understanding—all make mistakes." See posthumous correspondence file, Folder 21, Box 2, Ben Robertson Papers, Special Collections and Archives, Clemson University Libraries, Clemson, South Carolina.

3. "B. F. Robertson," Retired Chemist of S.C. Dies in Ga.," *Index-Journal* (Greenwood, S.C.), July 2, 1943, 17; Busha, "Ben Robertson of Pickens County" (1982), 9; Klaas, "Lest We Forget," 43–44.

4. For an overview of the Liberty Ship program, see John Gorley Bunker, *Liberty Ships: The Ugly Ducklings of World War II* (Annapolis: Naval Institute Press, 1972). Another Liberty ship was named in honor of Frank Cuhel, Robertson's fellow *Yankee Clipper* passenger.

5. Mary B. R. Longley, "The Clemson I Remember," *Messenger* (Clemson, S.C.), February 8, 1978, 6-A; Bryan, "About Ben Robertson," xiv.

6. Ernie Pyle, "Moving Up with Company X," *Honolulu Advertiser,* February 29, 1944, 5.

7. Ernest N. Kettenhofen, letter to Jeanne Gadsden, June 24, 1946, Folder 107, Box 11, Ben Robertson Papers, Special Collections and Archives, Clemson University Libraries, Clemson, South Carolina. The S.S. *Ben Robertson* was sold in December 1946 to the Gratsos firm of Greece and renamed *Kastor.* The ship continued in commercial service until it was scrapped in Hirao, Japan in 1968–69. Special thanks to Ian Wrenford for supplying this information.

8. Busha, "Ben Robertson of Pickens County" (1982), 9; Klaas, "Lest We Forget," 43.

9. "Lady Astor, in Atlanta, Asks to Meet Ben Robertson Kin," *Anderson Independent,* March 31, 1948; Klaas, "Lest We Forget," 44.

10. Wright Bryan, "About Ben Robertson," i.

11. See, among others, "South Carolina Author Pays Tribute to State," undated clipping, Folder 12, Box 1, Ben Robertson Papers, Special Collections and Archives, Clemson University Libraries, Clemson, South Carolina; Bessie Mell Lane, "Robertson's Book is a Testament

of Love," undated clipping, Folder 12, Box 1, Ben Robertson Papers, Special Collections and Archives, Clemson University Libraries, Clemson, South Carolina; and Longley, *The Pilgrim.* Columbia Pictures briefly considered a film version of *The Pilgrim* but passed on it. See correspondence in Folder 22, Box 2, Ben Robertson Papers, Special Collections and Archives, Clemson University Libraries, Clemson, South Carolina.

12. From the Ben Robertson Society website, http://libpartner.clemson.edu/benrobertson society/ (accessed November 2, 2017).

13. Ford, "The Affable Journalist as Social Critic," 370.

Bibliography

Published Sources

Ashmore, Harry S. *An Epitaph for Dixie.* New York: Norton, 1958.

Bryan, Wright. "About Ben Robertson," in *Red Hills and Cotton: An Upcountry Memory,* by Ben Robertson, i–xix. Columbia: University of South Carolina Press, 1960.

Bunker, John Gorley. *Liberty Ships: The Ugly Ducklings of World War II.* Annapolis, Md.: Naval Institute Press, 1972.

Busha, Charles H. "Ben Robertson of Pickens County, Part I." *Old Pendleton District Messenger* 27, no. 10 (December 2013): 4–9.

———. "Ben Robertson of Pickens County, Part I." *Old Pendleton District Messenger* 28, no. 1 (January 2014): 6–11.

Cash, W. J. *The Mind of the South.* New York: Knopf, 1941.

Claridge, Laura. *The Lady with the Borzoi: Blanche Knopf, Literary Tastemaker Extraordinaire.* New York: Farrar, Straus and Giroux, 2016.

Clemson College Catalogue, 1918–19. Clemson, S.C.: Clemson College, 1918.

Cloud, Stanley, and Lynne Olson. *The Murrow Boys: Pioneers on the Front Lines of Broadcast Journalism.* New York: Houghton Mifflin, 1996.

Cook, Tony Stanley. "Remembering the South Carolina Upcountry. Ben Robertson's *Red Hills and Cotton.*" *Southern Studies* (Fall 1987): 217–38.

Cooper, William J., Jr., and Thomas E. Terrill. *The American South: A History, Volume 2.* 2nd ed. New York: McGraw-Hill, 1996.

Farrar, Ronald T. *A Creed for My Profession: Walter Williams, Journalist to the World.* Columbia: University of Missouri, 1998.

Ford, Lacy K., Jr. "The Affable Journalist as Social Critic: Ben Robertson and the Early Twentieth-Century South." *Southern Cultures* 2, no. 3–4 (1996): 353–71.

———. Introduction to *Red Hills and Cotton: An Upcountry Memory,* by Ben Robertson, ix–xlv. Columbia: University of South Carolina Press, 1990.

Gardiner, Juliet. *Wartime Britain 1939–1945.* London: Headline Publishing, 2004.

Halberstam, David. *The Powers That Be.* New York: Dell, 1979.

Harrison, Rosina. *Rose: My Life in Service.* Worthing, U.K.: Littlehampton Book Services, 1975.

Hoopes, Roy. *Ralph Ingersoll: A Biography.* New York: Atheneum, 1985.

Kennedy, David. *Freedom from Fear: The American People in Depression and War, 1929–1945.* New York: Oxford, 1999.

Kluger, Richard. *The Paper: The Life and Death of the* New York Herald Tribune. New York: Knopf, 1986.

Knightley, Phillip. *The First Casualty: From the Crimea to Vietnam: The War Correspondent as Hero, Propagandist, and Myth Maker.* New York: Harcourt Brace Jovanovich, 1975.

Lankford, Nelson D. *The Last American Aristocrat: The Biography of Ambassador David K. E. Bruce.* New York: Little, Brown, 1996.

Longley, Mary B. R. *The Pilgrim: Voyage 37.* New York: Vantage, 1965.

Manchester, William. *The Glory and the Dream: A Narrative History of America, 1932–1972.* New York: Bantam, 1973.

Milkman, Paul. *PM: A New Deal in Journalism, 1940–1948.* New Brunswick: Rutgers, 1997.

"Model 314, Where Are You?" *Boeing Magazine* (June 1965): 3–6.

Overy, Richard. *Russia's War: A History of the Soviet War Effort, 1941–1945.* New York: Penguin, 1997.

Raghvan, Srinath. *India's War: World War II and the Making of Modern South Asia.* New York: Basic Books, 2016.

Reel, Jerome V. *The High Seminary, Vol. 1: A History of the Clemson Agricultural College of South Carolina, 1889–1964.* Clemson, S.C.: Clemson University Digital Press, 2011.

Robertson, Ben. "A Hero of the Frozen South." *New York Herald Tribune Sunday Magazine,* February 9, 1930, 3.

———. "Australia's Labor Prime Minister." *New York Herald Tribune Sunday Magazine,* October 12, 1930, 15.

———. "Hamlet Lived at Elsinore." *Travel* (March 1937): 15–17, 55.

———. "The Hawaiian Melting Pot." *Current History* (June 1932): 312–15.

———. "He Never Went to College." *New York Herald Tribune Sunday Magazine,* November 23, 1930, 10.

———. "Heavy Traffic in Surabaya." *Travel* (July 1929): 35–37, 58.

———. *I Saw England.* New York: Knopf, 1941.

———. "King George Strives to Please." *Saturday Evening Post,* February 4, 1939, 5–7, 69.

———. "King of the Bush Country." *New York Herald Tribune Sunday Magazine,* July 3, 1932, 6.

———. "The Lucky Girls of Aruba." *Saturday Evening Post,* July 8, 1939, 8–9.

———. "The Mattress-Stuffing Tree." *Asia* (August 1931): 492–93, 533–34.

———. "No Sunday School Town." *Asia* (August 1929): 612–17.

———. "Our Sailors Sleep in the Palace of the Czar." *Scribner's Magazine* (May 1932): 298–99.

———. *Red Hills and Cotton: An Upcountry Memory.* New York: Knopf, 1942.

———. "That Yellow House in Surabaya." *Asia* (May 1933): 314–16.

———. *Travelers' Rest.* Clemson, S.C.: Cottonfield Publishers, 1938.

Robertson, Ben, with McCoy Hill. "At the Heart of Desolation." *Travel* (February 1929): 38–39, 48.

Sheean, Vincent. *Between the Thunder and the Sun.* New York: Macmillan, 1943.

Sorel, Nancy Caldwell. *The Women Who Wrote the War.* New York: Arcade, 1999.

Speer, Lonnie. *Portals to Hell: Military Prisons of the Civil War.* Mechanicsburg, Pa.: Stackpole, 1997.

Sperber, Ann M. *Murrow: His Life and Times.* New York: Bantam, 1986.

Taps, 1923 ed. Clemson, S.C.: Clemson College, 1923.

Williams, Arthur. *Tales of Clemson, 1936–1940.* Clemson, S.C.: Clemson University Press, 1992.

Unpublished Sources

Alfred A. Knopf Papers. Harry Ransom Center, The University of Texas at Austin.

B. O. Williams Papers. Special Collections and Archives, Clemson University Libraries, Clemson, South Carolina.

Bailey, Beatrice Naff. "Losing a Life to Find It: Ben Robertson, Jr.'s Freedom Quest." M.A. thesis, Clemson University, 2012.

Ben Robertson Papers. Special Collections and Archives, Clemson University Libraries, Clemson, South Carolina.

Busha, Charles H. "Ben Robertson of Pickens County: A Brief Biographical Sketch." Paper presented at Pickens County Historical Society, Pickens, S.C., November 19, 1982.

Giesen, James C. "The South's Greatest Enemy? The Cotton Boll Weevil and Its Lost Revolution, 1892–1930." Ph.D. dissertation, University of Georgia, 2004.

John Dewey Lane Papers. Special Collections and Archives, Clemson University Libraries, Clemson, South Carolina.

Klaas, M. D. "Lest We Forget: Ben Robertson, Foreign Correspondent." Seminar paper, San Francisco State College, 1966.

Luce, Dianne. "Ben Robertson's Red Hills." Paper for academic presentation, undated.

Peeler, Jodie M. "BR: The Life and Works of Ben Robertson, South Carolina Journalist and Author." Ph.D. dissertation, University of South Carolina, 2001.

Sawyer, Nathania K. "Harry S. Ashmore: On the Way to Everywhere." M.A. thesis, University of Arkansas at Little Rock, 2001.

Walker, William S., Jr. "Ben Robertson, War Correspondent." M.A. thesis, University of South Carolina, 1971.

William Wright Bryan Papers. Special Collections and Archives, Clemson University Libraries, Clemson, South Carolina.

Index

About the Author

Jodie Peeler is professor of communications at Newberry College, where she teaches journalism and specializes in media history. A Greenwood County native, Peeler earned her master's and doctoral degrees from the University of South Carolina.